Legendary Leitrim

- exploring north west Ireland

Alanna Moore

Python Press

Alanna Moore is the author of:
Divining Earth Spirit - 1994, 2nd ed. 2004
Backyard Poultry–Naturally - 1998, 3rd ed. 2014
Stone Age Farming - 2001, 3rd ed. 2025
The Wisdom of Water - 2007
Water Spirits of the World - 2012
Sensitive Permaculture - 2009
Touchstones for Today - 2013
Plant Spirit Gardener - 2016
Peasant in Paradise - 2021
Fairy Haunts of Ireland - 2023

Legendary Leitrim - exploring north west Ireland

ISBN - 9780645285475

Published by Python Press,
Ireland and Australia.
www.pythonpress.com

Text, design, maps and photos by Alanna Moore © 2025

Illustrations by David Gascoigne, pages 8 coin & 10 map, 64, 94; and Yolande Hyde (the others).

All rights reserved. No reproduction, copy or transmission of this publication may be made without written permission of the publisher. No person should rely on this book as a substitute for specific advice and the author disclaims any liability in connection with the use or misuse of the information herein. Historical facts and dates, and directions to sites may not be fully accurate. The publisher takes no responsibility for this. Do your own research. Travel and explore at your own risk. Enjoy taking risks!

Many thanks to all the authors, local historians, libraries and community groups who have kept alive the living history of Ireland, Leitrim in particular, and provided much material for this book via their publications and their willingness to share cultural knowledge and provide assistance to this book project. And thanks to the Folklore Commission for their fantastic resource, the digitised folklore of Ireland at www.duchas.com

Contents

Introduction - Time Travelling Leitrim   5

Chapter 1 - Setting the Scene

History and Pseudo-History 7 St Patrick 8 The Myth of Tara 9 Rathcroghan Mythos 9
Archaic Connaught 10 Linear embankments 11 Black Pig's Dyke 12
The Doon of Drumsna 12 Cattle Raid of Cooley 13 Dagda's Track? 14

Chapter 2 - Through the Gateway to the North West

Drumsna Village 17 Rue 20 Cornacorroo 20 Jamestown 21 Tully 23 Lisduff 24
Castlecarra 25 Clogher 26 Foxborough 26 Aughintobar 27 Headford 28

Chapter 3 - River crossings

Developments in the Late Iron Age 31 Early Christian sites 31 Early medieval Leitrim 33
Annaduff 34 Carrick on Shannon 36 Summerhill and Townparks 37 Attirory 38
Inishmucker 39 Portaneoght 39 Port 40 Leitrim Village 41 Drumhierny 41
Battlebridge 42 Drumboylan 42 Tumna Church 42 St Eiden's Tumna 43
Church Hill 44 Visiting Tumna 45

Chapter 4 - Kings of Hospitality

Moy Nissi 49 Kings of Hospitality 49 Kiltoghert 50 Experiencing Kiltoghert's Monastic
Site 52 House of Hospitality at Mong 53 Drumheckil 54 Passage Tombs 54 Sheemore 55
Pilgrimage to Sheemore 57 Kilclare 58 Edenmore 59 Sheebeg 60 Lough Scur 61
Kiltubrid 63 Drumany, Churchfield and Lough Nacarriga 65 Castlefore 65
Keshcarrigan 66 Laheen 67 Lisdromarea 67 Annaghearley 67 Effrinagh 67 Corlisheen 68

Chapter 5 - Saintly Envy

Conmaicne Maigh Rhein 71 Fedaro 71 Labbyeslin 72 Mohill 73 Plague Saint 74
Mullaghbrack and Belcarra 76 Cloone 77 Drumharkin Glebe 79 Cloone surroundings:
Sunnaghmore 81 Aghavas 82 Miltron Glebe 82 Carrigallen 82 Clooncorick 83 Killegar 84

Chapter 6 - Lakes of the Holy Cow

River Mermaids and Cow Lakes 87 Derrycarne 88 Furnace 88 Fearnaght 89 Aughry 89
Dromod 89 Lough Rinn 90 Farnaught 92 Gortleletteragh 94 Lear 94 Cloonee 94
Drumconny 95 Keeldra 95 Annaghmore 96 Clooncumber 97 Johnsons Bridge 98
Cloonmorris 98 Edercloon 100 Clooneen 100 Roosky 100 Killinaker 101

Chapter 7 - Land of the Dagda

Pagan Fenagh 103 Fenagh Lough 104 The Abbey and the Serpent 105
Fenagh Graveyard 105 The Bell of the Kings 106 Two Abbeys and a Book 106
Ballinamore 108 Oughteragh 109 Oughteragh Holy Well Experience 110
Miskaun Glebe 110 Lough Garadice 110 Woodford 112 Tullyhaw and Magh Sleact 112
Ballymagauran 114 Derryragh 115 Derryragh Experience 117 Kilnavert 118
Killycluggin 120 Lissanover 122 Jampa Ling 123 Ballyconnell and Ballyheady 123
Tomregan and Mullynagolman 124

Chapter 8 - Iron Mountain

Coming of the Iron Age 127 Acres 128 Drumshanbo 129 Lough Allen 130
Sliabh an Iarainn 131 Pulty 132 Sweathouses 133 Ballinagleragh 135 The Playbank 135
Dowra 135 Glangevlin 136 Tobar Muire 137 Shannon Pot 137 Cavan Burren 139

Chapter 9 - Wild West Breffni

Tarmon 141 Spencer Harbour 142 Corry 143 Drumkeerin 143 Belhavel Lough and
Ben Scardaun 144 Tawnylea 144 Killarga 145 Dromahair 146 Creevylea Abbey 150
Killerry 152 Killerry Healing Stones Experience 153 Parkes Castle 153
Deer Park 154 Glencar 154

Chapter 10 - Bastions of the North

Glencar Valley 157 Lurganboy 158 Benbo 159 Manorhamilton 159 Tullyskeherny 162
Glenfarne 163 Lough MacNean Upper 163 Corrocloona 164 Kiltyclogher 165
Rossinver 166 St Mogues Holy Well Experience 167 Rossinver area 168
Lough Melvin 169 Sheenun 170 Sheenun Energies 171 Kinlough 171
Rosfriar 172 Tullaghan 172 Glenade 173

Introduction

TIME TRAVELLING LEITRIM

When we visit the cultural heritage of north west Ireland we time travel in relatively unspoilt landscapes, touching a distant past. At monuments that have survived over millennia, we can connect into an awesome continuum. Human history stretches back far in Leitrim. Archeological evidence goes back to Mesolithic times, some 9,000 years ago.[1] Since the first people arrived in Ireland following the Ice Age and after ecosystems had re-established, the population swelled and declined at different times. Their fortunes fluctuated from catastrophic changes - the impacts of plagues, climate change, war and invasion, Icelandic volcano eruptions blotting out the sun for years and bringing famine, and the like. Scientists have seen clues to these changes in markers such as ancient pollen. *"Pollen analysis has suggested widespread forest regeneration in the second half of the first millennium BCE, which may indicate a significant decline in population during this time"*.[2] This de-population time occurred around the start of the Irish Iron Age. Later, new groups of people started to arrive and fill the gaps. They brought new technology, gods and goddesses, icons and ideas. It was a cultural revolution. Centuries afterwards, their history and stories, orally transmitted, started to be recorded by medieval monks onto vellum manuscripts. The mythic era had began!

Breifni, the old name for north Leitrim, was regarded as one of the 'rough thirds of Ireland' - mostly unsuited to farming. Dominated by mountains, hills, lakes and boggy marshland, much of it was heavily forested. This allowed the ancient Gaelic culture to remain undisturbed, despite colonisation, until relatively recent times.[3] Despite the landscape challenges for farming, Breifne has long been important for its high concentration of mineral resources. With the bulk of Ireland's iron ore located here, it was a hot spot in the Iron Age. In an origin myth of the coming of the Tuatha da Danaan, this mythical invader tribe first appeared on Leitrim's Iron Mountain. It was a good choice, because here they could forge their superior iron weapons, under a cloak of cloud and forest. Iron can be sharpened much better than the bronze tools and weapons of the day, and it has deadlier potential. Forests are quicker to clear with iron axes too. This myth describes the coming of the Iron Age to Ireland.

As people sought control of the metal resources, there was much to fight about. As a result, borders were exceptionally fluid until Gaelic control was ended, with the Plantation of Leitrim from the early 1600s. (It was the last area in Ireland to be colonised.) So, too, the meanderings of Legendary Leitrim also strays over modern borders at times, to Deeply Map out and showcase many of the amazing ancient places and legends in the mythic fabric of this beautiful region.

Since the time of the Great Famine, Leitrim saw a huge population decline. It went from 155,000 in pre-famine times, to just over 35,000 today. As a result, there was little desire to develop the land or remove monuments of the past. The people were gone. Thanks to official recording of sites, first by the Ordnance Survey (OS) mappers in the 1830s, we know of a great many monuments located here, and also see ones noted that have since disappeared. Amazingly, an estimated 90% of the monuments in Leitrim still remain, in some degree! [4] There are lots and more are being found. Mostly in ruinous condition, many are still recognisable and it's amazing there's anything left after so much time. A taboo to not touch sites usually prevailed, until colonial times. Then they were at the mercy of Plantation landlords, who did preserve some, or 'enhanced' them as ornaments for their demesnes.

When exploring Leitrim's ancient past, don't expect to see grand 'castles'. Gaelic lords traditionally lived, or bunkered down, on crannogs, artificial islands with wooden buildings that they could retreat to, ensuring seclusion and safety in wartime. Castles are more Anglo-Norman in style and typically just un-glamorous stone tower houses, two or three stories high. The fortified homes of the elite were prime targets and were usually destroyed by rebel groups.

What is a common sight in Leitrim (and not so much in the rest of Ireland) are the one thousand plus recorded ring forts, as seen on the right. These protected farmsteads were typically situated on hilltops, with wattle and daub, thatched roofed homes surrounded by circular mud or stone walls that kept them and livestock safe from wolves at night. There's not been much archeological examination of them, however the Leitrim Fort Group has lately been conducting a survey, of what were the ideal home sites of their day, between the Bronze Age and the Middle Ages. [5]

Exploration of sites can be done on many levels. Sites without stories can be barren and boring. If we visit sites, soak up the atmosphere and reflect on their stories, we bring them back to life in our imagination. This helps us to resonate more deeply and richly with the landscape. It can also provide clues to past site history, for distinguishing natural landscape features from man-made, where energy signatures can be strikingly different. This is because of the remanence factor, where sites long ruined, hidden or levelled can still have palpable feelings that we might sense if focussing sensitively. Maverick English biologist Rupert Sheldrake came up with the name Morphogenetic Fields to explain this phenomena. I call them Fields of Memory, that can often be charged with intense emotional content from the past. A sensitive researcher or pilgrim can access these Akashic Records, as the ancient Indians called them. I have sprinkled in some of my own psychic site impressions, for good measure. After more than forty years of interaction with the energetic dimensions of landscape through professional dowsing and geomancy work (initially in Australia), I'm qualified to speak about subtle aspects of sites.[6] And I think anyone and everyone can benefit from seeking their own experience of the Deep Mapping of landscape.

For serious investigation, as well as fun and fruitful touring, you might want to get Ordnance Survey Discovery maps, numbers 16, 17, 33, 34, 26 and 27A, to see all of Leitrim and surrounding areas. They show monuments and sites, plus the little laneways that get you to them, and the lie of the land. You can also go online for Ireland's fascinating historical maps and time-travel on this free-to-see map website at https://osi.maps.arcgis.com

I hope you enjoy the journey as much as I have!

Chapter 1
Setting the Scene

History and pseudo-history

There's often a romanticised view of the past, even when it was rent with blood and gore. Old literary sagas of warring 'goodies' and 'baddies', have enemy tribes sporting hideous deformities, while the 'good' people are always beautiful and on the high moral ground. There's an obvious bias. The grim reality was messy - ruling regents often being challenged and kings killing rivals (and vice versa), while the concept of 'high kingship' was a fantasy and aspirational at best. Genocidal activities were the norm and truth was the usual victim of war.

Historical traditions were typically written centuries after events allegedly occurred. From the 7th century the monk scribes were kept busy compiling and copying 'histories' by hand, in books known as the Annals. Ambitious abbots often distorted facts for their own gain. Their stories are riddled with discrepancies and absurdities, but they also contain fascinating insights and lyric magic in them. But you definitely can't accept the medieval manuscripts at face value. These days academics consider them as 'pseudo-history' and 'pseudo-mythos'. However, they do reflect the political dynamics of the times. There was often conflict amongst churches run by elite hierarchies. Monastic federations fought amongst each other and raided enemy churches.

Recorded mythos can also lead us astray. For example, the most popular Pagan Irish deity, harvest god Crom Dubh. His memory survived until quite late in Leitrim. Elsewhere mostly forgotten, his memory was silenced by spin doctors, who cast Crom in a bad light. The claim of human sacrifice made to him, for one, is fabricated and without evidence. Contrary to what the church said, he was warmly appreciated as a benign force for the people.[1] And early Christian folklore sometimes even cast him as a benelovent 'landlord'.

Mythos describes glorified 'saints', who somewhat stepped into the roles of the local deities. They were not always saintly, however. (St Colmcille in Donegal, for example, was banished from Ireland for tribal warmongering and went on to fame at Iona in Scotland.) In literary tradition, saints did impressive magic tricks to rival the Druid establishment in the sensational fiction used to counter peoples' natural disinclination to having their perfectly good culture rubbished. Saints were many, Leitrim had fifteen on the record, but most are long forgotten. Eventually the status quo shifted to them, or else hid under a flimsy facade of conformity.

Unlike the peasantry, whose oral histories are of a more authentic nature, the monk scribes were 'literate'. This means they were well read in Greek and Roman classics, the Bible and church literature. They admired the writings of their colleagues in France, who, for example, creatively penned a posthumous re-invention of St Martin of Tours. So they followed suit and re-invented the humble St Patrick centuries after his death and had him gloriously roaming the countryside making converts, as per St Martin's fictitious travels.[2] But worse, they condemned historical figures and whole tribes at the stroke of a pen. Those scribes were plagiarists and character assassins peddling false narratives and propaganda. Just doing their job.

St Patrick

Consider the prime example of extravagant fiction - St Patrick's expelling of the snakes of Ireland. It's a story concocted for a foreign audience and not much talked about here. Within Ireland, he was more known for allegedly expelling the bird-serpent goddess Corra from various locations.[3] The snake story is obviously code for putting down the Pagans and exorcising the serpentine forces of the Earth, which he did not achieve. (After over 40 years of professional geomancy experience by the author, I know that such beings are still out there!)

The implausible, and zoologically impossible, tale could well be a dig at the reverence of Celtic ram-headed-serpent god Segomo, whose mythic lineage must have stemmed from Vedic India, with its Nagas, the horned serpent spirits. Nagas, as well as Segomo, were considered beneficent beings who fertilised the land and acted as war gods when their territory was threatened. *"In most iconography the ram-headed serpent is...evocative of plenty and fertility – representing a dualistic scheme illustrating the interdependence of life and death, and encapsulating the theme of regeneration intrinsic in Celtic religious belief."* [4]

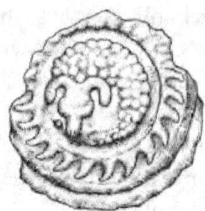

Segomo (or Segomom) was a god of the Celtic Belgic tribes (called Fir Belg in the Annals), O'Connor says.[5] The name, or honorific title, means Powerful Victor and Mighty One, and he was worshipped across ancient Gaul, Britain and Ireland. Segomo's images appear on Iron Age coins (e.g. like this one from southern England, on the right, from the years 10-15CE) and they continue to be seen into the Roman period. In other representations, he accompanies several Gaulish gods. On the Gundestrap Cauldron, he's under the control of nature god Cernnunos, as below, who triumphantly holds him by the throat in one hand, the other hand displaying a torc, symbolising his authority. Here is a probable precursor to the myth of St Patrick over-powering the serpents.

An image of Segomo shows up in ancient Ireland, in the pedigree of the Eoganachta royal dynasty in Munster, says O'Connor. These descendants of the Manapi tribe served Ireland's sea ports and used mon, man etc in their place names, eg Munster, the Manapian province. The Irish Sea was then called Muir Mean, the Manapian Sea, with its Isle of Man and sea god Mannanan Mac Lir. The Eoganachta replaced the indigenous Brigantes and their spiritual capital was at Knockaine in Limerick.

"The early Irish name Nia Segamoin [Servant of Segomo] clearly echoes his one-time presence". Nia Segamoin was said to be the name of an ancient 'high king', the title also means Champion of Segomon."[6]

Fast forward to Christian times and modern plastic statues of Mary (such as the one on the right) have a serpent subjugated under her foot. Times might change, but things stay the same!

Setting the Scene

THE MYTH OF TARA

The Church of Armagh set a prime example of how Irish myth, history and truth can be crucified for selfish ends. Craving supremacy as a survival strategy in a church-eat-church world, they created a tapestry of fake news. *"Armagh's monastic propagandists cooked up a scheming stew of sheer political brinkmanship to win the patronage of powerful war-lords,"* as author Tom O'Connor puts it. Those Ui Neill warlords were an offshoot of the Fir Belg who controlled a small kingdom in Donegal and had far reaching ambitions to conquer all of the north. When they finally succeeded and wrenched Tara from the cruthin Ulaid in a battle in 637, Armagh's scribes had the Ui Neills re-created as "High Kings of Tara since time immemorial", when in truth Tara was just a minor royal centre of Ulster.

Actually, Tara was one of several Taras, it's the typical name for an Irish royal hill. Tara, Turoe or Tory, are the name forms derived from Temhair in Old Irish. An example being Tory Hill/Temhair Ri, the royal hill near Croom in Limerick. Tara basically means a prominent hill with panoramic views, O'Connor notes. Tara in Meath was never the premier centre of 'high kingship' in a land of multiple warring kingdoms. Not until 637. Even then it was a tenuous position. But the Tara supremacy myth lingers on. *"Facts of history were suppressed by pseudo-historians of the Ui Neill war lords and the monastic federation of Armagh in favour of their own concocted glorification,"* as O'Connor calls it. Yet the so-called histories were taught as literal truth to Irish school kids until not so long ago.

RATHCROGHAN MYTHOS

Similar happened in relation to Rathcroghan in Co. Roscommon, the supposed centre of Connaught royalty "since time immemorial". Yet in the 6th century, when St Patrick purportedly went to meet the Connaught kings, he didn't go to Rathcroghan, but instead to their power centre at Magh Seola. Fir Belg descendants, the Ui Bruin Seola clan lived on their royal crannog on Lough Seola (now Lough Hackett), west of Tuam in Galway. They set up there after Maine Mor's Ulster clan invaded the earlier Connaught capital, in the second half of the 5th century. The Ui Bruin Seola later set their aims on conquering nearby Rathcroghan, with its excellent pasture land for cattle. But it took them centuries to overrun the native cruthintuatha there.

The Sil Muiredaig branch of the Ui Bruin (followers of Muiredaig) would have outgrown their capital at Magh Seola by then. After nine years of bloody skirmishes, in the year 752 they completed conquering the Calraige tribe at Rathcroghan. As the new rulers there, with no ancestral connections to it, they adopted the Bronze Age monuments as their own and inaugurated their kings at Carnfree mound. (Their last king, Rory O' Connor, ruled from 1156 to 1186.) From there, they gradually battled their way further north from Ui Bruin Ai, as it became known, to claim what became Ui Briuin Breifne, the northern reaches of modern counties Sligo and Leitrim. They were the ancestors of the O'Rourke clan of warlords.

The Ui Bruin Ai dynasty of Rathcroghan connived with Armagh to represent their capital as the original centre of Connaught, because a rival dynasty ruled from Rath Cruacha at Athenry at this time. Those usurpers had to be silenced in the media. So, ancestral traditions of the invading Fir Belg tribes and the royal centre of Lough Seola were surreptitiously transferred to Rathcroghan in official pseudo-history, while the Cain Padraig, the rule of Armagh, was subsequently proclaimed across Connaught as the church's reward. Their manipulative mission was virtually completed when names and stories about Rathcroghan's monuments were assigned by 19th century archeologists, who borrowed them from medieval pseudo-legends, as they did at the Tara in Meath and elsewhere. Misplaced tales were accepted because the old folklore was gone, swept away by colonisation. Only displaced peoples lived around there, it was reported in Folklore Commission records from Rathnaglye School - *"Most of the people in this area are migrants who have been brought in from Galway and Mayo and, consequently fields and hollows are not named as one finds them in other districts. [Unlike] In the Tuam district of Co. Galway [where] almost every field in the small farms has its name."* [7]

The Rathcroghan cruthintuatha, who may well have been descendants of Bronze Age tribes, were tenacious at holding onto their sacred territory against relentless attacks by the Fir Belg for so long. One wonders if perhaps some special protection was at work, some sacred sovereignty powers invoked to keep their territory unviolated for so long? Was the power of the old earthy gods and feisty sovereignty goddesses protecting them? Did they have the advantage that landscape barriers offered? Was their army big? Or did they they have another trick up their sleeve? Probably it was a mixture of all, as we shall see.

ARCHAIC CONNAUGHT

Mighty River Shannon provided a fixed barrier between the provinces of Ulster and archaic Connaught to the south, where the Fir Belg tribes had been pouring in from south-west England as refugees from the genocidal march of the Roman Empire. One of their most illustrious kings, Congentiatus (or Gan, aka Commius), whose minted coinage provides us with dates, had disappeared from the British records after the year 26 BCE. It's surmised that he surreptitiously led his tribe, the Gangani, as a folk movement across to the safety of western Ireland. They swarmed in via the mouth of the Shannon ('Sennos') River and set up their new territorial enclave, with their first capital at Temhair a' Ri, or Tooraree, the royal hill of north west Limerick.

Later, an expanding population of the Gangani gradually pushed north to set up a new capital around Turoe Hill, Rath Cruacha and Knocknadal (the Hill of Parliament), in modern east Galway. At the time of Ptolemy, who was mapping in the late first to early second century CE, Knocknadal was reported to be *"the most illustrious city in all Britannia and the most considerable in size, set in the west of Ireland"*. He calls this royal centre on the map - Regia e Tera. This was Cnoc Temhro in Old Irish, the Hill of Turoe.[8] It explains the context of the famous Turoe Stone that was found there (seen on the left).

For political purposes this history was suppressed, while a new motorway to Galway city constructed a few years ago was allowed to plough through some of this important area.

The waves of migrants who poured in from around 200 BCE to 200 CE, often clashed with the cruthintuatha they encountered. In order to gain sword land, they plundered, killed and enslaved the indigenes. The Ulaidh in the north were constantly being pushed and squeezed by the

Fir Belg expansions. Monumental frontier border control lines were made to keep them out, but borders kept receding north-eastwards. An early line of defence in this Iron Age saga went as far south as Athlone. Some of it was along the Esker Riada, an ancient road just south of Athlone. This esker is the famous ridge line created by Ice Age glaciers that once covered the northern half of the country.

As they melted away, along the southern edge they left a linear gravel ridge line running roughly east-west. Along this edge were tunnel formations where meltwaters had flowed out. Soon after the ice had melted, some ten thousand years ago, people began to arrive in Ireland. Eskers provided them with convenient pathways. They must have wondered about the awesome power of nature that formed the eskers. One can imagine how stories of Great Worms tunnelling through the land might have been conceived, from their observations of esker structure.

LINEAR EMBANKMENTS

Fast forwards to year 1 of the Current Era and territorial fighting and pillaging was rampant. Tuatha, and their elite classes in particular, were seeking land, power, cattle-wealth and survival in a competitive world. Danger lurked everywhere, but the Belgic peoples, who originated from the Rhinelands and elsewhere, had developed strategies for keeping safe from the Germanic tribes and Roman armies who easily overpowered their hill forts. They were numerous and well organised enough to build massive linear earth embankments to enclose their settlements and farmlands. [9] Fossed earthen embankments prevented cattle raiding. The protection of cows was paramount, as they were the wealth-that-walked. With wooden palisades added on top of the banks, warring armies might be kept at bay and boundaries defended too. Caesar called these enclosed settlements oppidum and there are many examples still visible across Britain and Europe. They were the original gated communities.

The original name for Fir Belg territory in central-modern-Connaught was Coiced nOl nEgmacht, the Province of the Isolated Embanked Enclave, as it was surrounded by hostile cruthin lands, O'Connor reveals. Linear embankments in Ireland represent a mighty legacy. *"The extensive lines of large banks-and-ditches...are the amongst the oldest, largest and most celebrated land boundaries in prehistoric Europe. Yet they are also the most elusive.... The linear earthworks represent the most extensive civil engineering tasks of their day and involved earthmoving on a vast scale,"* researchers have written.[10] But the banks haven't received the attention they deserve. Many sections have been levelled and their trace grows ever fainter as the years pass.

Ireland's linear embankments were first referred to in literary accounts as Worm Ditches, a creation of the Great Pest, the Oll-Phéist, Great Worm or Serpent. I wonder if that name was not inspired by the shape and structure of the eskers after the Ice Age ended? And did they go on to inspire Philip K. Dick, when he wrote the science-fiction novel Dune, about a world inhabited by giant, tunnelling, menacing worms? The Vikings may have had similar ideas. Their word 'worm', that must be a loan word in Old Irish, as in Old Norse worm means serpent or dragon, indicating a powerful force of nature, rather than the humble earth worm.

These mighty Iron Age dykes were not continuous, but stretched between natural barriers such as mountains, bogs, marshes, lakes and rivers. Several of the frontier lines of this Great

Wall of Ulster, as proposed by William F. M. De Vismes Kane over a century ago, stretched from the north-west, down to the south-east near Dublin and Dundalk. Typically they were positioned to protect important political centres and were often near ancient monument complexes too.

BLACK PIG'S DYKE

Later, the boundary embankments were mostly referred to in Irish as the Cladh na Muice, or Black Pig's Dyke. The magic boar legend had a transformed Druid or school teacher who raced around the landscape rooting up the ground to make huge fosses and banks. Folk tales of magic black pigs were still vividly remembered in the 1930s, with similar themes in disparate regions recorded by school pupils for the Folklore Commission archives. It may have been the shape of the banks that inspired the boar connection, given their resemblance to the profile of the broad shouldered back (drum) and rotund rump of the pig (muc), plus the prodigious rooting ability of powerful tusked boars. Lands of the Ulaid that were secured behind this great wall would be referred to as being in the Valley (or Plain) of the Black Pig.

The annalistic tale of a battle, Cath Magh Muc Dhruim, relates an origin story for a place name, for where Fir Belg regents of archaic Connaught, Queen Medb and King Ailill, chased magic pigs around their regia, a reference to the rooting up of the foss and banks of their royal oppidum, now modern day Athenry. But Magh Muc Dhruim, the Plain of the Magic Pig, where this battle occurred, had its name subtly changed to Magh Mucrima, the Plain of Pig Counting, by medieval spin doctors intent on obscuring the memory of the true capital of early Connaught. Local oral history around Athenry has preserved the original spelling of Maigh Muc Dhruim, O'Connor relates. The correct version of the name also survived in a poem in the 12th century Book of Leinster. Queen Medb was a sixth generation (or so) descendent of King Gan/Commius, which puts her reign in the late 1st or early 2nd century CE, when Ptolemy was producing his map of Ireland.

Another clue to the truth behind literary distortions, it slipped out in the famous Ulidian tale The Cattle Raid of Cooley. After Queen Medb's warring with Ulster, she retreated back home to Cruacha of Connaught via Athlone. This was nowhere near Rathcroghan and it has perplexed many a folklore enthusiast. But if you consider that she lived in Galway, at Magh Muc Dhruime (now Athenry, Ford of the Kings), which is more convenient to Athlone, it all makes sense! [11] By taking this route, Medb was keeping well away from enemy cruthin territory.

THE DOON OF DRUMSNA

The most massive section of the linear boundary banks, that some call the Great Wall of Ulster, cuts across a loop in the River Shannon at Drumsna, where stony shallows allow easy crossing when river levels are low. It was long an important trading route to access northern regions for trading and mining. Going into Leitrim, people sought out minerals such as iron, silver, lead and copper, as well as coal near Lough Allen. But first they had to go through this imposing rampant, the most important gateway to the north west, the 'checkpoint charlie' of its day. But today they give it a less significant title - the Doon of Drumsna.

Why is it here? We have to go back to when Queen Maeve ruled archaic Connaught from her base at Athenry. She had long eyed off territory to the north, especially around Croghan in modern Co. Roscommon. Here was a vast fertile territory that stretched across most of the modern day county and beyond, with a southern boundary of the River Suck. With cattle raids a feature of land grabbing, in her culture, *"the imperative to raid became central to the maintenance of Celtic social order,"* noted scholar Barry Cunliffe. [12]

An old name for the fertile plains of north eastern Roscommon was Moy Lurg, which, in the Annals of the Four Masters for 1597, was called Mag Luircc an Daghda, the Plain of the Track of Dagda's Club.[13] The Dagda, or Good God, was known for sporting a huge club that he dragged behind him to create a major boundary track, a substantial fossed embankment suited to a provincial boundary. That their boundaries were considered sacred and under the protection of the gods, is inferred by this name. So, where on this part of the edge of Ulster was it worth putting boundary embankments of such a divine nature?

In the first century CE, Queen Maeve's father Ferach More was king. (The famous Turoe Stone was originally set up within his fort in Galway.) Ferach had already invaded lands to the east of his archaic Connaught capital, crossing the Shannon River at Athlone and pushing into modern day Co. Westmeath, winning territory along the eastern banks of Lough Ree. In Maeve's time, part of this territory was re-taken by the cruithin of Rathcroghan and Maeve was badly defeated at the Battle of Airtech (modern day Frenchpark in Roscommon). This was chronicled in the Cath Artig, the Book of the Battle. Maeve later fought for this land again and re-took it.[14] She was a real warrior woman with plenty of blood on her hands, but no worse nor better than other regents of her day, I'm sure. She suffered malicious character assassination in the literature, but should be considered on a par with British Celtic queens Cartimandua and Boudicea (who were maligned by Roman writers). You get a feel for those times in the classic story of the Cattle Raid of Cooley, the Táin bó Cuailnge.

CATTLE RAID OF COOLEY

The Táin may be pseudo-history, but it does preserve the general state of play of its time, in that Ulster had to constantly defend itself against the onslaught of the invading Fir Belg of Connaught. At that time Ulster extended south to Athlone and south east almost to Dublin. In the Táin, Queen Maeve was warring over cattle in Ulster, then made her battle retreat, going back to Connaught by way of Athlone, to her home in east Galway. This shows the extent of the boundary of Ulster in around the first - second century CE. However, medieval spin doctors relocated her home to Rathcroghan in the literary sources, which makes her moves implausible.

Maeve was a real queen who followed the usual social code of her times. Cattle raiding was part and parcel of those times and it's the major theme of the story. But the Tain is not an original Irish story, because it likely comes from the Gauls of the Atlantic seaboard. It's a story that's been carried far and long by Celtic tribes and it was adapted to the locale and the current situation wherever it went. Some academics assert that the archaic basis of the Táin is depicted graphically on the silver panels of the fabulous Gundestrap Cauldron, unearthed from a Danish bog in Jutland in 1891. The silver cauldron is thought to originate from Armorica, being made around 75 - 55 BC by the Armorican Veneti in northwest France. It was in separate pieces when unearthed and various reconstructions have been suggested for the panels that are bestowed with images of mythical beings and events.

Professor Garrett Olmsted, who for fifty years studied Celtic myths, has concluded that - *"Altogether, the Gundestrup plates, taken in the order determined in Copenhagen by Nielsen et al (2005), relate the major events of fifteen episodes of Táin bó Cuailnge, in the order they occur in the tale."* This did not surprise him, because of the continuum of the Celtic concepts, which he discovered to be spread far and wide, and to also go back to archetypal myths of ancient Greece, Rome and even Sumer. *"Cultural connections between Armorica, south-west Britain, western Wales and Ireland, have been manifest over much of the last six thousand years…[and] during the Late Bronze Age western Iberia also was part of this zone…[they were] all sharing in the same material culture and all speaking Proto-Celtic dialects… During the Atlantic Iron Age, round houses, often with attached souterrains, small-enclosure round fortifications of stone, and peninsular fortifications are common to Ireland, Cornwall, and Armorica, with carved decorations on stone (such as those found at Turoe in Ireland and at Kermaria in Finisterre) connecting Ireland and Armorica directly."* [15]

"The myth on the silver cauldron… displays the narration of a springtime myth related to the cycle of rebirth…[that] gave rise to the Old-Irish saga Táin bó Cuailnge. The scenes of the portrayals on the cauldron correlate image-by-image with the beginning and end of the Táin and with the major episodes outlined in the seventh-century poetic narrations of the Táin. Plate E of the Gundestrup cauldron, in particular, displays the major events of the Aided Fraich episode. Here Cú Chulainn drowns his only son Fraech. The dead Fraech is then carried off into the otherworld by mourning women (bancuire) of the goddess Mórrigan and returns alive and well to the blare of trumpets three days later. … [Its] art style is unique to northwest Gaul and is largely confined to the region between the Seine and the Loire." Olmsted wrote. [16]

"There can be little doubt that in the Táin, the earliest written version of which dates to the eleventh century AD, we see a reflection of a Celtic epic which may, in many different versions, have been told from one end of Europe to the other. The survival of this oral tradition is one of the miracles of the Celtic tradition", Barry Cunliffe concurred. [17]

Dagda's Track?

The cruithintuatha of Rathcroghan found themselves as an isolated remnant of Ulster surrounded by enemy tribes. So, to avert the threat of more invasions from the south-east, they went to an enormous effort to fortify their borders against the Fir Belgs. What they created became the largest earthwork on the island of Ireland. It seems to have been super effective too. Because it was not until the year 784, long after it was built, that Rathcroghan finally fell to a northern Ui Briuin king, Tiprait mac Taidg. (This king went on to erase earlier capitals of Connaught, then assert that Rathcroghan alone was Connaught's capital "since time immemorial".)[18] The key to their defences must have been the Doon of Drumsna, strategically located at the eastern corner of Moy Lurg's southern border. Here, at a loop in the Shannon where it's rocky and shallow, is the best fording point north of Athlone. Some 23 km from Rathcroghan, it was a major entry point into Moy Lurg. A doon usually signifies an important, high-status fortified place, while some suggest that Drumsna's doon was a promontory fort or oppida. It would also surely qualify to be called the Dagda's Track of Moy Lurg.

The doon was protecting a much less-grand weir for fording the River Shannon, as described by local school students in the 1930s. *"The Shannon was crossed by means of fords before bridges were made. There was one near the town of Drumsna built of clay and stones."* [19] Here was a key trade and communications nexus point, that also allowed cattle raiders to wade or swim animals across when river levels were low. Barry Cunliffe speaks of *"The development of oppida controlling route nodes, and thus the movement of goods, as one of the more visible results of the complex socio-economic changes under way in the Celtic world."* [20]

A well defended Great Wall or oppida was of vital necessity and it was constructed close to the ford (around 1.5 km away), with boggy ground to the fore and the river deep at each end. The scale is massive. Three 1.6 km long north-south parallel earthen ditches and banks that run across the south side of the Charlestown promontory, opposite Drumsna, from a deep point of the Shannon in the south east, to another deep point at its other end. The banks were up to 6 m high, with timber palisading on top and deep ditches flanking it. There were two openings, in the form of out-turned, pincer shaped entrances extending east-west. There's evidence for massive gateposts 2 m² for gates spanning across 26 m. Plenty of room to bring a herd of cows through quickly. And to be first scrutinised by the garrison on the banks above!

The full width of all the banks and ditches is 156 m. This is really huge, compared to similar examples. Two farm tracks run between the banks and traces of ancient camps were noted in archaeological discoveries. As well, there are stretches of single ramparts to the north, on the left (west) bank of the river, at other shallow fording points before Jamestown. Menacing looking pointed timbers, called "iron-shod wooden piles" by Kane in 1915, acting as a chevaux de frise style defense, were found both at the eastern entrance of the Doon and beside the river on the east end. It would have been formidable!

Archeologists Tom Condit and Victor Buckley estimated that it could have taken 10,000 people two years to build the Doon. Up to 60,000 trees are estimated to have been incorporated into its structure. Of the purpose of the banks, they concluded that - *"Their defensive aspect is against the north and in particular defending the multiple fording points and shallows around the loop of the Shannon between Jamestown and Drumsna"*. [21]

Whether it was a defensive wall or fortress made by a great worm or dragon, a furious black pig, or by the Dagda's magical powers, the Doon of Drumsna represents an almighty effort. It remains today in shadowy form to remind us of the community determination to keep themselves safe. Those warring times were traumatic enough, but they must have also strengthened tribal unity and resolve. No other monuments are such dramatic signatures of the Irish Iron Age.

The history of subsequent centuries is sketchy and without such powerful markers, but we can discern a few grains of truth from pseudo-historical manuscripts, while archeology has provided substantial clues about what was, and what was not, going on in those epic times. Whatever it was, we need to keep the memory of significant places alive and our senses enriched by active appreciation of them. Otherwise, who is to know that they havent been bulldozed into oblivion, due to lack of interest?

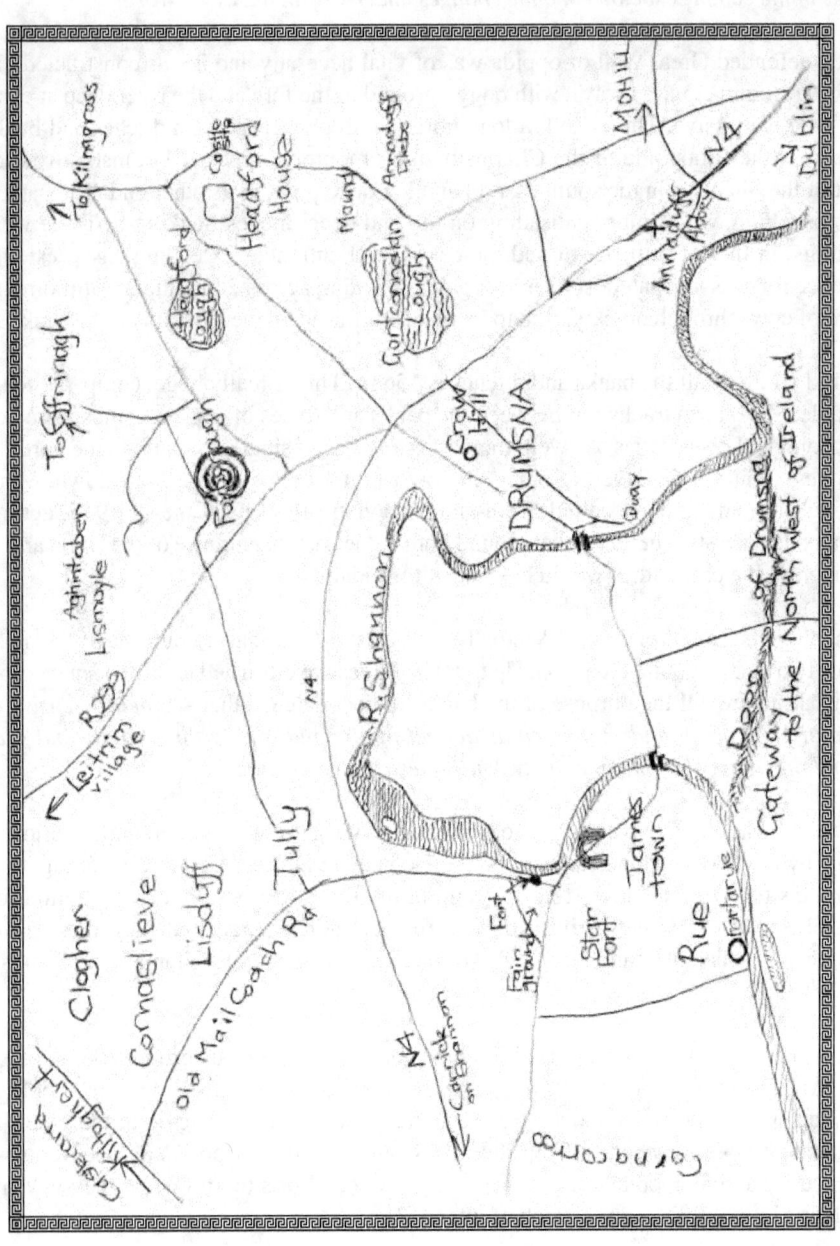

Chapter 2
Through the Gateway to the North West

Drumsna

Drumsna is a sleepy little village today, but it has a grand history. Designed around the entrance gates of Mount Campbell Estate, that lead to Charlestown House (seen right), the largely intact 18-19th century Georgian streetscape of the old village is largely unspoilt. Elegant stone buildings line the streets down to the harbour and bridge, where peaceful river vistas add to the charm. Some fine buildings *"display features of accomplished design that reflects the guiding hand and patronage of the resident landlord. Many of these premises adopt the characteristics of small classical country houses, expressed as symmetrical two-storey compositions with attractive door cases and a variety of fanlights of either a simple radial design of timber spokes or more elaborate leaded examples with intricate petal motifs,"* says Ireland's National Inventory of Architectural Heritage.[1]

Drumsna was a dynamic place when it was the most northerly port on the Shannon and Leitrim's main trading town. A substantial size, it had a variety of shops and its own courthouse. A small gaol house was created inside one of the arches of the bridge. The fine stone harbour at the east end of the village was completed in 1817. But in 1850 a navigation canal to Carrick on Shannon was opened and goods were brought up from there along it. Boats could then bypass Drumsna altogether and continue up the river, so the town began to decline.

However Drumsna was still on the old mail coach road from Dublin. Italian entrepreneur Charles Bianconi (1786 - 1875) came to Ireland and set up his transport company for mail and travellers, using horse drawn carriages. Drumsna was one of their stopover points and people would stay in what is now Taylors Bar. Locals found the Italian name hard to say, so they called him Brian Coney.

A highway bypass completed in 1996 stopped most traffic going through the village and it's quiet and peaceful now. In the process of building the 5 km road no less than five fulacht fia (Deer Cooking Places) were unearthed and recorded by archeologists, doubling the known number in the county (but they were subsequently destroyed).

A graceful stone bridge spans the old fording point. It's one of the few not to have been rebuilt by the Shannon Commissioners, as it was beyond the reach of navigation. At around 250 years of age, the bridge has stood the test of time, despite being on the main road to Sligo with lots of traffic. Some of it did collapse in the 1960s and an unsympathetic reconstruction was done with concrete blocks. But it has fared worse.

"In the year 1922 the bridges of Drumsna and Jamestown were blown up. It happened early in the morning on the first of July and the stones flew in every direction. It made big holes in the roofs of the houses and broke many of the windows, it knocked chimneys down. There was twice as much done to Jamestown. It knocked the tops off the houses. The men that blew it up were from around the locality and some of them were put to jail and the others went out of the country altogether." [2]

Until the bridge was restored, to cross the river people had to clamber up and down remaining sections of the bridge by ladders, local historian Des Guckian told me in 2024. (Sadly, Des passed away in May 2025.) The river around the bridge was the site of the discovery of a small Irish Elk skull. The giant species has been extinct for some 11,000 years and preserved skeletons have been occasionally dug out of peat bogs.[3] The skull may have possibly been placed there as a votive offering to the river gods.

Drumsna is mentioned a few times in the Annals under older names. The Annals of Connaught for the year 1261 record that Aedh O'Conchobar, king of Connaught, had a fortress here that was destroyed. The Ui Bruin clan raided and burnt it, because they didn't want the O'Connors as their overlords. The location of this ringfort is probably where the ruined old Methodist church and graveyard is, that's signposted next to the garden centre on the main road, up from the bridge and behind the monument to Surgeon-Major Thomas Heazle Parke. Parke (1857 - 1893) was the first Irishman to cross Africa and he famously found explorer Henry Morton Stanley in the Congo.

Standing in front of the entrance to the church ruin, if you look to the left, you'll see the shape of a low circular earth bank going around the site and close to the back verandah of the house

beside it. It surrounds the church ruin (seen on the left) and encompasses a massive Linden (Lime) tree. Brambles overgrowing much of it, typical of neglected sites, make for difficult viewing. On the south side, the ring fort extends into the garden centre, where the curving shed in the yard follows its contour. The overgrown ring fort has an interior diameter of 39 m. The width of the bank is 3.3 m, the height 25 - 75 cm and there's an external V shaped fosse 2 m wide and 30 cm deep. An entrance causeway is at the north, north-east side. [4] The rath is larger than average, suggesting an elite residence or fortress was indeed here.

Another ringfort is located on top of Crow Hill, above Drumsna village. Local school students reported in the 1930s that - *"There are not many fairy forts around this locality. There is just one I am acquainted with. It is on Crowhill beside Drumsna on Mr Duignan's land. There is a round mound surrounded by a ditch with bushes around it. Outside there is a pass round it like an avenue or footpath. I have heard people say that long ago [ghostly] horsemen used to gallop round and round it like an avenue for hours every night. Other days there was music and whistling heard at unreasonable hours."* [5]

The last shop left in Drumsna, Duignan's store is run by the family whose ancestors used to be the local hereditary bards, historians, doctors and noble literati of their time. You can see the fabulous O'Duignan family crest on the facade of both their shop and pub next door. It shows a sacred tree of knowledge, with a pair of snakes winding up it, a book on one side and a harp on the other, while a wise owl crowns the top of some versions. A most wonderfully archaic image!

Grab a guide map in the store and you can take a walking tour of this lovely town and its environs. Enjoy the river harbour, two riverbank parks, swimming spot, ringfort on Crow Hill and other historical features, including the Doon of Drumsna. Walking or cycling are the best ways to see them all.

To see some remnants of the Doon, go 1.5 km from Drumsna bridge to where there's a bump in the road and just past it, a farm gate on the left. From there you can see the wide, flattened down bank stretching away to the south. Across the road to the right you can see the line of the substantial bank going to the north. The house a little further up, also on the left, is the only home situated within the banks of the Doon. Previous owners, at a talk on the Doon that they attended, described to us how the place was badly haunted. When the couple were living there, at night they'd sometimes hear terrifying sounds of people battling.

RUE

Heading up the River Shannon northwards from Drumsna, there are several shallow fording points before the village of Jamestown. At these points, two linear banks are located on the south bank, before the river turns north to loop around the Charlestown peninsula. The first one is opposite the townland of Rue, with a significant ring fort located on the river bank on the Leitrim side, called Fortarue. T F O'Rahilly wrote that roe/roo and doe/doo meant a fossed embankment in Old Irish.[6] Perhaps Rue is cognate with this 'roo', proclaiming what used to be obvious?

Beside Fortarue, a curiously wide roadway graced by old Beech trees runs from the old fording point, shown on the right, straight up to the top of the hill. It has big banks on each side and it runs through what looks like a ring fort, though it's not recorded archeologically as such; while in Folklore Commission stories the circular enclosure is described as a *"full moon."*
[7] It ends at the top of the hill with a large enclosure and ring fort [8], which makes me guess that it would have functioned as a cattle fording set-up, with enclosures as temporary holding yards. Fortarue's past residents probably controlled cattle movements across the river, extracting fees and taxes for their services. In later times it was used as a pleasant 3 km circular walkway for the gentry, who no doubt planted the avenue of big Beech trees flanking its sides. Indeed, it's described as *"a walk for the use of the O'Beirne family who lived in the 'Big House'* [in Jamestown]". [9] It remains a lovely lane for a scenic stroll down to the old river ford.

The high banked Fortarue, on private farmland, is visible at the end of the road on the left. It has a 41 m diameter interior with banks 6 m wide and from 2.2 m - 2.6 m in height. Quite a size. A 3 m wide entrance causeway is located to the north, north-east.[10] When I visited in springtime, it was a wild jungle and bluebells carpeted the ground floor of this substantial ring fort. In the 1930s Fortarue had a supernatural reputation.

"Fortarue...derived its name from a local belief that the fairies are to be seen there on bright nights. Lights are seen nearly every night and some people are believed to have seen small red men dancing about in the fort. Some people believe it unlucky to row boats at night near this place. One night a man was out fishing near it when suddenly a wind called the whirl-blast arose and swept the boat to the shore. Luckily the man was uninjured and did not fish there again." [11]

CORNACORROO

This townland is a little north of Rue, on the opposite bank of the Shannon from the northernmost segment of the Doon. The 'roo' part of its name could well indicate embankments. In Cornacorroo a sword blade was found in 1845 on the bed of the river. It was described as a small, perfect rapier blade, 45 cm long by 4 cm wide. People were probably making ritual depositions at this fording point, perhaps in gratitude for a safe crossing. Also found in this townland were a medieval brooch and a bronze pan. In the next townland of Curries was found a medieval plain bronze tube, that probably formed the ferule-end of a spear, measuring 22 cm in length. [12]

JAMESTOWN

Jamestown's rectangular walled town and castle at a strategic minor fording point on the Shannon were built by Sir Charles Coote in 1621-22 and named after the Stuart King James. As the river loops around it, the town site is naturally defended on three sides and the walls completed the defence, well - that was the plan. It was founded as a Plantation town following the decision in 1620 to plant Leitrim with loyal English settlers. Coote was one of them, due to being well connected, as a friend of Charles Villiers, who was a favourite of the king. The walls he built were 6-7 m high and 1.8 m wide; they enclosed an area, including his castle, of about 2 ha. Non-residents, the Catholic population, were not allowed inside its walls between sunrise and sunset. It became a defendable refuge for the settlers in times of war and was more important than Carrick on Shannon in its day.

To cross the river, Coote built a wooden bridge south of the town, that was replaced by a stone one in 1730. The current stone bridge was re-built about a century later. O'Rourke besieged the town in 1641-42, causing much starvation, but did not capture it, however a Catholic Ulster army did take it in 1648. [13] In 1683 it was described as having around 60 families living there, mostly outside the walls since the hostilities of the 1640s left it in ruins. [14] In 1689 it was captured for King William but Colonel Lloyd Sarsen, in command of a Jacobite force, re-took it in the same year. [15] As a result of the warfare leaving the town wrecked, it never achieved the hopes of its creators. *"Numerous cannon balls from this period were extant in Jamestown...*[and they were] *donated to the Diocesan Museum in Longford,"* local historian J J Guckian wrote. [16]

The town walls are mostly gone now, all that remains are the north gate, two sections of wall and a church ruin. The old fording point was perhaps where the weir is now. Sluice gates supported on five masonry piers were built in 1882. It's a fine piece of Victorian engineering that continues to help regulate water levels for navigation.[17] Situated on a rise above the weir is the extensive old corn (flour) mill, a building from 1730 that ran off river water power and later becoming an auxillary work house, during the Great Famine.[18] A weekly market used to be held along the wide main street and a fair ground was located in the triangular area between the main road (near The Cottage restaurant) and Lisduff Rd, near their junction, in the townland of Tully.[19]

Beside the mill and weir, the remains of the small 17th century church (17 m by 8 m), purportedly a Franciscan friary, stand in a graveyard beautifully situated beside the river, outside of the town walls. Its masonry is mixed and a few older cut stones are included in it, probably originating from an earlier church.[20] A dreadful event is recorded for this site in the year 1492, when Hubert Mac Rannell, the son of the heir to the chieftainship of Conmaicne Rein (south Leitrim), and sixteen others were slain and burnt in the church of Cell Srianain either by Eoghan Ua Ruaric (according to the Ulster Annals) or by Cathal Oge Mac Rannall and Muinter Carolan (Annals of the Four Masters).[21] The ruined church is probably on top of an earlier church of Kilshrianan, or Kiltrennan, in Irish Cill Srianáin, the Church of Trennan, a mystery saint. Its origins are lost in the mists of time. Some think that here was the location for the convent mentioned first in 1310 and described as a parish church in 1477. Archeologists are not convinced.[22]

Within the walls of Jamestown, the Sacred Heart church was built in 1812 as a small private chapel for the O'Beirne landlords and their tenants. It was enlarged in 1847 and the old church abandoned, however the old graveyard continues as a main burial ground for the region.[23]

The other notable feature at Jamestown was a star shaped fort overlooking the town from the top of a drumlin 170 m to the west of the village, on privately owned farmland (and not shown on maps). If you stop in the linear car parking area that overlooks the river and weir, behind you is an overgrown wilderness area on a hilltop. The thickly vegetated rectangular site area is 40 m by 46 m in size. The location gave it wide views over the ford area, making it an essential part of the defences of Jamestown. We don't know when it was constructed, however in 1622 it gets a mention as being already there, in a complaint that *"the king had already erected a fort at great charge"*, making the building of a walled town (Jamestown) seem an unnecessary duplication of funds.[24] It must have been a substantial fort as there's a reference to a garrison at Jamestown in 1543 and in 1646 of a hundred men and their officers.[25]

Archeologists describe the remains of the star fort as a rectangular earthen platform 20 m by 17.5 m and up to 1 m in height, with slight banks to the north 2.5 m wide and .70 cm high on the outside and to the south its banks are 4.3 m wide and 1.2 m high on the exterior. Rectangular corner bastions around 10 m by 6 m in size are offset in two directions at each angle and are defined by scarps 60 cm -1.2 m high. It's surrounded by a slight fosse (all overgrown) and bisected by a north-south field boundary wall that's near the west edge, west of which is grass covered, while it's overgrown on the east.[26] (More about star shaped forts in chapter 10.)

The true location of Jamestown's old parish church may have actually been further away, up the mail coach road a short distance, at a site of more ancient significance and elevated above flood levels. Referred to in the Annals as the Convent of Muintir Eolius in 1644, it was dedicated to St Mary and aligned with the Creevylea Franciscan Friary in Dromahair, north Leitrim. In 1648 Jamestown was taken by Catholic Confederate forces[27] and the friary was made famous in the year 1650, when a synod of bishops issued the 'Jamestown Declaration'. J J Guckian had local knowledge of the actual whereabouts of this synod, writing that - *"A local tradition...has it that a 'meeting of Bishops took place in a ringfort on my grandfather's land...in...Ballinwing,"* [beside Sheemore], he wrote.[28]

By 1653 the Franciscan community was dispersed and the last recorded Franciscan chapter meeting took place in 1658. The friars returned to Tully in the late 1700s but there were only four left in 1801, their building was dilapidated and they didn't stay much longer.[29] During the penal era many went into hiding around Gowel, Kiltubrid and in caves on the slopes of Sliebh an Iarainn. Some local place names record this.[30] *"The last friar of Jamestown was probably Fr. Anthony Dunne, who died before 1825. The Franciscan Brothers of the Third Order Regular had a school there at about the same time. This school seems to have closed by 1835"*. [31] Another source said that *"Bishop MacNamee describes [it] as the oldest school then in the diocese."* [32]

Apart from being a defendable bolthole for Protestant settlers in it's early years, Jamestown never came to much as it lay in ruins. But the main road from Dublin to Sligo continued to pass through it into the early 21st century. The arched medieval gateway through the old walls was a bit narrow for a major highway. Not surprisingly, it was damaged by a passing lorry in 1973 and so its top was removed.

TULLY

The townland of Tully, bordering Jamestown to the north, is believed to have been the true location of the Franciscan Friary. Indeed, on the 1836 1st edition of the OS map it does say 'convent', where there's now a farmhouse. J J Guckian called it a *"small convent on the old mail coach road and near the north west angle of the townland."* [33] The farm here was owned by generations of the Clyne family. In 2004 a plaque was erected on the house gable to commemorate the past friary (however the dates on it are misleading, in that the friars were only here on and off). [34]

Tully townland goes down to the Shannon River and it continues around to the edge of Jamestown village. It must have once had a high population, because a lot of ancient monuments have been found here, including a mystery mound, cashel, a possible enclosure and five ringforts. The cashel, in a wooded valley between drumlins on a rock outcrop, is defined by a revetted stone wall. The subcircular wall encloses an area 31 m by 27.5 m, but only the base courses survive, being 3-4 m wide and 50 cm high.[35]

As well, Tully was the site of a fulacht fia (ancient Deer Cooking Kitchen).[36] Fulacht fia, are mysterious structures dating from the Bronze Age. No-one knows much about them, although their use continued up to the post-medieval era. They typically take the form of a low, horse shoe shaped mound that's filled with heat shattered stones and charcoal. This mound surrounds a hearth and a wooden trough. Stones were heated in the fire and dropped into the water-filled trough to boil the water. And cook the deer. They are thought to have had other uses too, such as for brewing, dyeing cloth, or leather making. A hot bath, perhaps? Always located close to water, this one was close to the River Shannon, with an area of burnt and broken stone spread over 10 m by 5 m. This covered a pit and hearth, where excavators in 1994 found a barbed and tanged arrowhead.[37] In the nearby area five more fulacht fia were uncovered, recorded and destroyed in the making of the N4 Drumsna/Jamestown bypass, over a mere 5 km riverside stretch.[38]

The mound mentioned earlier is just south of the N4, on the west bank of the river. The subcircular grassy mound, 25 m by 20 m by 40 cm high, has not been excavated.[39] It could be a robbed out tomb perhaps, although the location doesn't match a typical tomb site. There is also a large overgrown ringfort on the riverbank too, that rises up from the western shore on the border of Tully and Jamestown, at a narrow point of the river where it was probably easily forded. Probably the earliest control point and defensive centre, it's across the road from the triangular old fair ground and near the fulacht fia site. It's no doubt older than the star fort above it on the hill to the south. This ringfort is quite large, at 41 m north - south by 25 m east west. The earthen bank, 6-7 m wide and up to 2 m high, surrounds a D shaped overgrown area. The west bank is truncated by the Lisduff road and its fosse recut as a deep road drain.[40] From the road you can view a section of the rath's curving bank, of what would have been an original 'checkpoint charlie' of its day, beside the old fording point on the Connaught and Ulster divide.

LISDUFF

The old mail coach road goes from Dublin to Sligo, via Drumsna and Jamestown, and north-westwards on to Carrick on Shannon via Tully and the next townland of Lisduff. Lisduff has a well built, but semi-ruined church ringed by an old enclosure. This enclosure is a marker for its antiquity - *"The existence of an ecclesiastical enclosure is arguably the key indicator of an early medieval ecclesiastical foundation. Sub circular and oval enclosures are synonymous with early ecclesiastical foundations and were used to demarcate sacred space,"* as archeologist Susan Curran notes.[41]

Leitrim has ten examples of this, with the Abbey of Annaduff the most impressive. Drumsna also has the possible site of Aed O'Connor's fort now enclosing the Methodist church ruin. Another and little known example is found here in the townland of Lisduff, perched up on an eminence that rises out of the low, boggy land, with views over to Sheemore, Sliabh an Ierainn and other prominent hills. Its antiquity is evident in a reference from the Jamestown school folklore collection, that also tells of a sonic place memory. *"There was a church in Lisduff near Jamestown before there was one, either in Jamestown or Carrick on Shannon. It is said that the bell can be heard ringing sometimes at night."*[42]

The archeological record states that the circular enclosure has a diameter of circa 20 m, with banks of one metre in height. Within this ring is a rectangular, roofed building with an interior 18 m by 5 m, that was originally a Catholic church and later a school.[43] J J Guckian wrote that an 1825 report on education in the region stated that the Lisduff school house was *"a good sized chapel and 102 pupils."*[44] The site is now used as a farmyard, but it's beside a small public road that comes off the mail coach road, so you can look at the outside.

When I thought this was all there was to discover, I'd only just scratched the surface! JJ Guckian believed that the original Catholic parish church was at Lisduff, before it was moved to Carrick on Shannon, taking the name St Mary's with it. He also thought that the adjacent townland of Cornaslieve housed part of the original Franciscan Friary, as well as an ancient burial ground, and that there was once a chapel in Cornaslieve, now all vanished.

A local resident showed me around. Looking over a fence across Cornaslieve townland, that rises up to some 100 m in height, higher than the surroundings, I saw broken stones poking through the grass in the backyard of a house. Many of them were cut stone pieces, indicating an old building may have been there. Perhaps this was the location of the Franciscan chapel? The townland name itself is intriguing. A glib translation from the Irish gives the Hill of the Mountain Land. Which seems a bit silly. In old Irish the prefix Cor can have another meaning - the Highland of the Crane, the sacred bird associated with death and escorting the spirit to the afterlife.[45] That seems appropriate to an ancient burial ground. But locals believe it to mean the Little Rocky Heights / Hillocks, I was told. This could also be a reference to stone piles of friary ruins. The vanished Cornaslieve chapel, St Mary's, was *"likely used as the parish church since Kiltoghert was confiscated"*, with Carrick's old parish church not erected until 1870 and taking the old name, St Mary's. A trace of it, in the form of a holy water font stone, existed when JJ Guckian was writing. *"This could be the Franciscan church of St Mary"*, his research concluded.[46]

CASTLECARRA

Continue up the tiny road north-westwards and you reach the Castlecarra crossroads, from where you can go to the left a short distance before turning right up to Summer Hill and Carrick on Shannon. To the right, the Castlecarra road, Bothar na Caiseal Chairrhe, goes east to Kiltoghert, site of the early parish church, an important early road connection from Carrick.

Turn left and you'll see the gates of a previous big house, at Castlecarra / Aghacarra on old maps, that's across the road. The name indicates a castle on a rocky site, but there's no sign of it now, though it would have been a significant location in its day. Perhaps it's under the junction with the road to Summer Hill. The old rusting entrance gates, recently replaced by bland modern gates, looked like rows of spears - a suitable statement of intent. Interesting confirmation of its significance is seen on an old OS map of Leitrim, where the only other place name shown anywhere near Carrick is Castlecarra. We know almost nothing about it now, but it may have been associated with the Plantation of Leitrim. Folklore Commission records mention a - *"a tyrant that lived at Castle Cara beside Carrick on Shannon"*. [47]

CLOGHER

Turning right along this Castlecarra road from Lisduff, you're heading eastwards and soon going around a small hill on the right. On the wooded hill above was the site of Grange Lodge, a big house with ancient origins. The townland name is Clogher, suggesting a convent. J J Guckian's book tells of old literary references to this townland, one of the earliest notable places. The remains of a ringfort, a corn mill, mill race and corn kiln lie on the northern townland border, close to the Castlecarra road. All in ruins or vanished now. [48] Around the back of the Clogher drumlin and near the big house site, a ringfort is seen on the OS map. It has a large internal diameter of 35 m and was planted out as an estate ornament tree-ring, with mature trees growing around it. [49]

The name Grange Lodge gives us the clue that the 18 -19th century house was located on fertile land that was originally a convent farm. Indeed, it was once part of the Boyle Abbey, run by the Cistercians. *"The Grange of Monterolis [contained]…four quarters of land belonging to the abbey, that is to say Liscally, Drumloman and Lismacagan, Clogher and Dromore."* [These are adjacent townlands.] [50] The Cistercian monks worked on their granges, farming, brewing ale and carrying on all manner of trades. They aimed to be self-supporting and when lay brothers were in short supply they hired labourers, locals who would have learned new farming and craft skills from the monks. [51]

Clogher can have several meanings. R. B. Warner, of the Department Antiquities, Ulster Museum, Belfast, was writing about the name of another Clogher, a town in Co. Tyrone. The simple translation of Stony Place didn't match the geology to justify such a name, as is also the case with Lisduff. So he concluded that -*"It seems probable that the name Clogher predated the early historic settlement, or rather referred to some feature which was already in existence at the time of its foundation. This feature may well have been some sort of ruinous stone structure."* [52]

FOXBOROUGH

A little north, north-west of Drumsna, Foxborough has a well preserved trivallate ringfort on the summit of a hill, one of only four in the county. It's the most well preserved and substantial of the four and, with an overall diameter of 75 m and 38 m within its banks, much larger than the other examples, that average around 24 m in diameter. Its presence, taking in expansive views, indicates an elite residence was here, while another three ring forts are located in the next townland north, just 200 - 300 m away in Lismoyle. [53] This suggests a large population in the past. Indeed, a school student reported of Foxborough in the 1930s, that *"there is only one house in it now, owned by John Beirne. Years ago there were about fifty families living in it during the famine time."* [54]

Ringforts can be seen in many locations because it's traditionally taboo to tamper with them. Over time, many people may have perished in them as a result of warfare. This is why they often had a hiding place, a stone lined underground chamber dug beneath them called a souterrain, where people could hide from danger and butter could be kept cool. Ringforts may have some restless ghosts in them or be haunted by sad memories. Tragic death locations were typically avoided by the living afterwards. Empty ringforts were thus left for nature and became wilderness places. Eventually the forts became the favoured haunts of Otherworld beings. They developed quite a supernatural reputation and are often called fairy forts now days. [55] Such is the evolution of a sacred site, in this case a site that's sacred to the fairies. The following accounts are typical of what people have traditionally encountered around forts.

"Fairies used to dwell in forts and there used to be lights seen from one fort to the other fort. There is a fort in Foxborough with three large rings around it. Long ago there was music heard and horses heard trotting in it". [56] *"Every night a light is seen going from Lisduff fort to Lismoyle fort, it is sometimes very small at other times it is large and three lights are seen at various times."* [57]

AUGHINTOBAR

North of Foxborough, the next townland of Aughintobar is the location of a holy well called St Brigit's. Famous for many cures, the well is a muddy hole in the ground. Beside it there's a remnant of a stone cross standing upright in the the ground. Fred Gill was the hereditary custodian of this well, before he passed away in 2021 in his late 80's. His father and his father before him were its custodians too. I helped him load up bottles at the well one balmy summer's day.

Traditionally reputed for its power of healing[58], Fred (RIP) told me that the well water is used for blessing oneself with when sick and is not for drinking. (It did not look wholesome for drinking.) Fred assured me that sick people of all ages were happy to receive a bottle of its water from him. His cheerful disposition would have been a great salve, as well.

Today the well is hardly known and it's not marked on any OS map. But the townland name proclaims it (tober meaning well) and it remains there yet, protected in a farm field. A little tree grove encircles it, with added barbed wire to keep cattle out. There is a subterranean mystery to this townland as well, a mythic tunnel mentioned in several Folklore Commission accounts, such as this one.

"In ancient times there was an underground channel, running from Charlestown (Sir Gilbert King's) straight to Ai an Tobair [now Aughintober)] near Lismoyle, where it came out. It is said that this channel was a place of refuge and retreat for armies and it is supposed that O'Rourke and his army retreated through it. It is now closed up with dirt and mud, but water can be seen, to the present day, spouting out on a hill near Lismoyle". [59]

HEADFORD

From Drumsna, go due north from the village, cross over the bridge above the N4, turn left at the roundabout and take a first right onto the tiny ridge road, to get to the townland of Headford. This was part of the ancient pedestrian route from the Drumsna ford over to the holy hill of Sheemore, via ridge tracks and a bog trackway. In a valley below the ridge near Headford Lough are the scant traces of Ballycloran Castle plus the tall leafy ruins of Headford House, as signposted on the 'Anthony Trollope Trail'.

The original castle here was associated with the MacDermott clan, who were rulers of Magh Lurg in Roscommon, so it wasn't their territory. Fort of the Heads is the literal translation of the Irish name and this refers to the decapitation of one's enemies, a popular past time for warlords drunk with power. Perhaps there were a series of buildings here, as it changed hands often, or heads. For Headford House, adjacent to the now vanished castle site, an 18 - 19th century date has been suggested, but the house was a ruin in the 1840's, so it can't have existed for long. Only the east and west gable walls of this possibly three-story house survive, reaching to their full height and mostly ivy clad. [60] In a sheltered location behind the ridge and held together by ivy roots, the walls have escaped being toppled by wind. For now, the green towering walls merge with more modern cattle yards. From elite class building, to cattle class stockyard.

The big house ruin was an inspiration for the first novel of acclaimed English novelist Anthony Trollope, who lived briefly in Drumsna as he investigated a crooked post master. His moonlighting as a nascent novelist isn't that notable from a literary point of view, but it does give insights into the lives of the peasantry in the 1840s, just before the Great Famine began, and shines a light of those dark feudal days.
[61]

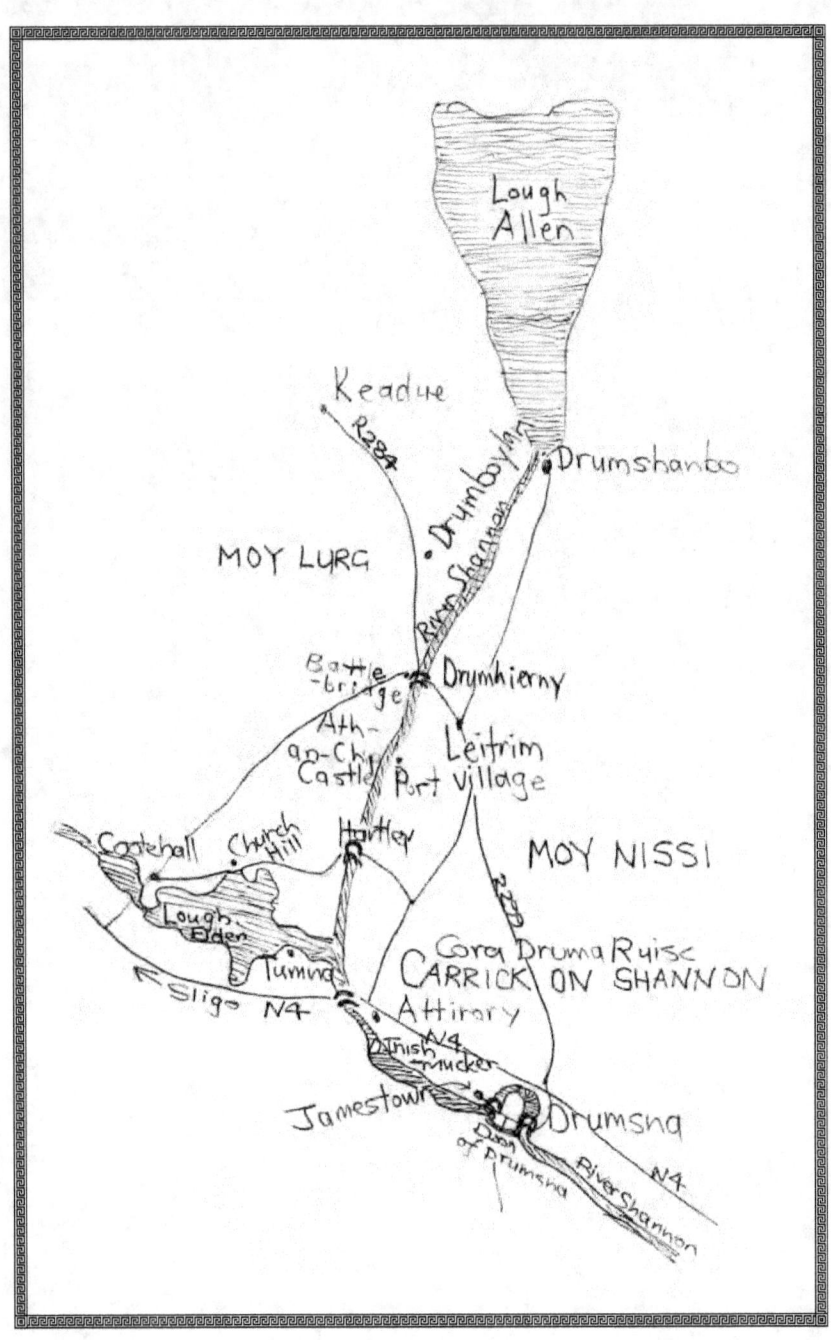

Chapter 3
River Crossings

Developments in the Late Iron Age

Fir Belg tribes of archaic Connaught in Galway had thrived and multiplied. By the start of the current era it must have got crowded. Seeking sword-land to spread into, they rewarded allied tribes for their military services by giving them dominion over buffer states on the edge of the Ulster/Connaught divide. The job of these Collas (bands of fighting men) was to defend those lands and thus vassal states eventually ringed the Ulster border all the way from the north-west to south-east. These groups were collectively known as the Airghialla, anglicised to Oriel. Airghialla is Old Irish for Eastern Subject Peoples, a reference to the power base of the Fir Belg to the west, to whom the vassal states paid their dues.

The buffer states were peopled by various tribes. The Manapi was one, a late coming group known for its seafaring and sea trading, who first settled along the western coastline. Their top god was Mannanan Mac Lir, Lughaid Conmac was his son. Septs of the Manapi were planted at bases along the coastal inlets, where they became known as the Conmaicnamare - the Young Sea Hounds. This shortened to Connemara (and from it evolved the McNamara surname) and they became an important presence in an arc stretching from Na Forbacha (Fir Belg), west of Galway city, north to Mannin Bay, named for the Manapi, near Clifton in Mayo. The name also evolved into Conmhaícne (pronounced con-mac-nee) and this tribe eventually spread further north, including into modern day Leitrim, from around the 6th century, it's thought. The Sil Muiredaig branch of the Connaught Ui Bruin of Magh Seola in Galway, after battle with the Calraige tribe, where they won lands north of Croghan in 752, expanded into Leitrim and Sligo's northern parts and these areas were then called Ui Bruin Breifni.

The southern part of Leitrim became known as Magh Rein and this was Conmaicne territory. In his 1938 History of Leitrim T. M. O'Flynn calls this tribe the Cormacs. This might be explained by entries in the Annals that refer to the country of the eastern Conmaicne, being Annaly, of the O'Farrells in Co. Longford, and Muintir Eolais of the Mac Rannalls, that was ruled by these two families who descended from Cormac, son of King Fergus. [1]

Muintir Eolais, meaning the Land of the Descendents of Eolais, was the name for what later became the Barony of Leitrim and Maothail/Mohill in south Leitrim between circa 800 to 1600. Muintir Eolais was the political dynasty of the Reynolds, Shanley, Mulvey and Farrell, the main nobles of Conmaicne Rein, whose overlords were the Mag Rannaills. The territory of Muintir Eolais is a sub-unit of Conmaicne Rein, as it excludes Carrigallen Barony. The name Eolus also means knowledge in Irish.[2] In the medieval era territorial boundaries were often fluid, reflecting the constantly shifting power bases in those edgy times.

Early Christian sites

In the early days of Christianity there were few towns in Ireland, but this changed as ecclesiastical settlements were established. Missionaries had a huge job in overturning the dominant Pagan paradigm. So they gravitated to sites of importance, where they might be granted land and power. And, as O'Connor puts it - *"It was missionary policy to choose sites for principal churches near the seats of secular power in order to exert maximum influence."* [3]

There were practical considerations of good access, water and farmland, too. These were to be had at the many royal sites where they established. They were typically fertile places that often featured megalithic funerary mounds and monuments, the churches of their day, that bear witness to the ritual activities of countless generations of the cruthin, indigenous peoples. This clustering of monuments followed a continuum back to Neolithic times, up to some 6,000 years ago. Various types of megalithic monuments include the passage, portal, court and wedge tombs. Some important sites have all three tomb types in their vicinity, showing continuous habitation across millennia, Fenagh being a great example.

Geology had a strong bearing underlying this occurrence. *"While each tomb type generally has its own particular siting criteria, Cooney (1979, 85) discovered that all the tombs in Co. Leitrim are on, or are in close proximity to, the small proportion of the county with relatively good podzolic or rendzina soils."* [4] Leitrim's monastic sites were also typically found in the few limestone soil (or sandy) areas, amidst a sea of heavy clay soil and challenging terrain. There's good reason for this, when the properties of limestone are considered. *"Soluble phosphate, the principal vegetational contribution to the calcium compounds from which growing animals make bones, is between two to four times higher on limestones than on most other rock types and only the limestones offer adequate trace elements for animal growth, such as copper and cobalt,"* Ian Stewart wrote. [5]

To maintain clan hegemony in fertile locales, earlier monuments that proclaimed territoriality were incorporated within the sacred enclosures of subsequent septs, as a *"visible illustration of the potency of ancestral forces"*, as John Waddell puts it. *"There is little doubt,"* he continued, *"that royal sites like Tara were exploited as symbols of ancestral territorial claims and were manifestations of primordial pedigrees in early historical times."* Or, as Conor Newman suggested - *"the need to assert hereditary legitimisation…[was] a compelling force in later pre-history too, when a desire for ancestral validation is proclaimed in the assimilation of older monuments in the fabric of new ones."* [6] Many a fake family tree was created to cement the claim, as well.

In Pagan times, elite families worked closely with Druid advisors, the law men and cultural experts of the tribe, to maintain cultural heritage and social harmony. The new religion was a huge threat to indigenous authority and was greatly resisted. Intricate manoeuvring would have been needed to neutralise the Druid's influence on the tribe, if the Christians were actually able to. I imagine the Druids only paid lip service to the new regime. Usually a chief gave over lands for the early Christian establishments and they often took on administrative or priestly roles in them, thus receiving new streams of income. So, by donating their important 'palaces' they bolstered their positions of power and authority. (In archeological assessment these 'palaces' are not as grand as the medieval descriptions would have them.)

Early monasteries were often located along the edgy zones of provincial borders and Annaduff Abbey is a good example. Strategic posts of elite warrior clans were also often placed in such locations, to defend borders in their fortified homes and garrisons.[7] Monasteries keyed into the territorial function as well, not only providing religious training and services, hospitality and health care to travellers and the infirm - they also hosted armies on the move. This has been encompassed in the words hospice, hospital and hospitality. Their first allegiance would have been to the military might of the land.

With roles of quasi-clerics and administrators of the monasteries, erenaghs (aireannach) and coarbs, the hereditary lay guardians, were from clans of the literate class, who promoted scholarship, helped to administer to the sick and provision their houses of hospitality. Their services were paid for with income raised in the church's termon / airchennach lands. [8] Following the Plantation of Leitrim, churches and termons (meaning Sanctuary Lands) were confiscated and granted to the new Established Church. The Glebe lands, as they were then called, were kept for financing the upkeep of Protestant ministers.[9] In those dark days, Catholic people were forced to pay tithes to the new church, as well as rent for what was often their own ancestral homelands. They endured a slavish, feudal existence, when feudalism had long ended elsewhere.

EARLY MEDIEVAL LEITRIM

Commonest monumental features of the time, and still evident in the landscape, are the ringforts, also known as liss / lios, rath, dun/doon, fairy fort etc. These circular or sub-circular walled enclosures for their farmsteads protected people and livestock from predatory wolves at night. The earth bank walls, with prickly trees planted, or timber palisades, on the top, had an outer fosse (ditch) around them. In rocky areas, circular enclosures of drystone walls are called cashels. They were in use from the Bronze Age until late medieval times, when wolves were all exterminated. In the wilds of Leitrim, wolves probably hung on longer than elsewhere. A report from the 1680's stated that *"the wolves which were very numerous in this county are now very few"*. They was still a big bounty paid for killing them at that time. [10]

Most folk lived in wooden houses within ringforts, 90% of which are univallate, having one bank and ditch only.[11] Often sited on hill tops for defensive purposes, they were connected together both visually and by walking tracks. After abandonment they become sacred sites, in effect, known as fairy forts, that were respected and preserved, keeping their resident fairies safe.[12] (A student of the author in a dowsing class, an archeologist, once commented - *"I didn't know that the fairies actually exist, but if they protect the ancient sites - I'm all for them!"*)

Leitrim was a hotbed of ecclesiastical activity in the early medieval era, from 400 - 1100CE. Of the 1,978 recorded archeological monuments in the county, 70% are from this era. Many more lie hidden and lost under grass and brambles, though new surveying techniques, such as Lidar (ground penetrating laser mapping), are revealing more, with another 36 early medieval sites added to the register following a Lidar survey of south Leitrim in 2012.[13] Church founder saints were numerous in Leitrim, with around fifteen of them; while St Patrick and St Bridget made guest appearances too.[14]

Irish place names can alert us to sites. Names with 'kil' in them can be a good indication of a church site. However, it can also be a misinterpretation of 'coill', the word for forest. Visual clues on the ground include traces of clustered settlements. As these were not the norm until perhaps the 9-10th centuries, they might indicate monastic sites. As well as religious activities, the early centres featured craftworkers, artists, scholars and teachers, etc. Aristocratic family allegiances ensured their security and protection. This fostered the evolution of urbanisation and was a model for economic development.

Some monasteries attracted students and pilgrims who boosted the local economy too. Over time these establishments accumulated property, treasures and prestige, and sometimes a huge lust for political power too. Their great wealth made them targets for raids from the Vikings, as well as from other rival tribes, so some defensive features were built into them. Circular walled enclosures around the monasteries evoked sacred protection and they were considered holy sanctuaries, even for people on the run.

ANNADUFF

Beside the Shannon, south of Drumsna, Annaduff Abbey is just before the end of navigation on the river. Accessible by boat, it had a strategic location at Annaduff (the Dark Marshland), where its core part was founded on an island amidst marshes, making it easily defendable. Once an important abbey, today there's little trace, only the fast deteriorating, heavily ivied ruin of a late medieval church. As local historian Des Guckian (RIP) told me, if something is not done soon to save this ruin, a big wind might just blow it down.

The once-prestigious graveyard is mostly grass today, with few stone markers, but lots of bumps in the ground. Where are all the grave stones? you might wonder. *"A gravestone may sink into the soil by as much as 2ft [60 cm] per century. That, in itself, is an appropriate symbol for the sinking into oblivion of many one-time prominent monastic sites. To the fore amongst these would have to be the ancient Abbey of Annaduff,"* lamented Guckian.[15] Yet in its hey day, this place would have been full of chapels and huts, a forge, hospital and scriptorium; people carving stone crosses and memorials, etc. Ancient sites in the wider vicinity show that the area has long been well populated, too. Perhaps there was a Pagan or Druid centre at this site before?

Abbey tradition goes back to its founding by St Coimin Ea in 650. (However, some accounts say it was founded by St Patrick, before he crossed the Shannon at Drumsna and founded the nearby Kilmore Abbey.) The ea in Coimin's name tells us that he was associated with St Colmcille's monastery at Iona, some say he was an Abbot there. Coimin, (or Comin), went on to live at Iona and died there in 669. Aligned with the monasteries at Kiltoghert, Kiltubrid, Fenagh, Cloone, Mohill and Kiltrennan/Jamestown, the abbey thrived until the early 13th century. From 1270-1470 it was served by the Augustinians of Mohill Monastery, but after then it was it's own independent Parish. [16]

Annaduff Parish is one of the oldest in the Diocese of Ardagh and Clonmacnoise, with its present boundary identical to what it was before 1155. The long and narrow parish is around 10,000 acres in size, with 66 town lands. It was once covered in thick Oak woods and bogs with a mostly low population, except for fertile pockets on sandy soil (old red sandstone) and limestone. It is partly bounded by rivers, the Shannon to the west, to the east the Eslin, running down to the Shannon at Rooskey, and a river that flows into the Headford Lough, to the north. This suggests ancient tribal boundaries being re-purposed for the parish, as it closely co-incides with the territory of the MacShanley clan. [17]

Geophysical and Lidar studies in 2016 by archeologist Susan Curran have revealed some of the archaic character of the site. *"Combined, the surveys revealed three potential concentric ecclesiastical enclosures at Annaduff, the southern most parts having been subsumed by the road in front, but they must have taken the outer enclosure close to the original river bank"*, she wrote. [18] Triple banks show the size and importance of the site, however, like most other sites, it has not had much archeological investigation. In its day it was packed with buildings, their fabric all recycled now. As Des Guckian puts it - *"The original buildings would have been built of timber. The central building would have been small, probably no more than 12 ft by 10 ft. Other small buildings surrounded it. The monks would have built themselves small wooden cells. There might have been 30 scattered buildings in all... Typical of an important abbey...there were three concentric, almost circular banks around the core. These embankments were longest on the outside and shorter on the inside. A monastery was a place of refuge. Anyone, even those who had done bad things, was allowed inside the outer ring. You had to be a much better class of person to be allowed inside the second ring. Only the holiest were allowed inside the inner ring. These would have included monks, the abbot and the kings."* [19] Behind the adjacent St Mary's Church, built in 1839, you can see remnants of the curving banks that once enclosed the abbey.

Breifne overlords, the O'Rourkes, were associated with Annaduff Abbey. They buried their clan at the monastery of Clonmacnoise, founded 549, and they donated this abbey to them, in exchange for the privilege. (So famous was Clonmacnoise that, if buried there, you were said to go "straight to heaven".) But when the graveyard at Clonmacnoise closed, from the late 18th century they were buried in the O'Rourke family plot at Annaduff, the next best location.

Annal entries tell us of how, in the year 1011 Brian Boru, one of Ireland's "greatest princes", sailed his fleet of boats on a conquest mission up the Shannon to raid Ulster, staying at Annaduff Abbey en route, along with ally and rival King Malachy (the second most important Irish king at that time) and a contingent of Viking boats. From his base further down the Shannon at Kincora (now Killaloe), Co. Clare, he was a regular visitor to Annaduff Abbey. A house of hospitality is noted for here in 16th century sources. [20] One can imagine the necessity of a pleasant and sustaining stop-over here. There would have been political importance to their visits too, for, as Curran points out - *"the trivallate and bivallate raths in particular can point to the location of political centres."* [21]

Brian was successful in his battle and he took as hostage a local king, clad in chains, back to Kincora. Apart from warmongering, Brian was known for his enlightened rule as a high king and he *"confirmed Armagh as the ecclesiastical capital of Ireland...churches were rebuilt, bridges were erected, roads were improved and education was cultivated."* [22] He died fighting the Vikings at the Battle of Clontarf in Dublin in 1014.

In King Brian's days the shore line of the Shannon was much closer to the abbey. But after drainage works for land reclamation in the 19th century, the river became much narrower and so the shore is now some distance away. The old main road runs along the front of the site, parallel to the main N4 road. The turn-off to it from the new N4 road is opposite the Mohill road turnoff. Then take the turn first right soon after.

The ruined medieval parish church of Annaduff is hard to see under its heavy mantle of ivy and it is not safe to go inside of it. Best to just look at the outside. The doorway has been modernised and there are two corbels at roof level with carved heads. A few stones from the early abbey were incorporated into the church's south end, local historian Tony Ward noted. [23] In the east end is preserved an acclaimed 15th century decorated window that was inserted into the original window. It's quite special and possibly depicts the heads of a king and a queen, one on each side of it. It's design is said to be a perpendicular style that's rare in Ireland,

that may have been influenced by the north doorway at Clonmacnoise cathedral. [24]
"This delicately-executed masterly sculpture has two spears above the royal heads. This represents the Tain War, across the Shannon...As part of that conflict the Doon of Drumsna, an enormous fortification, was built in present day Co. Roscommon, just across the Shannon from Annaduff," Des Guckian suggested in a newspaper article. [25]

In the graveyard are West Breifne chiefs Bryan O'Rourke and his wife Margaret, with a grave slab sporting their coat of arms from 1767. There's a tradition that a church bell is buried in soft ground somewhere 200 m from the old church.[26] Annaduff has a few ancient sites in the vicinity. A megalithic tomb features on a height, on the archeological record described as a barrow (Iron Age tomb) located on the north facing crest of a hill in Annaduff Glebe. [27] The following story, from Folklore Commission files, seems to be a reference to it.

"Once there lived on Sheemore three giants and it is said that they challenged each other in weight throwing. The first giant threw a stone which landed in Notley's Hill in Annaduff. The second giant threw one the same size, and it landed a short distance from the first one. The third giant threw one which rested across the other two, forming the shape of a house. These stones are still to be seen in Annaduff and cattle take shelter under them. It is said that the stones were 14' long and that they stuck down 6' in the ground, when thrown". [28]

CARRICK ON SHANNON

The main county town, and the smallest in Ireland with just under 5,000 inhabitants, Carrick was another important ford on the Shannon, at a narrow point of the river. The Irish name Cora Droma Ruisc has been translated as the Stony Ford of the Ridge in the Marsh. But this could be a mistranslation, as we'll see later. It's a scenic town firmly focussed on the river, that attracts visitors from far and wide for fishing and boating on it, as well as the 42 lakes within 10 km of the town. The St George Heritage Centre and Workhouse can be visited there also.

After Drumsna ceased to be the terminus of river traffic, with navigation improved from the 1840s, Carrick became the major depot for river trade, with boats transporting timber, cement, hardware and Guinness stout between Carrick, Dublin, Athlone and Limerick. After the closure of the Grand Canal Company in 1960, transport shifted to the roads and later, from 1862, onto the new railway service. The graceful stone bridge across the Shannon was built in 1846, as a famine relief work scheme. It allowed more boat traffic through and replaced the earlier nine arched stone bridge, that was built in 1718. Before that one there was a wooden bridge with a castle at each end on the opposing banks and this castle was depicted on the Seal of the Carrick on Shannon Corporation (1613 - 1826).[29] A section of stone ruin left standing beside the eastern approach to the bridge is a remnant of it (the sign is below). The Castle of Carrickdrumruske and the town were the territory of Brian Og O'Rourke until his dispossession in 1603, after which it was granted to Sir Maurice Griffith. It later passed into the hands of the St George family, who were landlords of the town for 300 years, living in Hatley Manor, beside The Dock, a stately home of the 1830s.

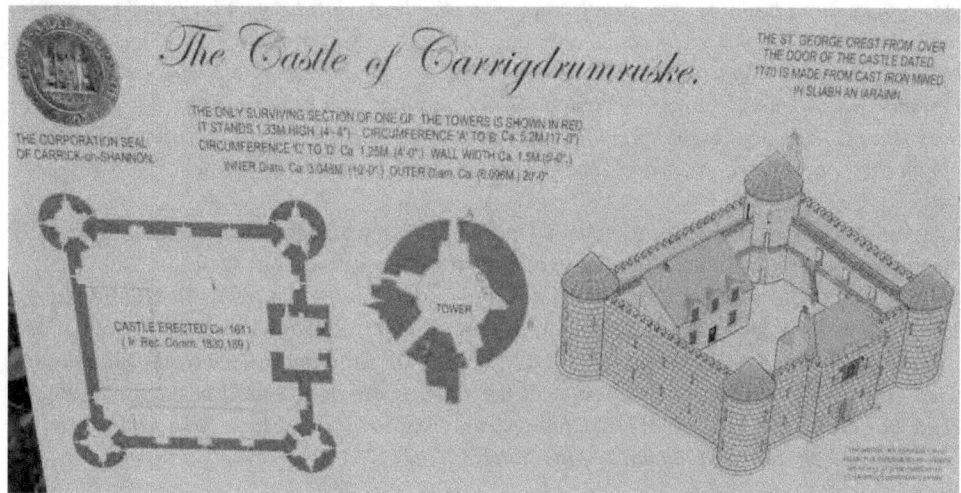

Carrick was the county's first urban settlement that developed by 1611 around the newly built castle and it gained borough status in 1613.[30] The wooden bridge gave a vital link on the Dublin to Sligo road and also to Cortober, the suburb across the river. That was fortunate for the Irish, because Catholics were banned from living in Carrick for all of the 17th and most of the 18th centuries. They had to live on the other side of the river at The Liberty, outside of the borough boundary and now called Cortober, the Hill of The Well. The Liberty is just across the bridge and if you walk up the hill road beside the pub on the river, the streetscape of more vernacular style homes has a very different feel to ex-Protestant-only Carrick on Shannon.

SUMMERHILL AND TOWNPARKS

The fording point in modern Carrick used to be called Ath Cora Conaill, the Ford at Conaill's Weir, now Townparks townland. It would have been in the form of a stone and clay weir across the shallowest point. On a fatal day in 1270, the Duke of Ulster William D'Burgh would have brought his army over it and headed eastwards, where, as MacLochlainn explains, *"some of Aedh O'Conchobar's forces attacked and killed some English in Feda Conmaicne* [a forested area near Carrick]. *Dinenn confirms Rúisc means skirmish – my research shows Druma Rúisc, Hill of the Skirmish, is Summerhill, the true Irish place name for this place. Before 1270, Townparks was called (Ath) Corra Conaill, but after the battle it was Corra Druma Rúisc"*.[31]

Summerhill in Carrick on Shannon has also gone by the name of Gallows Hill, for the gruesome public hangings that the English inflicted. Summerhill was the jolly new name eliciting an aura of pleasure. Or, perhaps there's a sinister undertone here, a Pagan association with the Other world, the old eternal Summer Land of the dead. The earlier name Hill of the

Skirmish, where the natives fought the invaders back successfully, is perhaps a better memory to be retained in a place name, showing that the Irish were not always under-dogs during colonisation.

Nearer the river, Leitrim County Council chambers are situated where was once the most hated building in town. *"The jail in Carrick on Shannon, now in ruins, was built in 1822. It was a very large building and struck terror into the hearts of the people. There is a tunnel leading from the old jail to the courthouse and the prisoners were brought through the tunnel, to 'face' the judge who used to arrive in a carriage surrounded by mounted police. The death sentence was frequently pronounced and the gallows may still be seen. Several are buried in the grounds. There was great rejoicing a few years ago when the old jail was abandoned* [and] *a man flung the first slate off amid loud cheers."* [32]

Like many crossing points for travellers, Carrick has a long established tradition of friendly hospitality which continues to this day. Indeed, it is transformed on weekends with swarms of 'hen' and 'stag' parties. The Bush Hotel is perhaps best known for its hospitality. In the 1930s it was recorded by local school pupils that - *"Some years ago this building was a long thatched one storey house having about ten windows in front and was surrounded by a low wall. Outside the hotel grew an enormous Chestnut tree which spread its branches across the road as far as the chapel. It was deemed unlucky to destroy that bush which was in consequence replanted at the back of the hotel"*. [33]

Carrick town and vicinity had several ring forts in it. But from the 17th century they became unnecessary and out of fashion. Many were then levelled and built over as the town grew. This must have been catastrophic for the fairies that had moved in and felt safe in their circular grounds of sanctuary, that for generations were taboo to be disturbed. The Folklore Commission recorded some consequences of the destruction of ring forts in local lore collected in the 1930s. *"The present Marist Convent, Carrick-on-Shannon is built on an old fort.* [The Marist Sisters Order moved into this convent at Mount St Joseph in 1891.] *The old people say that long ago the fairies used to live in this fort and every night they are supposed to have come out on the roofs of the houses on Gallows Hill and Jamestown Road where they remained till daybreak singing. ...The site on which eighty two houses have recently been built at Lisnagat, Carrick-on-Shannon, is supposed to have been an old fort and, quite recently strange noises have been heard and lights seen in the old fort."* [34]

ATTIRORY

A southern suburb of Carrick, Attirory was the site of a once important burial ground that overlooked the river and may have pre-dated Christianity. Marked as Caldragh on the old maps, this name designates an ancient burial site. In the Archeological Inventory it is listed as being on the top of the prominent drumlin there, but there isn't much to be seen. The roughly circular earth platform has a diameter of 180m and the best preserved piece of bank and a slight external fosse is at the north west. In the centre is a rectangular platform with a radial bank. There's also a D shaped bullaun stone somewhere.[35] It's all covered with grass and barely visible, but a Lidar survey, conducted by Susan Curran shows evidence of the enclosure and rectangular platform. [36] In 2015, when roadworks were undertaken there, human remains were found, a local landowner told me.

INISHMUCKER

Perhaps named for the Black Pig of the provincial boundary, this island sits in the middle of the River Shannon, a little south west of Attirory. It's now connected to the mainland, but previously the river was deeper and it was a true island. A highly strategic boundary location, no ancient sites on it are mentioned in the Archeological Inventory, however folklore suggests that it did have past import.

"There is a hidden treasure up in the middle of the river Shannon... about two miles from the Quay in Carrick on Shannon, towards Limerick. There is an island near the place which is called the Seven Acre island. There was a fort on the island and there were fairies in it. The fairies had gold and they hid it in the river. Sometime after, monks built a monastery on the island...The ruins are still there, even up to the present day. The treasure is hidden someplace among the ruins. Some strange man went looking for it twenty years ago and a horse appeared to him three times. Through the fright he got he died from his nerves. No one is allowed to go near the treasure now because they might also die". [37]

And, in records from 1604, there were other establishments there. Inchmucker is described as *"having a 'castle or fortress', and it was to be granted to Tadhg O'Rourke, brother of Brian Og, along with all the castles, lordships and manors in County Leitrim in perpetuity,"* notes J J Mac Dermott. [38]

PORTANEOGHT

Further up the Shannon there were several other shallows where river crossings were possible at minor fording points, as the name Port in Portaneoght suggests. This townland was also a secret location for religious gatherings in the Penal Days of Catholic oppression and an illuminating report comes from a local school. *"There is a Mass bush on the land of my uncle John Hunt at 'the Ford' in Portaneoght, Carrick on Shannon. Mass was said there in the Penal Days. He has, in the house, a quern, with a cross on it; it is said that it was used to grind the wheat for the Altar Bread which was used at the Mass Bush".* [39]

Archeology recognises the presence of bullauns - boulders with 'cup marks', hollows carved into them that are often found at early Christian sites or in important duns and cashels - but offers no explanation for their function. Some of the folklore from the schools collections have them called 'holy water fonts'. But some look likely to have been used to grind substances in. Medicinal herbs perhaps? However in this story's case, we find a continuation of pre-Christian rituals of reverence for the sacred corn, the Old English word for their staple grain. Spiritual connection to the grain could be described as a totemic religion, similar to Australian Aboriginal tradition. Bullauns may well have been used to ritually grind corn for the making of sacred cakes, when the wheel of the year turned to harvest festival time. Here, in this simple report we find a quern, a grinding stone of probable pre-Christian date, that's been re-purposed with a cross and used for grinding corn for church altar bread. A breaktaking leap across the paradigms, showing that aspects of early Christianity in Ireland were a continuation of indigenous Pagan practises.

Going back to the ringforts around Carrick on Shannon, a school pupil in the 1930s reported that there were - *"a chain of forts in the Liss - Corryolis - Portaneought district. My Grandmother told it to me - They are near each other, each one on a hill and are of a similar description. They are all circular in shape with an outer earthen fence and trench and an underground chamber. Each was guarded by three white horses who paid a round of visits to the other forts every night. They were seen travelling with fiery breath and 'fleet as the wind'.*

"Lis na gcag is the next townland. It got its name from three huge black cats who are supposed to guard it still. On the next hill stands Lios na bree ['fort of the badgers']. Badgers ruled this fort. Fiery shapes have been seen moving from one fort to another and crying and wailing heard. My great grand-father cut the bushes in one of these forts. Shortly after he fell ill. Only for Father Mick Hanly of Ard an Aifrinn he would have died; but he lost all his cattle that year. The owner of another of these forts, levelled it, so as to improve the appearance of his field. The man he employed to do it was dead within the year, while he himself was found dead, the next Holy Thursday with his throat cut by his own hand". [40]

The name of the townland of Corryolus, just north of Carrick, on the river junction where the Boyle river meets the Shannon, has great antiquity - the Weir of Eolus, the Conmaicne ancestor.

PORT

On the banks of the Shannon and upstream from Carrick, Port is believed to be the site of the legendary castle of Ath-an-chip, in Irish Caislén Átha an Chip ar brú Maighe Nisse, that included a house of hospitality for Moy Nissy. This Old Castle at Port, as it was called in 1660 (aka Port Shan Castle), was built by Norman invader Miles MacCostello around 1245, as he wanted to expand out from territory on the west side of the Shannon (Moy Lurg, that became the Barony of MacCostello). But he didn't last long, the sons of Aed O'Connor helped Cathal Mag Ragnaill expel him and the castle was then mainly used by the two premier clans, the O'Rourkes and MacRagnaills. No trace of it remains today.

Like many important establishments, it was preceded by an earlier one. Largely forgotten now, there was previously an abbey at Port that was founded sometime in the 6th century. It was called Leitrim Abbey (even though Leitrim village is a few kilometres distant) and St McLeighus is named as its abbot in several historic references. McLeighus had his festival day on February 8th and his father was said to have been an attendant of St Patrick. The Abbey closed down in 1218, as did many others around that time.

Port is mostly known for its association with the only victorious battle of a ruling Gaelic clan over the Anglo-Norman army, between Aed O'Connor the Connaught king and Walter de Burke, that occurred on 28th of July, 1270. After the deadly skirmish in Carrick, De Burgh's forces moved northwards into Moy Nissy, where they rested overnight at Port before the battle, no doubt enjoying hospitality at the Port castle. Then they fought the documented Battle of Connaught at Atha an Chip castle and Aedh O'Conchobar had his glorious victory. *"The location of this has alluded researchers, until recently. Research concludes Port Shan Castle (Downs Survey) on Port townland is the site of the castle. O'Rian et al (ITS) agree Ath an Chip is Drumhierney townland, beside Battlebridge, proving this is Ath an Chip Castle".* [41]

In Port townland archeologist Susan Curran found indicators of the site's past importance.

Remote sensing surveys revealed the presence of a pair of bivallate forts, a highly unusual occurrence enough and they are only 25 m apart.[42] The bivallate rath was associated with high society and only 10% of all raths of Leitrim (perhaps eight) have two concentric banks and ditches around them.[43] Being situated beside the Shannon River, the western border of Moy Nissy, it probably hosted a garrison of high status military defenders, perhaps hereditary warrior clans, planted by the Moy Nissy chieftain in exchange for territorial defence at the minor fording point.

The western rath is largest, with a 36 m internal diameter, the other rath a bit down the slope is about 25 m in its internal diameter. Traces of rectangular structures were also noted inside and attached to the perimeter of the raths.[44] To the south, the townland beside Port is Caldragh, a name that bestows the ancient designation of a burial place. It may have serviced the original abbey at Port and perhaps it also received the slain from the 1270 Battle of Connaught.

LEITRIM VILLAGE

Leitrim village developed in association with the canal and quays from the early 1800s. But there were settlements here earlier. In a report of the county made in 1683 it was remarked that Leitrim had once been a considerable village, but there were no signs of a town then, only the ruins of an old castle.[45] Nowadays the village is a good stopping point for refreshment, food and the hiring of electric bicycles, which provide perfect travel options in this region, where there is lots to see in a small area. There's a lot of boat traffic here as well, since the canal system was re-vamped.

The original castle was built here in the 15th century by the ruling Mac Ragnaill clan. Built to repel the O'Rourkes from taking Muinter Eolais, it was destroyed in 1530 when the O'Donnells of Donegal desolated the area. It was the O'Rourkes who re-erected it ten years later, circa 1540, then burnt it down in 1580 to prevent the English from acquiring it, but they took it anyway. Brian Og O'Rourke re-took it again and after the Battle of Kinsale in 1602, O'Sullivan Beare was hosted there, after a horror journey of escape to one of the last Gaelic lords' strongholds. It was besieged by 3,000 English soldiers in 1603, as a result. O'Rourke managed to escape, but only a single length of mortared limestone wall remains of the castle, after the English systematically destroyed it.[46] The site, which had a police station built over it, is sign posted from the centre of the village and is near the canal.

DRUMHIERNY

In 2020 there was a celebration made for the 750th Anniversary of the Battle of Ath an Chip. Drumhierny (the Ridge of the Master) was a thick woodland when the Folklore Commission stories were recorded. It became the estate of Drumhierny Lodge, which has been lately transformed into an eco-resort. On the eastern shore of the Shannon, *"Battlebridge was for many years the main road to Sligo from the East, placing Drumhierny in a very advantageous and strategic position."* [47]

A clue to the importance of this townland is the presence of no less than seven enclosures situated here, ranging in diameter from 25 m to 33 m in diameter. One has a mature Oak tree in its centre, no doubt planted as an 'estate ornament' by the idle elite. [48]

BATTLEBRIDGE

You can take a scenic, circuitous route from Leitrim village to get to Tumna, our final location this chapter, by going around Lough Eiden/Drumharlow. You travel first through the tiny village of Battlebridge, that's opposite Drumhierny, on the western shore of the Shannon. In Irish its name is Béal Átha an Chatha, the Ford of the Battle. Pupils at Ardcarne school in Roscommon in the 1930s wrote that Battlebridge was named for a battle fought "long ago" - perhaps the Battle of 1270 - and they recorded what may well be physical evidence for this. *"There is a quarry near the bridge and a couple of years ago when the workmen were engaged in blasting, some bones were turned up, believed to be human bones"*.[49]

DRUMBOYLAN

Further upriver there are more minor fording points. The next most important one was at Drumboylan, where, in the 1930s, school students reported - *"Tradition says that when Saint Patrick visited Connacht he crossed from Leitrim into Roscommon at the ford in Drumboylan."*[50] Drumboylan is an ancient fording place. A wooden footbridge crossed the river here, while on the Leitrim shore there's a large island, Inis na gCon, that once had a stone causeway for fording eastwards. River dredging has since pushed its rocks up onto the shore of the island. This traditional ford was also taken by O'Sullivan Beare and his weary people towards the end of their awful trek from County Cork in 1603, fleeing for their life after the Battle of Kinsale.[51]

"It is believed that St. Patrick in one of his crossings of the Shannon near Drumboylan was hissed at by an enormous serpent in the river. It is related that St Patrick chained him to a rock in the bed of the river and there he remains. It is also said that every seventh year, he gives a plunge, and drenches any person, or object, within reach. He is supposed to be at a point that is called, where the three Shannon's meet."[52] [This location is presumably where the River Boyle meets the Shannon.]

TUMNA CHURCH

Turn left just after the Battlebridge pub and camp ground. On the right you'll soon be passing Tumna Church, once the parish church, not to be confused with Tumna Abbey, our next port of call. Here is a fine shell of a building (merely roofless) and worth a stop to wander up the track through the gateway to view it. (There's a parking spot just before it, in front of an unused farm gate.)

The Yew trees in this graveyard are huge and stately. Yew were once a premier sacred tree, associated with Pagan death rituals. I've read that the Druids who conducted ceremonies beneath them may have been affected by psycho-active fumes that the Yews emit. Thus they could have entered the Other-worlds on a fast track! You usually only see Yews growing in graveyards and around churches. On a practical level, the red flesh of the berries is poisonous and they could not be planted near livestock. But perhaps the sacred trees were considered to be guides and protectors, death doolas of a sort. It speaks to me of a continuity of Druid ritual practises of care for the dead. Whatever the case, my feeling at this church site is of the overwhelming sanctity of these ancient trees and the blessing to be had there when communing with them.

St Eiden and Tumna

Carrick's river precinct was transformed when the highway was upgraded some thirty years ago and a lovely riverside park was created. Recently the park was blessed with the installation of a wooden sculpture of St Éidín, near the entrance to the river boardwalk. I watched it in 2018 being deftly carved with a chainsaw by acclaimed sculptor Will Fogarty. It portrays Éidín somewhat like a river goddess, with fish swirling around her feet. She also has nine river washed round stones placed around her, to represent eleven pure gold, egg shaped spheres that were dug up in the vicinity of her church (two of which later vanished). You can see the original gold 'eggs' at the National Museum in Dublin. They have graduated sizes and suggest a possible necklace.

The ruins of Éidín's establishment can be visited on the banks of the Boyle River, beside Lough Drumharlow, previously called Lough Éidín. This is in the townland of Tumna, usually translated as the Tomb of the Woman. There was strategic importance to its location. Here the Boyle River is narrow and, before bridges, it was once a fording point. So it may have already been a centre for the elite when, in the 5th century, St Éidín's monastery was established there. Being a river crossing would make it an obvious location for a check point or hospitaller for travellers and for collecting taxes from trade by those who controlled the site. Later, as a monastery or nunnery, it probably continued to enjoy this privilege of gathering taxes or tithes, one can imagine.

What does the folklore have to say, from the school collections of the 1930s? *"Tumna was once great. It was once thronged by priests and nuns as well as great congregations of people who came there to worship God. At one time there was a church and graveyard there."* [53]
"St. Éidín is the local saint. Her grave is in Tuamna… There is a ford near her grave. The district Tuamna is named in memory of her. The derivation of the word Tuamna being tuam(b) an mná [woman], or tuam(b) an átha [ford], in either case referring to this saintly woman who ruled her convent on the gently sloping hillside." [54]

So, the Woman's Tomb at the Ford. When river water levels are low you can see the beginning of the ford on the river edge, just below the church site, as in the photo overleaf. Local man Nick Kaszuk (proprietor of Trinity Bookshop in Carrick) has told me of stories of local school kids who long ago enjoyed walking along it far out into the river and then giving a surprise to passing boaters when waving to them! The bottom of Nick's boat was once scraped by passing over it, but since then the middle of the ford has been dredged out deeper.

Of St Éidín, precious little historical folklore remains, but it is recorded that she *"probably belonged to the earliest order of nuns, those established by St. Brigid at Boyle. Very little is known of her locally. The feast day of St. Éidín or Naoim Cadaoine is celebrated on the 5th July. No people are called after St. Éidín, neither are there any prayers said in her honour. There is a holy well in Tuamna near the ruins and monastery... No patterns or fairs or pilgrimages were ever made to the well, to the knowledge of any people. The water of the holy well at Tuamna is not used for any purpose. Cattle do not drink it either."* [55]

Archeology, however, has much to inform us. Susan Curran conducted a Lidar survey of the site, that was shown to me by landowner Olaf Siegmund. It is wonderfully revealing. In the farm field behind the church site you can see patterns of clustered building foundations, showing how densely populated it once was. What's more - three concentric rings of roughly oval shaped enclosures radiate out from the centre and cover a large area. Such a trivallate enclosure signifies a site of great significance, as at Annaduff Abbey. This was obviously a major monastic foundation.

CHURCHILL

St Éidín didn't restrict herself to Tumna and we don't know if she was buried here at all.

Folklore tells us of another establishment nearby, a nunnery by the north western shore of the lake, south east of Cootehall village on the Hartley to Cootehall road. Place names here give us the clue, while a bullaun stone recorded on the OS map is another, with Folklore Commission tales confirming the tradition, as in the following accounts. *"Cilleen is…a place in the townland of Churchill. It means a 'little church'. There was a church there at one time…Clogher or Clotar meaning a convent. The river is called by this name because there was a convent near the river."* [56]

"Killean (Churchhill)…contains great ruins of an ancient church that was little known in this neighbourhood until the owner of Killean farm began to build a new house when he dug the field for the foundation of his house he laid open the ruins and they showed the site of the church and the cells for the monks." [57] *…"There were a great number of nuns in this convent. They used to cross from Killeen to Ardcarne. There is nothing left to commemorate this church except a small heap of stones and a water font."* [58] *…"There was a ball of gold found there once, near a man's grave. The nuns are supposed to have buried gold crosses, chalices and other valuables, for safety in the churchyard. When any man in that neighbourhood began to prosper all the neighbours said he must have found the nuns' treasure."* [59]

"When the road was being made in 1846, the stones were taken from Killeen for road material. In those days there were no horses or carts and the men had to carry the stones on their backs or on hand barrows. Every morning the stones used to be back in their own places. This went on for some time until the men abandoned their task. Killeen, however, crumbled in time and apart from the stones, originally noticed by Mr. Thomas O'Gara, Killeen, no one at present knew about the 'Killeen' stones. [However]…The 'Clochare' Bridge and river bear testimony to its existence…

"One night a man was passing by Killeen Convent. He observed three lights ascending from it. They travelled along the river, gliding on its surface and stopping opposite Tuamna. Here the lights spread into a big blaze and vanished in the graveyard of Tuamna." [60] *… "Balls of fire and light are often seen travelling across Loch Eiden from Killeen and resting at Kilmacarril fort. No one likes to cross the ancient pass after nightfall lest they should cross the fairies path."* [61]

VISITING TUMNA

Visiting St Eiden's church site is worthwhile and it's handy to Carrick on Shannon. Take the N4 highway westwards towards Sligo and after 3 km turn right onto the R5131 laneway. The brown sign to the site is just there, turn right and go a kilometre or so, then there's a tiny car park, where the last brown sign at a gate points you to the site, which overlooks beautiful Lough Drumharlow/Eiden. The site is on private property which is kindly made accessible to the public by land owner Olaf Siegmund. From the car parking spot there is a gate and a walk over some 500 m through farm fields, following the signs, and descending down a low hill towards the ruins beside the river. It is somewhat steep and rough terrain to get down to the site, but the views are worth it. Close all gates after you and watch out for cows.

As you descend the hill to the abbey site with views of expanses of water surrounded by mountain scenery, including cairn topped hills and Slieve An Eiran, it's a spectacular and relatively unspoilt setting. The lake is a haven for Greenland White Fronted Geese in winter, and is an important feeding area for Whooper Swans also. A large island on it, Inishtirra has the remains of large ancient enclosures that suggest a possible moated site was there. On the north shore an area of callows, wetlands that are inundated seasonally, provide important wildlife habitat, while there's a semi-natural woodland south west of the lake at Hughestown.

Close to the riverbank, a sub-rectangular stone wall encloses the central abbey site. Within its bounds are two crumbling building ruins of no great age. No doubt, earlier buildings preceded them. These days, the most intriguing aspect present is small and in the centre of the graveyard. It's a stone altar table, as some call it, one of only very few existent. On top of a stone slab a collection of attractive water washed stones sit. These are known as Wishing or Blessing Stones, also as Cursing Stones. Both effects can made here, in accord with a favourite occupation of the early saints, who freely cursed as well as blessed people and places.

This is a ritual place for focussed magic. Here, by turning the stones clockwise, one can bestow blessings and wishes from afar; conversely, by turning stones anti-clockwise, a curse can be sent out. Cursing was considered appropriate when it was targeting injustice, for people who were otherwise powerless to get redress from oppressors. If a curse was not considered a just one, it could rebound on the curser.

The condition of the stone altar looks curiously fresh and intact, compared to the crumbling church ruins. This could reflect peoples' strong connection to the ancient past and a testament to the belief in their personal power to influence fate via prayer. In a far cry from the hierarchical mode of the church, the survival of people power would have been essential for a population otherwise reduced to a state of powerlessness in a colonised society, and thus they preserved the possibility of magically influencing events.

Some clairvoyant visitors to Tumna have reported to landowner Olaf of their encounters with the spirit of St Éidín whose benign presence has remained here. Others have come across the traumatised ghosts of nuns who were slaughtered there in the past, he told me.

You can visit the Tumna Abbey site with a church congregation who go annually every July 5th to celebrate St Éidín and conduct a blessing of the graves. Contact the Carrick on Shannon Historical Society for more information about this. Or you can go visit it on your own on any day.

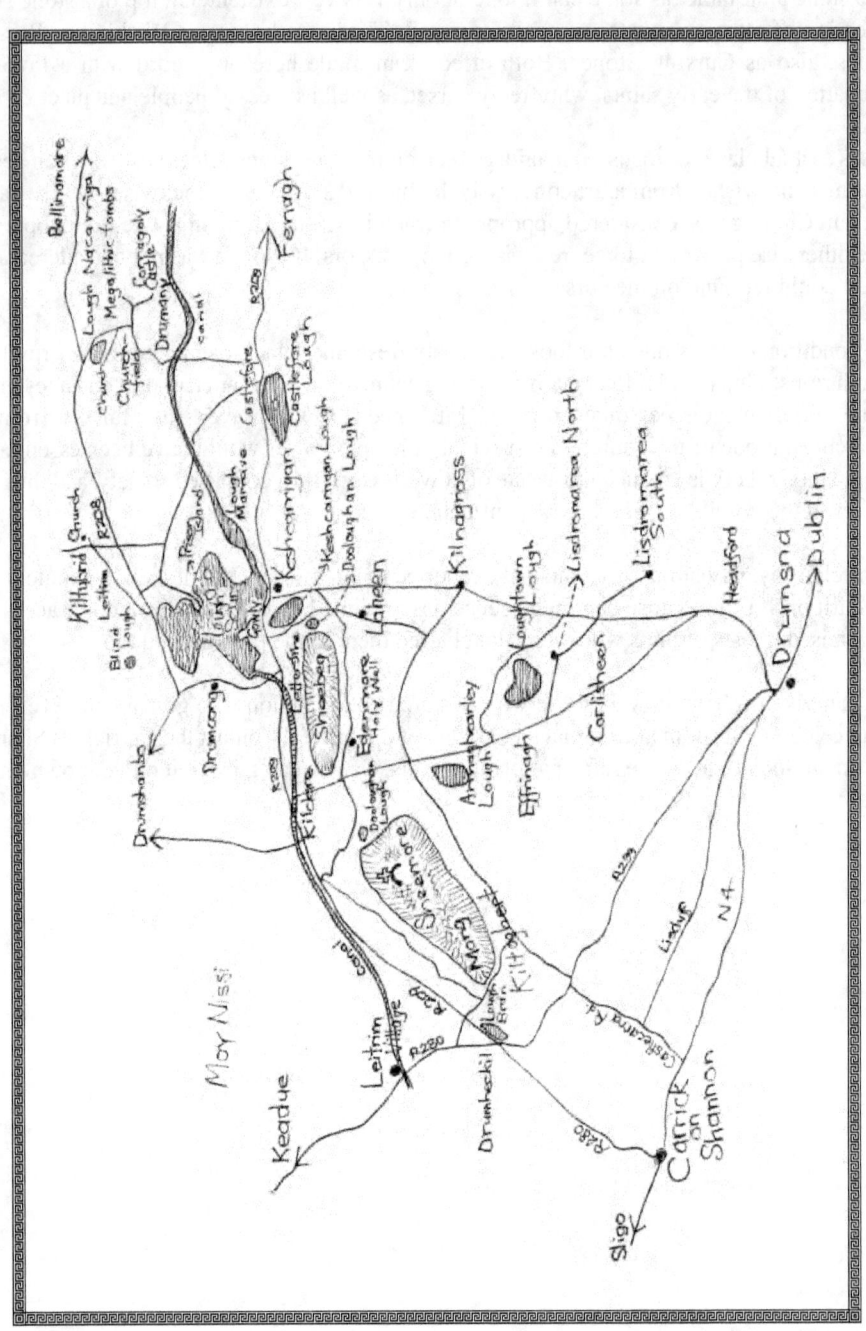

Chapter 4
Kings of Hospitality

Moy Nissi

The old medieval territory of Moy Nissi is adjacent to Carrick on Shannon. This was the level tract of country on the east side of the Shannon, bordering Moy Lurg in Roscommon. Moy Nissi corresponded to the later Barony of Leitrim, however it excluded forested areas such as Feda Conmhaícne (the Wood of the Conmacnee, now the Carrick on Shannon Electoral Area) and Drumshanbo, that was also heavily forested until the late 1600's. [1]

Once the territory of the Gilhooley clan, Moy Nissi included the parishes of Kiltubrid and Kiltoghert, and it was centered on An Sli Mhor (Sheemore), and An Sli Bheag (Sheebeg), the sacred mountains of south Leitrim. The name Sheemore, popularly translated as the Big Fairy Hill, also indicates the presence of ancestral burial mounds on the summit, rare monuments of great antiquity and prestige. The limestone-soiled terraced hill is well drained and fertile, with layers of features that indicate the continuing presence of an elite farming community through the ages. It's located on a fertile strip that JJ Guckian described as spanning from the townland of Port (Shannon River) and going east, north-east via Leitrim village, through the hills of Sheemore and Sheebeg, and on through to Fenagh and Newtowngore.[2] Not far from the ford at Drumsa, Sheemore has long been an important site. Perhaps even a royal ritual centre, site of the inaugurations of tribal chiefs, the so-called kings.

Kings of hospitality

Just what was it to be a king in Ireland and what was their role in society? It's estimated that there could have been around 150 'kings' across Ireland at any given time and to keep the job, they had a big responsibilities towards their people. The majority could be considered chieftains of their clan. In popular Celtic mythos, a would-be king had to ritually marry the goddess of the land in order to assert his authority and gain co-sovereignty of the land. Kings were co-responsible for the fertility of the land and tribal welfare. It was part of pan-Celtic tradition from across the Atlantic seaboard. Celtic societies had strict hierarchal structures, as Jean Markale explains it. At the top was the High King, beneath him/her, the regional kings and beneath them, the local kings, the chiefs of their clans. A social ranking that was almost as high as the local king, and about the same import as an abbot or Druid, was that of the hospitaller. These people, or families, as it was an inherited position, were required to keep an open house for the refreshment and care of all comers and at all times. For this provisioning they were allocated big areas of good land and a host of servants. Hospitality was always sacrosanct to the Celts and Markale says that this highly respected office appears to have originally been held by the king or queen.[3]

Ancient Babylonian legends describe the sacred origins of this role, of king as provisioner . *"The Babylonians believed the purpose of the human race to be the service of the gods.... Before mankind's creation...the cities of lower Mesopotamia were inhabited by the gods who lived alone and had to feed and clothe themselves by their own efforts"*. The gods laboured as farmers and dug rivers, such as the Tigris and Euphrates. But it got too much for them so Ea/Enki, made a substitute worker from clay, this was the first human. After then, the gods had their own workforce and the *"Babylonian pantheon lived, embodied in anthropomorphic statues, in palatial houses, surrounded by their divine families, courtiers and servant...the chief temple of the city functioned as his house or, better, his palace."* The city and its hinterland belonged in principle to its patron deity, whose temple statue was fed, clothed, bejewelled and entertained. Temples were centres of economic activity. *"Many...possessed vast herds of cattle and flocks of sheep and goats. Some temples were also involved in manufacturing, scribal training and other social and commercial activities* [and] *employed a considerable workforce."* Temples supported widows, orphans and foundlings as part of that workforce. Apart from maintaining defence and law and order, the Babylonian king's role was to oversee the stocking of the gods' temples with foodstuffs and treasure, wrote George.[4] Their sacred duty of provisioning hospitality was a concept that travelled far and wide and lasted for millennia in various forms.

Following this vein in Celtic Ireland, it was also the case that the largesse of the elite confirmed their regency. The tradition of the House of Hospitality carried out this important function, being called in Irish a bruidhean, as in Brú na Boinn (Newgrange today); as well as Leitrim's Caislén Átha an Chip ar brú Maighe Nisse at Port. Another name was teach aoide. Houses of Hospitality continued to operate until the end days of the Gaelic lords, but the tradition didn't die out. It eventually evolved into the ever-popular Irish pub, where comfort, nourishment, social connection, culture and merriment provided people with a milieu of community to savour and salve them. (While nowadays, rather than being supported by the authorities, it is the pubs that are being taxed and regulated out of existence.)

KILTOGHERT

Kiltoghert is a fertile townland and one of Leitrim's largest in size. It has an ancient cultural heritage with a cluster of early medieval monuments in the north western end. These include a church, graveyard, holy well and a high status bivallate fort, on the summit of a drumlin, with three lesser univallate ringforts nearby. Recently detected in Susan Curran's Lidar survey was the new *"notable discovery"* of a huge sub-circular enclosure, defined by a bank with slight traces of an outer fosse, at the base of a hill in the north west of the townland, near its boundary. Of an unusually large size, at about 78 m diameter, it has a number of internal divisions and could indicate a local centre of administration or military use, Curran suggests.[5]

This political power centre beside Sheemore attracted Christian missionaries who also wanted to enjoy the fertile surroundings. The earliest monastic settlement was nestled into the foot of Mong, a name describing lush pastures, literally meaning Long Haired/Horse's Mane. It's about 500 m from the cluster of older sites mentioned above.[6]

"Kiltoghert Cemetery... [has] *the ruins of an old Church. Once it belonged to Saint Patrick and was used for Catholic worship until the penal times. It then became the property of the Protestant community - and was occupied by the latter until it fell into ruins about a hundred years ago. Those ruins are still standing. There was also an under ground tunnel from the Church to the Guest House in the immediate vicinity of the Cemetery...* [that] *was the property of the Franciscans, where travellers were provided with food and lodgings."* [7]

Not only were Kiltoghert fields fertile and well drained, Kiltoghert was amply watered as well, as in one account. *"In the year 1911 there was a great drought. There was no rain from 30th May until the 16th October. All the wells were gone dry except Kiltoghert and a well in the Kilclare district. One day eleven horse carts met at Kiltoghert well at the same time".*[8]

But who was the mysterious St Toghert of this first church foundation, the so-called Virgin of the Conmacnee. Did she even exist? There is no record of her. (Parish records only began in the mid 15th century.)[9] Despite vague origins, the Kiltoghert establishment became the parish church, until this honour was removed to Carrick on Shannon. One can imagine it was previously a Druid centre that was re-purposed for the church.

The cluster of ancient monuments in the west of the townland include a high status, bivallate rath on top of a drumlin.[10] The internal diameter of this bivallate fort is 28 m, while a neighbouring rath is much larger at 44 m. This may have been where a minor lord lived, while the bivallate fort was used as a defendable refuge when needed, it's suggested. The other smaller sites may have accommodated lower ranking freemen (ocaire class in the hierarchal system) who farmed the lands of the upper classes. It all suggests that a high status settlement was here long before the abbey.[11]

Kiltoghert Abbey was mentioned in the Registry of Clonmacnoise as a monastic church and community in the 10th century, its coarb collecting taxes for it - being three cows and three pigs paid annually. The principal families of the parish of Kiltoghert were the MacRannels, Mulveys, MacShanleys and Morans. Within Kiltoghert graveyard there are numerous old tombstones of these families, as well as O'Rourkes, MacKeon, Peyton and MacGovern families, many having elaborate coats of arms on them. It was obviously a prestigious burial place in the 18-19th centuries, also for people from further afield.

In the centre of the cemetery there's the curious grave of Bishop O'Moran, who died in 1169. He was one of the Morans of Mong. The grave, seen right, includes relics from the old abbey, with a possible keystone of a door or window carved with the head of a bishop, that probably came from an early church. People must have revered the man, as they once considered the clay from around his grave as a powerful curative.[12] In front of the Bishop's modern grave pedestal is a recumbent gravestone with deeply incised carvings, which some have discerned as symbols of hospitality: a bannock of bread, a measure of butter, knives, spoons and a candle stick. It is an *"an illustration of how they fed the hungry"*, wrote J J Guckian.[13]

The grave of Father John MacKeon, the parish priest here who died 1832 was also once a place of pilgrimage. Clay was removed from it and used by people for cures and it was littered with votive offerings, coins, tokens etc, by supplicants. The Bishop of Ardagh was also buried here, in 1587.[14]

The Big Well of Kiltoghert, 100 m north of the graveyard and beside the road and a house opposite, was once included within the bounds of the monastic enclosure. From the Penal Times, when church ceremonies went underground and the importance of holy wells as sites for religious observances rose, an annual 'Pattern Day' was enjoyed here on the last Sunday in July. Locally called Patron Sunday or Garland Sunday, an echo of the Pagan celebration of Lughnasa, it was considered the last day of Summer and the start of harvest, celebrated with the first meal of grain, or new potatoes. On Pattern Day people visited the graves and said prayers beside them. They also visited the well, bought drinks, fruits and sweets from stalls and played sports. On this day many would take soil from around the bishop's grave and add well water to it, to improve the efficacy of its cure. [15]

J J Guckian describes how he was taken to the very last Pattern Day, held here in the early 1930s. MacNeill believed the well was not considered holy, but the patron was well remembered. There is a memory of dancing and specifically the Cake Dance, she noted. [16] This dance has been revived in recent times by Leitrim's most famous dancer Edwina Guckian.

Traditions and foot-fall from other festivities were transferred to the Big Well from other wells. Tobereendoney (meaning Sunday Well, for Garland Sunday), half way between Leitrim village and Kiltoghert and some 1.6 km away, had become infamous for 'party fighting' and

about 1850 someone was killed during the annual fighting of clans. This saw a stop to the event and it was then transferred to Kiltoghert. The Patron Day at Drumharkin Glebe, near Cloone, was also shut down and transferred to Kiltoghert. Here was south Leitrim's last outpost of Lughnasa type festivities, MacNeill wrote.

Experiencing the Kiltoghert Monastic Site

When I visited Kiltoghert one Garland Sunday the sun was shining gently and a couple of other people were also at the graveyard, quietly tending to their family graves. I was on my own and had no expectations of the site, except to take some photographs. It hasn't been a place of worship nor hosted Pattern Days for a century or two. My mind was suitably blank and thus perfect for receiving psychic impressions.

As I slowly descended the path from the top car park on the hillside I suddenly got the inner message to stop and tune in psychically to the place from this higher vantage point. So I stopped, breathed in the freshness of the day and 'checked in' to the other dimensions. I gazed out over the pleasant sunny scene below, the stone ruins and ancient grave slabs mouldering, crumbling walls of the medieval church thick with ivy, mighty Yew trees here and there, and lichened stone walls. Then, into my receptive mind's eye came the lovely vision of a cloud hovering above the site, a Field of Memories full of angelic-type beings, some blowing trumpets and making angelic sounds. A memory cloud of sublime historic energies imprinted onto this once vibrant place, where monks have sung, prayed and chanted over centuries of sacred time. I was not surprised to see and sense it, but the fact that it was still so strong was wondrous! I soaked in the scene and it was sublime! This lovely place has such a benign atmosphere, perfect for meditation and further exploration of the subtle reams. Much more than what meets the eye. I'll have to return.

HOUSE OF HOSPITALITY AT MONG

A House of Hospitality run by generations of the Moran family was located above the early monastery, on the slopes of the hill of Mong, their ancestral territory. A high status family, the Morans had the hereditary right of interpreting the law as Brehons, or judges. But they became more famous as hospitallers.[17] One of the Morans held the top hereditary office, ran the establishment and derived income to provide the social services provided. For this they controlled the church's termon lands. Their teach aoidh was a hospice for the poor and aged, as well as a place of refreshment for passers by. It was close to a cross roads and highly visible. Many such establishments stayed active until well after Plantation times. Later, the church and termon lands were transferred to the Protestant church of the Planters (who used the English name Glebe for termon lands). The teach aoidh at Mong is mentioned several times in Folklore Commission records from local schools.

"On the side of the hill about a quarter of a mile from the Ballinamore road was a guest house long ago. Poor travellers who were going on their journey throughout the country were given food and lodgings and would then be able to continue their journey... The doors of the house were never closed." [18...] *"There is the remains of a wind-mill on the highest part of Mong* [presumably for grain grinding.] *On the hill also in olden times there was a bruidhean or guest-house for travellers. Being situated as it is, so high up, its lights were visible far off and were a glad sight for hungry travellers, who knew when they saw so many bright doors and windows, that food and shelter were waiting for them there."* [19] ... *"Moran kept a light burning all night to guide wayfarers in this lonely district. All who came were welcome and received refreshment. There is a story over Moran's grave...which commemorates the good work done by this man. On the stone are engraved a loaf and a candle".* [20]

There are also numerous tales told of hidden treasure buried on Mong. They typically involve supernatural guardians, ferocious spirit animals like dogs. The people involved don't usually get the treasure and so it is in this tale. *"In Kiltoghert one time there lived a man the name of Billy Moran. He dreamt three nights one after another that there was gold hid under a big bush at the foot of Mong and there is a serpent minding it."* [21]

Sounds like myth, right? Actually there are many cases of valuable treasure being unearthed from around forts and abbeys, the economic hubs of their day. Abbeys were also considered sacred safe places to store other people's valuables in. No wonder they were constantly being raided. Vikings just had to sail up the rivers to pick them off. If raids were known to be imminent, treasures were hidden by the monks and nuns, who often buried them, but then didn't always survive the ensuing slaughter to retrieve them, as probably happened at Killeen.

DRUMHECKIL

Less than 3 km from the Kiltoghert establishment there was a much lesser known early monastery in the townland of Drumheckil. Marked as an 'abbey' on the 1901 OS map, it's located on a triangle of land overlooking Lough Bran, east of Carrick on Shannon on the R280 road, beside the junction where the R299 to Drumsna branches off. The adjacent townland of Grange was the monastery farm, as the name indicates. In the Annals, it was recorded as the Grange of Muintir Eolius; while in 1835 surveyors stated that Grange contained two forts and the ruins of the abbey called Sean Clochar na Ghrainsighe, or Grange Old Convent. An outpost of the Cistercian Abbey in Boyle, Roscommon, that abbey had several granges at a distance of up to 64 km away, most of them in Roscommon. The connection with Boyle is through the local elite MacShanley clan, who were aligned with the Abbey at Boyle in the mid 13th century. Boyle Abbey, established around 1161, was the second Cistercian foundation to set up in Ireland, and for the prestige of being buried there, the MacShanleys granted it some of their good farmland - the townlands of Drumheckil and Grange.[22]

Most of the stones of this abbey have been carted off now, but some crumbling remains of walls can still be seen in the rocky farm field that overlooks the Kiltoghert Creamery to the south, alongside the present cottages.

PASSAGE TOMBS

Over the millennia from Neolithic times, various types of megalithic monuments appeared in Ireland, ranging from passage tombs to later portal, court and wedge tombs, and then ring barrows in the Iron Age. The tombs required a large and stable population to assemble all the materials. Passage tombs are the oldest type, at around 5000 years of age and are the least common. They are mainly found along a south-east to north-west corridor running from the largest and star example at Newgrange in Meath, up through Leitrim (with three on the summit of Sheemore) and on through the great cemeteries of Carrowkeel, Carrowmore and Knocknarea in Sligo, where the oldest examples are found. This makes the passage tomb cemetery on the summit of Sheemore a most special cultural icon.

An intact Irish passage grave typically consists of a corbel roofed (domed) stone chamber that's approached by a narrow stone passageway lined by orthostats (pillar stones), with a passage length ranging from just 1.2 m, to over 40 m long in the case of Knowth. It's all covered over by an earth and stone mound. This is ringed by large kerb stones as a retaining wall. Mounds range in size from 10 m - 85 m (Newgrange) in diameter, but mostly they are 10 - 25 m across. Generally there is just one chamber inside, of circular, polygonal, sub-rectangular or trapezoid shape, but some are cruciform (cross shaped), with three chambers at the end of the passage.

The passage and chamber are typically roofed over with large quarried slabs or boulders of stone. Chambers have spectacular domed roofs, with horizontally layered courses of slabs. Some have their passage entrances aligned to the east, or to the winter solstice, as at Newgrange, suggesting an invocation of rebirth for the dead. Otherwise, where there's a cluster of tombs with one large focal monument, as at Newgrange, the smaller tombs are usually aligned to face the main tomb. [23]

Apart from the huge scale of these monuments and the massive size of many of the stones, another noteworthy feature is the presence of carvings on some of the stones plus the cremated human remains found on mighty basin stones, as at Newgrange. But a great many have been quarried for their stone and are now just a pile of rubble, or a ring of kerb stones, that were too large to haul away. Most have never been excavated by archeologists.

SHEEMORE

The sacred hill An Sli Mhor, or Sheemore, the Big Fairy Mountain, is the holy heart of south Leitrim and a probable royal centre of great antiquity. At a height of 178 m, it's really just a hill, but it towers over the other drumlins and is the most significant landscape feature around. The hill form is of limestone terraces and it looks so similar to Glastonbury Tor in the UK, another holy mountain that's also terraced. The summit is fairly flat and some 200 m across. Sheemore's three passage tombs sit prominently on the summit, as a great shout of territorial might. Other archeological features here suggest a diverse settlement of elite farmers, a village perhaps. Sheemore later became renowned as the residence for troops of fairies, witches, giants, dragons and mythic warriors, such as Finn MacCool, leader of the warrior elite gang known as the Fianna. Hence its name sets it in the Other worlds.

People get a little confused by the Irish word si (originally sidh, sid), pronounced shee. It can be interpreted as either a burial mound or as the fairy hosts themselves. The two things have kind of blended together in the popular folk mind. The root word for sidh/sid comes from the Latin situs and sedeo, a word that became seat, site and sedentary in English.[24] The original Celtic paradigm of the burial mound has it as the symbolic seat of ancestral power and glory, and, as the supreme territorial marker, it made an impressive land title statement. Mounds housed the revered bones of the ancestors, once considered power objects. But now when people see the word si - they just think of fairies.

Monastic tales cast such mounds as being where the Tuatha Da Danaan tribe were purportedly banished to after losing a battle and being demoted to being just fairies. The way this tribe is depicted in origin myths characterises them more as a family or pantheon of various gods and goddesses that migrated into Ireland and had to fight out territory between themselves using all sorts of magic tricks. Popular folktales of later times often mimic this with their warring fairy troops. If you consider the deities, as I do, to be glorified nature spirits who have co-evolved alongside humankind, then no wonder they were mirrors of human society. The Tuatha Da Danaan might have also been a literary representation of a group of elite warriors, or Druids perhaps, in tales warped and blended with much poetic license.

Typical Sheemore traditions go like this. *"On the top of Sheemore lies a huge heap of stones and it is said that under this heap a Fianna lies buried and some even say that Fionn himself lies buried there. Another warrior is buried on the top of Sheebeg and it is thought that the fairies of those two hills are two different tribes and that they keep continual war between each other. Long ago the heap on Sheemore was built in the shape of Fionn but one night in a great storm it was blown down and this storm was said to be sent by the fairies of Sheebeg."* [25]

The tombs that these folktales refer to are in various states of ruination and one has an enormous concrete cross planted on top of it. The northernmost cairn has a diameter of about 10 m with a kerb of upright stones inside of which a small burial chamber is exposed in the centre. The cairn over it has been removed. The central, unopened cairn is about 20 m across and 5 m high and the floodlit cross so incongruously placed on it, as if to crucify the past, was erected in 1950, while JJ Guckian assures us that *"the chamber was not disturbed"* in the process. It went up in the feverish Holy Year of 1950, to celebrate the *"definition of the Dogma of the Assumption"* somehow.[25] That act of vandalism of a noble monument that has stood proudly on the summit for some 5,500 years seems to me to have sadly displayed an astonishing lack of cultural pride, derived from a colonised, emasculated mind-set.

At an historical society field trip with archeologist J Reynolds in 1998, monuments and features on Sheemore were identified. The site is criss-crossed by archaic field boundaries and dotted with circular enclosures, *"one of which was thought to have contained stone moulds for bronze or iron casting… Also identified was believed to be a ritual pathway up to the passage graves on the summit"*, Guckian reported. Metal working industry would be typical of a post-Neolithic settlement and it's regularly found at royal complexes. The ritual pathway can be seen spiralling around the hill.

The eastern side is very steep and wooded and this is where its famous fairy caves are located. They are not really accessible to people, the entrances in the limestone cliff face are just narrow slits. The fairies prefer not to be disturbed by people, so it suits them. (But, being fairies, they don't need entrances to come and go as they please from within their mountain home.) These are deep caves that go far into the limestone hill and in one cave school boys in the 1930s found a stone axe that they took to school and recorded, but today its whereabouts are unknown. (I can't even re-find the account of it online.)

"The caves of Sheemore were the seat of all the fairies of Leitrim. It is full of fairies but they are not appearing now…I used to hear the old people describing all the fairies they used to see dancing around the caves. On one occasion there were people going to the fair of Leitrim and coming around near the caves didn't they see people on horseback and on foot and heard cracking of whips and swishing of saddles. There was a full pack of foxhounds and beautiful princesses amongst them…" [26]

In another story, a man found himself in a fairy cave in Sheemore after selling his horse to the

fairies. *"Those caves are like palaces inside!"* he told people afterwards. [27]
At the base of the hill to the north east is the deep and mysterious lake Dooloughan, the Dark Little Lough. *"A giant who is supposed to have dug the hill by taking two shovelfuls thus made the lake at its base. No bird, not even swans ever live in that lake. There is also supposed to be a hidden treasure in this lake"*. [28]

But if you want to look for it, as some must have tried, the lake may too deep to fathom.
"At the foot of Sheemore there is a lake and men have tried to find the bottom but have always failed. It is said that no matter what falls into it is never found or seen again". [29]

PILGRIMAGE TO SHEEMORE

There's now a new walking track to access the base of Sheemore, starting from Leitrim village. From this track you can enjoy viewing rural landscapes that have barely changed in the past 200 or so years, since the subdivision of common land created small fields with hedgerows between them. Gentle walking gets you back into Slow Time. You'll discover so much more that can be seen and appreciated at this pace. It's the perfect pace for getting to an anciently sacred hill.

To get to the summit you have a steep walk upwards and it can get fairly rough, muddy and rocky. Fitness is required, plus good shoes (or go barefoot, for a fuller, more sensual experience). Watch out for farm animals and it's best to avoid windy days for your visit. An occasionally damp day, with wonderful patterns of cloud and sunshine swirling around, can be delightful!

When you ascend Sheemore, remember that this a private farm, so be careful and respectful.

Enter via the farmgate, or go around beside it. There is no path, so I recommend taking the slow route on a spiralling trajectory upwards, in a sunwise/deosil direction. Ascend the limestone terraces and take in different angles of the magnificent views. On a clear day, other hilltops and their ancient cairns can be seen far and wide, as well as miles of hedgerowed fields, old cottages and circular tree rings indicating ring forts. Sometimes curious cloud formations whizz by and I once gazed down upon a rainbow coloured mist below. Awesome!

This would have to be the number one pilgrimage place in Leitrim. It uplifts your spirit. Here you can be transported from the mundane world, a time traveller traversing far into the ancestral past, or ready to access the inherent magic of the land and dive into the Dreaming of Country. If you walk up Sheemore silently and mindfully, in a spirit of sacred communion, you might have visions or revelations. You might access the Otherworld here. There are still fairies residing in the hill and they may grace you with a friendly connection, if they sense your suitability. The Fairy Queen herself has several times graced me with her presence and I've had the pleasure of introducing her to others. Always an enchanting experience! I wrote a song about the fairy world of Sheemore and I reverence her by singing it to her. She's greatly pleased by this and her joy can be palpable.

If you ascend to the summit of Sheemore, don't expect to find any fairies at the top, where comes the shock of the new - an array of internet antennas close to the largest passage grave, that's surmounted by the ugly concrete cross. A row of power poles brings electricity up to light the cross at night and power the antennas. All very insensitive to this place of ancestral power. Site energies are definitely not conducive to fairies resided there, nor to the peaceful enjoyment of this special place. Until the summit gets a respectful make-over, a better place to linger is on the terrace below it.

KILCLARE

Going back onto the R209, turning right and eastwards, you pass through Kilclare with the post office shop next to a lock on the canal. The area was once a dense woodland, as the name suggests - Coill Chlair, the Wood of the Plank Bridge or Plain. Stopping at the bridge and canal lock, you can go for a walk on either side of the road. The new walking/cycling track follows the old canal path. In farm fields south east of the post office are the small drumlin hills of Kilclarebeg townland, with a higher drumlin just to the north east, in Kilclaremore. Taking the next right turn onto the road to Drumsna, you immediately pass between these two hills. They may be farmland and plantation covered now, but under the vegetation lies the remnants of a rare ritual landscape, an archeological complex.

In Kilclaremore townland there are several forts and a rare embanked enclosure that is believed to be a ritual monument, the only example found in Leitrim. It's near the top of the north east slope of a small hill. The 20 m wide area is circular and slightly dished, it's surrounded by a wide bank, a grass covered stone spread of 5-6 m width and 20 cm - 5 m high. There is no fosse, because it's not a defensive structure. The interiors of these type of enclosure are a bit lower than the surrounding land and they are usually associated with a complex of other ritual monuments. [30]

That's the case here, for two cairns are nearby, one on a rise in a low spot 150 m to the north west in the adjacent townland of Scrabbagh. It's a possible passage grave.[31] A ring barrow lies

100 m to the south west of the enclosure, on a rise on a low hill top. It's described as a flat topped, grass covered circular stone spread in a ring with a 9 m wide interior area, 20 m on the outside, having an entrance at the south east end. Also in this probable ritual centre are a pair of standing stones, located some 100 m from the embanked enclosure. They stand on a low hill and are described as two glacial erratics 1.2 m high and 90 cm wide, that are 9m apart in a north-ish to south-ish alignment. [32]

Folklore remembers this pair of stones as having been flung there by battling giants, or mythic warriors of Sheemore and Sheebeg, or of Kilclaremore and Kilclarebeg. This may have been the case in the sense that they dropped "out of the blue", being stones brought from other places and dropped out of melting glaciers (stones that are now called glacial erratics). *"[In Kilclaremore]…is a very big field…in which there are two big stones. The people say that the Firbolgs and Tuatha De Danaans threw those stones from Sige-beg and Sige-Mór."* [33]

EDENMORE

Continuing along this little road to the next crossroads, a right turn takes you back towards Sheemore and a left turn takes you up a tiny, ancient road that connects Sheemore to Sheebeg. There are so many monuments hidden in the landscape around here, but they're mostly inaccessible. But if you go to the left up this road there is an easily accessed holy well and you can park near it too. It's signposted on the right. Go through the farm gate and walk the short distance down the grassy lane and you'll see the well beside a stream in a drystone enclosure. It's a peaceful rural setting with donkeys grazing in surrounding fields.

The well was dedicated to St Patrick, which signals the importance of the local complex of sacred sites that attracted the wrath of the incoming church. The well site was venerated up until the 1950s. The well water was reputed to be particularly healing for sore eyes and warts. It was called a spa well and the mineralised waters flowing from it are stained reddy brown.[34] Not suitable for drinking, then. A flagstone on a pedestal stone to the left of the well used to be a mass rock, where mass was celebrated during the Penal Times. To the right of the well another stone (in the photo right), a small boulder with a hollow on top that suggests an ancient ritual grinding stone, was installed there by the landowner who lives in the house overlooking the well. It was found when he was tidying up the site and was probably used for making altar bread.

There are several legends associated with the site, including several of the supernatural kind. *"There is a holy well in Edenmore ...It was supposed that Saint Patrick blessed this well. He also took a drink from it. The stone on which he sat is still there. On the same stone he wrote his name but it is so long ago it is hardly visible now."* [35] *"....In a townland called Edenmore there is a holy well with trees growing around it. Once a woman came and she stayed three days tidying around the well and planting trees. She stayed in a house named Kelly's. She then went to a house named Doherty's. One day she asked for a gallon of meal. Mrs. Doherty gave it to her. She then asked her would she take a cup of tea. The Dohertys were quarrying stones in Pairck Lantic at that time. The woman said "No" but she said "You are so good you should not be quarrying in Pairck Lantic because it is a grave yard." That same evening at night fall a light appeared where the Dohertys were quarrying and they stopped and put back the stones again."* [36]

At the top of a drumlin in Edenmore lies a large and overgrown oval ring fort, with a largish internal diameter some 28 m by 35 m.[37] It has quite a large reputation too, judging by the following folk tale. *"In the townland of Edenmore there is an old fort in which fairies were supposed to dwell. It goes by the name of Eden's Fort. ....James McNulty of Selton counted five hundred fairies leaving it one day. John Floyde and Patrick Mac Nulty, of Selton, saw lights on several nights about twelve o'clock. No one ever interfered with the fort because it was believed that the fairies would cast a spell on any person who would have anything to do with it...no one ever enters the fort."* [38]

SHEEBEG

Following this same old tiny road eastwards brings you directly to the Little Fairy Mountain of Sheebeg (originally An Sli Bheag). If you approach the hill from the other end of the road in Keshcarrigan village, it's a pleasant walk and you can pass the modern statue of legendary character Finn MacCool. He, as well as romantic duo Duirmuid and Grainne, plus the local elite, have been linked to this sacred hill and passage grave in populist mythos.

"A treasure was supposed to be hidden in Sheebeg ...It is a high hill surrounded by good, rich, green, level land. A King and Queen and a crock of gold were said to be buried in the mound. A man named O'Hara, a national school teacher interested in research work, heard of this and came to the hill and dug down very deep in the mound until he came upon a big flag which he could not move. At length he got an opening under the stone and he found to his surprise bones of a King and Queen and traces of gold but in a very small quantity. The bones were brought to a neighbouring house of the district. Crowds of people came to the

house where the bones were, also to the cave from where they were taken. My brother and I entered the cave one day, but it was very dark inside and we could see nothing. About a fortnight afterwards the bones were put back as they did not think it right to keep human bones and the bones were never stirred since." [39]

But another account suggests there were more than just traces of gold with the skeletons.
"With several companions we journeyed to the historic promontory of Sheebeg and got permission from the local guards to view the find, which was fortunately intact until the arrival of the officials from the Dublin museum. We were stricken with awe and admiration at what we saw. There lying in two stone coffins from which the lids had been removed, lay the skeletons of a male and female. The male was evidently a warrior, for clinging to his remains were fragments of armour and his trusty sword lay bare by his side. On his brow was a massive gold circlet quaintly carved which showed he was of princely rank and bracelets of the same precious metal adorned his arms. The female figure also had several beautiful bracelets of smaller design on the arms, and the golden ring around the head also bore lettering which owing to age and conditions in the vault could not be deciphered... The inscriptions on the golden badges of rank found on the skeletons in Sheebeg are thought by some to be in the Ogham writing... I made enquiries from one of the oldest men in the locality as to how this pair, evidently royal, came to be buried there. He told me that he heard from his grandfather, who heard it from his grandfather and so on, that the poor remains we saw that day were once a pair of the highest royal rank." [40]

When this unauthorised excavation happened in 1931, the locals became convinced that here were the actual remains of legendary couple Diarmuid and Grainne, and there was huge excitement. Crowds of sightseers poured over Sheebeg and news was conveyed far and wide, being reported to as far afield as Australia. It all got a bit unmanageable. The gards were called in to quell the excitement. No official archeology has ever been conducted and no found objects were handed over to the authorities. The bones were re-interred, damage had been done. Afterwards, people put statues of the mythic couple on top of the tomb. [41]

A small lough beside Sheebeg is similar to the one at Sheemore, being also to the north east, and also called Dooloughan. There are supernatural tales about both loughs too and I wouldn't be surprised if valuable items once deposited as votive offerings might be found in them one day. In Celtic paradigms it was a sign of status and power to make such depositions. The pieces were often booty, gained from raiding other tribes, a prestigious activity in its day.

LOUGH SCUR

If you continue up the old road towards Keshcarrigan, before you get to the village, turn left onto the R209 and you'll soon get to Lough Scur. At the centre of MacRagnaill territory, beautiful Lough Scur is set amidst sublimely picturesque landscapes, with a line of mountains in the background to the north. The earliest Mac Ragnaill strongholds were on islands and the five or six crannoga that they retreated to there. There are 93 known crannoga in Co. Leitrim. No-one knows their age, but dates coming from analysis of a crannog near Enniskillen showed a millenium of occupation, starting around 670 and ending in the 17th century. [42]

Near the western lakeshore and within the townland of Roscarban, a crannog on the lake was constructed with a timber foundation structure that's still partly visible. In the 19th century a large disc quern and a stone mould for metal fabrication were found on this crannog.[43] The Lough-Scur Quern-stone, is possibly the largest example in Ireland, according to Wikipedia. Overlooking the lake, on a mainland hilltop in Roscarban, a fort was strategically located, the closest fort to the lake. Perhaps this was the earliest Mac Ragnaill stronghold.

After his father Felim died in 1265, newly crowned king of Connaught Aed O'Connor built a castle on the Gowly peninsula of Lough Scur, called Castle Island. Then, in 1270, his troops camped in the idyllic fields of his Mac Ragnaill allies, before they attacked the Anglo-Normans in the Battle of Connaught. Defending the Conmhaícne from Norman conquest was his military objective, and in 1270 his Lough Scur regiment and Conmhaícne forces both participated in the decisive Battle of Áth an Chip. The lake's name Scur preserves the memory of his troops and horses being stationed there. (Meanwhile, the English forces were camped some 5 km away, at Annaghearley, the Marsh of the Earl, named after the event, no doubt.) [44]

They were a violent lot, probably demonised from being subject to colonisation and war. In 1570 Sean na Geann, Sean of the Heads, a MacRagnaill, set up beside the lake and carried out all sorts of atrocities. *"Sean na gCeann…built a castle on the shores of Lough Scur, and the mortar was mixed with the blood of cows seized from the people around. He also built a jail on an island in the Lough where he used to put Catholics whom he saw going to Mass or talking to a priest."* [45]

This fortified house was on the southern shore of the lake in the townland of Gowly. Also known as Sir John Reynolds, he was one of the Mac Ragnaills who submitted to English rule, anglicised his name and was re-granted ancestral lands, over 2,000 Irish acres, in around 1621. Castle John, regarded as a fortified house, survives as a rectangular, five bay, three storied house, almost complete apart from the roof and east gable. A semicircular spiral stair tower with gun loops comes out from the north wall. A tiny signposted road running off the R209 road approaches it from the south. A lake shore walking track takes you to it. Unless it's too overgrown, as it was when I went in March 2025.

On a rocky island in the lough, about 200 m north of Castle John, are the ruins of Leitrim's first prison, made by John Reynolds around 1612, when he became sheriff and gaoler of Leitrim, a carte blanche giving him power over life and death. The three storey rectangular structure structure on Prison Island has a few small windows, an arched doorway and fireplaces on the first floor and gun-loops in the walls. [46] It was possibly there before, as *"it appears to resemble a purposely-built Gaelic tower house"*, notes J J MacDermott.[47] People were hanged on the island, or made to walk blindfolded into the lake; Sean himself was murdered in revenge for a prisoner's death.

South of the lough, some 400 m from the shore, and not far from Castle John, a megalithic monument sits in an incredibly picturesque site, commanding a magnificent view of the lake and distant mountains. The site overlooks the already mentioned crannog and is accessible from the road. You can park next to a gate and walk to down to it a short distance via steps and a flagstone pathway through privately owned fields, but watch out for cows! Here are the

remains of a portal tomb, known locally as Dermot and Grania's Bed. There are two portal stones, a couple of collapsed side stones, a collapsed backstage and a huge roofstone that's broken into four pieces. Another couple of stone slabs 6 m away could be all that's left of a second chamber. [48] The story of Dermot and Grania, the lovers-on-the-run from the alpha male, comes from a much later era than this venerable tomb.

The MacRagnaill clan was split along religious lines when, during the Plantation, many sided with the English and changed their name to Reynolds. The following records their tragic expulsion. *"The Reynolds people that remained Catholic had to leave Lough Scur and to take up the wild bogs of Commagh and Annagh in the parish of Drumard, Co Longford"*. [49]

The local seat of power eventually shifted from Lough Scur to the nearby townland of Letterfine, where the Peytons, a Planter family, established their big house. The Reynolds' Laheen Estate wasn't far to the south. Both Laheen House and Letterfine House were built circa 1800. The two families were the prominent landholders there and they intermarried in the early 18th century, but their original big houses are long gone.[50] Their estates were located along the fertile strip of land previously described.

KILTUBRID

Going back onto the R209 from Lough Scur, head for Drumcong and from the R208 take a second left after the village. You'll soon be passing through the townland of Leitrim where, on your left is a mound of earth and stone, 13 m diameter wide and 1 m height, which may be natural, that's best seen from the air. Nearby is an enclosure, a 20 m wide sub-circular platform with some evidence of an earthen bank at the south, south-east, also best seen from above.[51] Continue up this road until you get to a T junction and turn left. Across the road a little to the north of this junction in Kiltubrid townland lies the ruins of the Parish Church of Kiltubrid, which means the Church of the Well. It must be an ancient ruin as it's called St Patrick's Church, for Patrick was supposed to have founded it while en route to Magh Sleacht. Here was probably a staunch Pagan place as well, I suppose. The building here could be from the 15th century, while Kiltubrid Parish was formed in the early 15th century.[52] Today, there's just a single wall left standing in the rectangular graveyard (60 m by 55 m). Older pieces of church are incorporated into features, such as the mausoleum and graveyard wall, including late medieval window mullions and a couple of cross slabs. At the entrance is a reconstructed holy well. There is a record of two grave covers from the 17th century.[53]

Behind Kiltubrid Church is a small lake known as Lough Caogh, the Blind Lake, the water of which was believed to possess medicinal qualities and was much resorted to, especially for erysipelas, or for swellings either on man or beast. A story goes that it was only a small well at first, but that St. Augustine came and enlarged it to its present size. After taking the cure, on leaving the place it's strictly forbidden to look behind one, or the effects will be lost.[54]

"In the parish of Kiltubred in the townland of Listermacron there is a little lake named Lough Eagh which is supposed to have a cure for swellings. Monday and Thursday are the two special days on which this cure is made and these are also the days on which the water is taken from the lake. For making this cure two bottles of water and some clay is used. The water has to be taken from the lake before sunset and cannot be taken into the house. This cure is made by pouring the water on the swelling while saying In the name of the Father and of the Son and of the Holy Ghost. Then the clay is rubbed on the affected parts while repeating the same words. It is supposed that many people have been cured by the water of this Lough". [55]

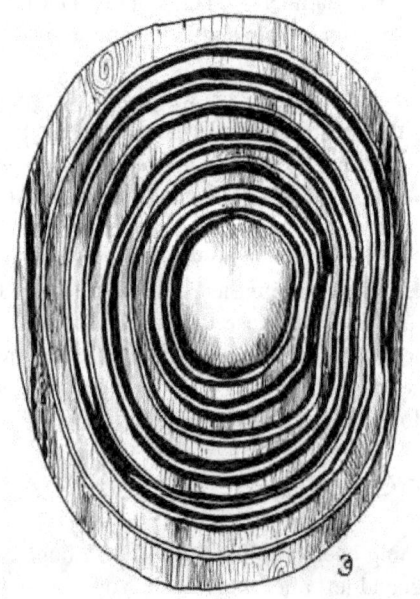

Kiltubrid townland was the place of discovery of the Kiltubrid Shield, an amazingly well preserved wooden shield from the Bronze or Iron Age. It's considered the most perfect example of its kind ever found in Europe. It was dug out of a turf bog in 1863, from a depth of 3 m. Turf, or peat, is said to take roughly a thousand years to form a one metre thick layer. So this could possibly date it to around 3,000 years of age. The acid conditions of the bog were perfect for its preservation.

The shield is oval in shape, with a perfect central boss 7.6 cm high, and seven slightly raised concentric circles (as ribs). On the reverse it is plain and has a handle. The whole thing is carved out of one piece of wood. The original measurements were 66 cm in height by 53 cm in width, with a thickness of 1.25 cm. A typical Irish wooden shield, it was grasped by the cross-piece underneath the umbo (boss) and could be projected to full arm's length during battle. The wood was probably alder. It may have once been covered with leather, painted and decorated. The ribs show an indentation on one side, possibly from shrinkage and warping. [56]

DRUMANY, CHURCHFIELD AND LOUGH NACARRIGA

Continue on this road and you will soon be passing through Drumany townland, possibly meaning the Hill of the Marsh. This area has a concentration of megalithic sites, an archeological complex of ritual centres. On either side of the road in the undulating low lying landscape are the remains of two tombs on slight rises, both marked as Giants Graves on the old OS maps. On the left is a wedge tomb, with massive uprights that form a roofless, over grown wedge shaped chamber, with internal dimensions of 2.7 m, 1.4 m and 2.1 m. On the right of the road is a portal tomb. A rectangular chamber 2.4 m by 2 m and 2.15 m in height is formed by two portal stones, a sill stone and two side stones, one has fallen inwards, that are now part of a field bank. A single roofstone, 2.2 m by 1.8 m has slipped. It's on a low platform 40 m across and 1 m high, with no sign of cairn material. [57]

Drumany also has a St Patrick's Well, known as a holy well, that's down low near a stream. It features a masonry corbelled structure 2.15 m across and 1.6 m high, within which is a circular chamber with the water, with a doorway to the west. A record from 1944 mentions the presence here of a bullaun stone with two basins, but this has not been recently seen. [58] In the adjacent townland of Drumroosk North is a possible ancient tomb, a mound near the western shore of Lough Nacarriga. It's a grassy circular bump in grassland with indistinct edges. [59]

Coolkill Church is 100 m to the west-north-west, in Churchfield townland. This is the ruin of the parish church of Fenagh. The name Coolkill mean the Church of the Woodland. The rectangular church ruins measure 13.7 m by 6 m inside and feature all four walls, except for the top of the west gable. It's situated inside a grassy oval enclosure some 75 m by 52 m, defined by an earth and stone bank 3.5 m wide and 1.1 m high. The enclosure is a sure sign of an ancient pedigree. A 3.5 m wide entrance ramp is at the south, south-east. No evidence of burial is recorded. St Patrick's Well is 260 m to the south west.[60] South east of Churchfield, in the townland of Corragoly is a ruined castle / tower house, on a light rise. Just a fragment of a low vault of mortared limestone survives, 4.5 m wide, 1.5 m wide and almost 2 m high. [61]

CASTLEFORE

Heading south from Drumany you can get back on the R209. Turn right and you are soon in Castlefore, Baile Choille Foghair. Empty now but for a few houses, this was once a thriving village, supported by the huge ironworks, owned by the Lord of Collooney. With thirty families living there in 1683, it was more populous than most places in Leitrim.[62] A crannog is located in the Castlefore Lough, some 100 m from the east shore. It would have served as a bolt hole for the local elite.

Castlefore once boasted a legendary bardic school that flourished for centuries. Not far from the royal power centre at Lough Scur, it was established by hereditary bardic family the O'Duignans. A member of that illustrious clan, Philip O'Duignan came over from Kilronan in Co Roscommon (20 km away), where they were historians of the ruling MacDermotts, to establish the school here. One of his clan has been described, in an obituary of 1440, as an *"ollamh in history"* for the Mac Donnchaidh, ruling elite of of Tirerrill. *"O Duibhgeannain scholars provided professional services to other families also and one of their formal titles was that of 'ollamh Conmaicne',"* Bernadette Cunningham has explained.[63] They kept a house of hospitality at Kilronan.[64] It's likely that they kept such a house at Castlefore also.

The Castlefore O'Duignan's became the historians of the local elite here, possibly for the MacRagnaill clan. Peregrine O'Duignan was one of the celebrated scholars known as the Four Masters.[65] A bardic school would typically operate from the beginning of winter, traditionally November 1st, and the school year ended when the first cuckoo was heard calling in the spring. In other words, it followed the agricultural cycle and allowed people to be back on their farms during the busy warmer months. (Nobody had 'holidays' then!) This was an acclaimed cultural establishment, but nothing remains of it now. The signposted site, beside the road leading the short distance to the lakeshore, is a leafy quiet location, in what was once a bustling village.

If you take the road at that junction away from Castlefore Lough and go towards the Ballinamore Canal, you soon come to the townland of Kilmacsherwell, the site of a fortified house and ironworks built by Colonel Coote in the 17th century. It was destroyed in the rebellion of 1641. Three walls with corner towers and gun loops were recorded 200 years ago, but nothing is visible at ground level now. On the old maps it's marked here as Castlefore, so this was the original elite central of the area. There's only the faint trace of what may be an entrance road to the tower house left to be seen.[66]

The Ballinamore-Ballyconnell Canal, once a river, is to the north and adjacent to the site. It was begun in 1846 and during the Great Famine was an employer of 7,000 people, working by hand over 14 years. But it was of poor quality and was hardly used. At the end of last century it was all revamped and revitalised, then renamed as the Shannon-Erne Waterway in 1994. Now it's possible to travel for up to some 400 km along it, all the way from Limerick city to Belleek in Fermanagh. It's the longest stretch of navigation in all of Europe![67]

KESHCARRIGAN

Go back onto the R209, head west from Castlefore and you'll soon be back near the southern shore of Lough Scur at the charming village of Keshcarrigan (Ceis Charraigín, the Wattled Causeway of the Little Rock), that's surrounded by lakes. In 1854 a beautiful bronze bowl was found in the wide river that flows into Lough Scur from nearby Lough Marrave, just north of Keshcarrigan.

The bowl, of approximately 14 cm diameter, is made of beaten bronze and was probably finished on a lathe. The soldered on handle is decorated with a bird's head motif. The bird's head has two eye sockets that may have originally held red enamel insets. There is a hammered zig-zag line along the out-turned rim.

It was made in the Iron Age and may have been a ceremonial drinking cup. Reminiscent of 1st century AD bowls from southern Britain, it may be an import. It would have been a prestigious item and perhaps its location in a watery place represents a ritual deposition. [68] The Keshcarrigan Bowl is considered to be the finest example of its kind in the La Tene style (curvilinear and zoomorphic) ever found in Ireland.

LAHEEN

From Keshcarrigan, if you go towards Kilnagross, you can take an interesting back road through the old desmesne of Laheen House, with its fine old stone farm buildings and mature trees (but the original big house is gone). Take the left fork at the Y junction below Sheebeg. This is an old road connecting Kilnagross with the estate and Keshcarrigan.

LISDROMAREA

Continuing on this lane from Laheen, when you get to the next junction, turn left and at the following junction turn right to the Kilnagross crossroads. If you continue straight heading south towards Drumsna on this road, you pass between Lisdromarea North, then Lisdromarea South, on the left and right of the road. These are the Forts of the Hill of the King. The two ringforts are on the summits of adjacent hills. (There were a lot of kings in those times!) If you take the second road on the right from Kilnagross (towards Effrinagh) you pass right beside the northern fort of the king. It's just past a sharp, right angle turn, in a commanding elevated position, beside a small derelict house, now a farm yard.

Further up this road there are lovely views towards Sheemore and of the large heart shaped Loughtown Lough. You will pass the old Protestant Chapel of Ease, built for a short lived Plantation community on the lakeshore and now a badly reconfigured barn. A side road just past the chapel takes you down to the ghost village of Loughtown, that's probably the best place to access the lake (through private land).

ANNAGHEARLEY

From the Kilnagross crossroads, a right turn puts you on the road back to Carrick on Shannon. You'll soon pass by Annaghearley townland and lough, just past the next crossroads. A peaceful rural location now, it was once a thriving centre of industry, although little trace remains. Jamestown's Franciscan Friary once had their farm here. The little river that flows into Annaghearley Lough was modified as a mill race and you can see its straight path defined by trees. The ruins of a water powered corn mill, corn kiln tuck mill and several houses were still existent in 1835, located beside the adjacent crossroads to the north west of the lough. The townland there is Drumliffen Glebe, the church lands that lie beside Sheemore. A Glebe House is marked on the 1901 map, in the north end of this townland. At Annaghearley, just before the 1270 Battle of Connaught, the English Earl was camped with his troops.[69]

Perhaps there was a House of Hospitality associated with the Friary around here too, for sustenance and a safe camp place? From those times of high drama, it's now a bucolic vista of lake and fields, overlooked by the sacred hill of Sheemore. If you turn left at the crossroads and head south, you end up back in Drumsna.

Effrinagh

En route to Drumsna you pass through the ex-village of Effrinagh, with just the pub left now. Across the road from the pub there's a monument to Jimmy Gralton, the only Irish man to have been deported from Ireland. Read all about it on his memorial stone there, that's situated in front of the Gralton homestead and with a fine view of Sheemore behind it. British filmmaker Ken Loach made a great film about Jimmy's story, called Jimmy's Hall. The Abbey Theatre also put on an excellent musical version of the story that premiered in Carrick on Shannon a few years ago. The monument here was unveiled by president Michael D. Higgins.

Less than a kilometre south of the pub at Effrinagh, you will be crossing over the path of an ancient togher, a bog trackway. It crossed beneath the Effrinagh-Drumsna Rd, around where the Drumnadobber Rd branches off it, in the townland of Corlisheen.

Corlisheen

This well made, one metre wide Oak plank togher was unearthed by peat diggers one metre below the surface. Radiocarbon dating gives it an age of around 1450BC, in the Early Bronze Age. A lot of Oak trees would have been needed to make this circa one kilometre long trackway. Not surprisingly, *"Peat samples from above and below the trackway were analysed and showed a steep decline in Oak shortly after the trackway was constructed."* [70]

The togher covered a large, wet, raised bog area, starting and ending on higher ground. At its north-west end it terminated at the base of a drumlin in the townland of Corlona. At the south-east end it converged onto a paved pathway that runs up to a ridge in Ardlougher, continuing the line of the togher.[71] Located in a large peat bog in Corlona/Effrinagh/Corlisheen that serviced people with their main fuel needs, it was unfortunately demolished, being in the way of the peat harvesters. A man born in my home at Corlisheen helped to dismantle it so they could get at the peat. He only later realised the significance of the ancient structure. No remnant is known of the trackway, however J J Guckian suggests that some could be surviving beneath the road junction, where Drumnadubber road meets the Drumsna - Effrinagh road.[72]

It's easy to think that the togher's purpose was to provide safe passage to the royal hill of Sheemore and to connect it to the ford at Drumsna and river networks. But it could also be interpreted as a ritual path, enabling death and rebirth rituals that involved the watery realms, providing access for the Druids of Sheemore to sacred bog holes. It's interesting that two of the townlands spanned by the togher have names that bear the possible crane pre-fix, 'cor' - Old Irish for crane - the bird most associated with death in Pagan Irish tradition. These graceful 'death doulas' were said to accompany the spirits of the dead to the other realms.[73] Becoming extinct in Ireland around 1600 (the Anglo-Norman invaders having eaten them all), a pair or two have been coming to the north-west in recent years to breed, a most welcome return! Moist, boggy areas are their favourite haunt.

This togher may have lead pilgrims, arriving at Drumsna from the Shannon River, across the treacherous bogland towards Kiltoghert and the early church of mysterious St Toghert, the supposed Virgin of the Conmacnee. But the name of the Church of Kiltoghert, some 1,500 years younger than the togher, could also mean the Church of the Trackway, rather than the name of an obscure saint, as Ordnance Survey researcher John O'Donovan asserted nearly 200 years ago. [74]

Kings of Hospitality

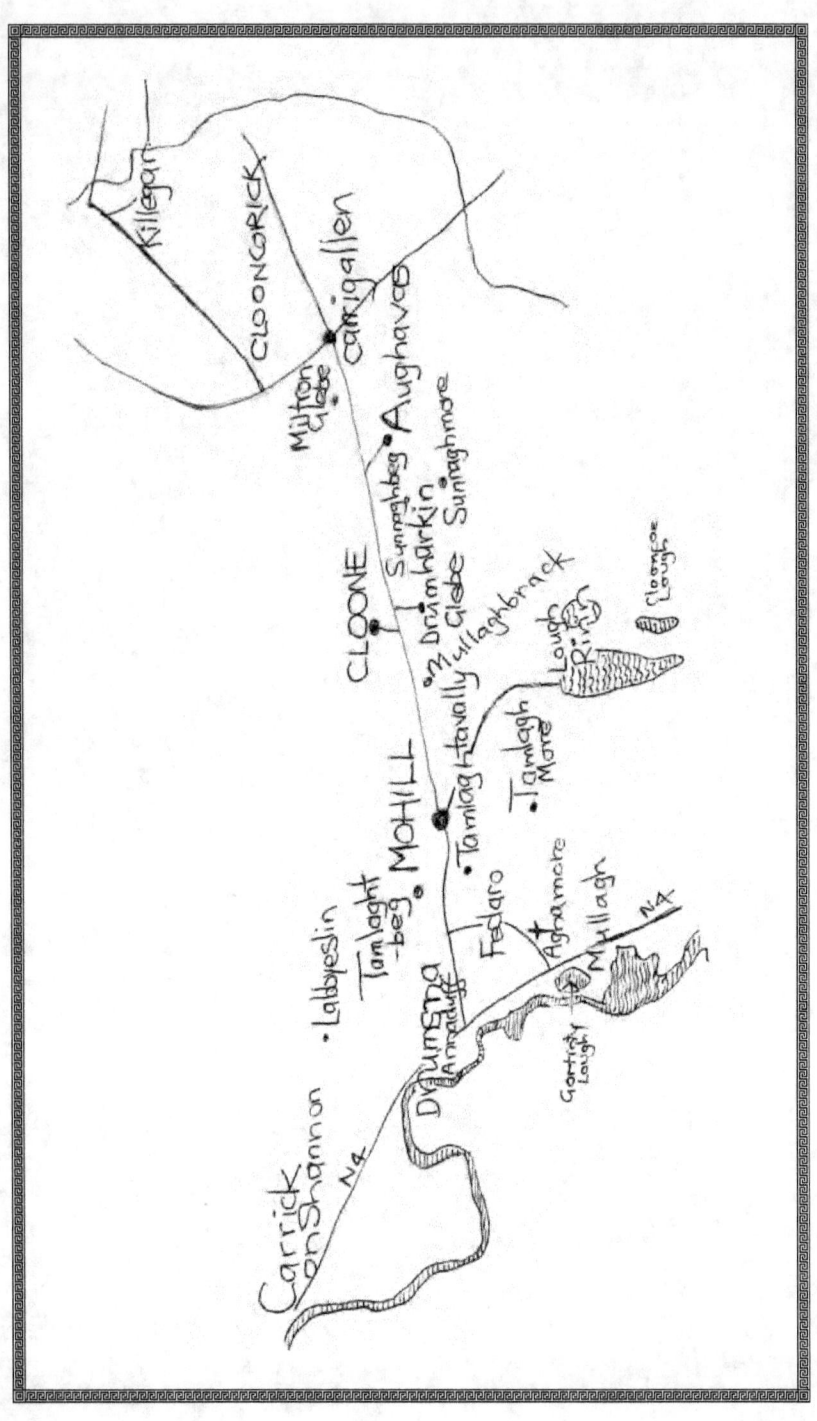

Chapter 5
Saintly Envy

Conmhaícne Maigh Rhein

When talking about medieval Leitrim, people often refer to the territory of Breifni. But, for much of its existence, Breifni was only the northern part of modern Leitrim. South Leitrim was called Magh Rein or Conmhaícne Magh Rhein in early histories, becoming the Barony of Mohill after the Plantation of Leitrim. It was populated by the Conmaicne (pronounced 'con-mac-nee'), an original Connaught tribe thought to have dispersed to these regions between around 500-700AD. Part of Magh Rein was called Muinter Eolais, Territory of the Descendants of Eolus. Eolais mac Biobhsach was the illustrious ancestor from whom the old clans descended - the MacShanley, MacGarry, MacRagnaill, O'Mulvey, O'Doonan, O'Keegan O'Murray and O'Moran. We see him commemorated in the townland of Corryolus, west of Carrick on Shannon - the Ford of Eolus.[1] North Leitrim was called West Breifne, or Breiffni O'Rourke. It included some of today's Co. Cavan to the east and some of Co. Sligo to the west. From around the 13th century, the O'Rourke overlords ruled all of Leitrim, but the MacRagnaill chiefs in Conmhaícne Magh Rein often rebelled and battled with the them.[2]

We journey now to Mohill, in the heartlands of Conmhaícne Maigh Rhein, the Plain of the Conmaicne, that's bordered partly by the Rein/Rinn River. The Conmaicne were said to be early converts to Christianity and there were several saints amongst them, but it was so long ago that they are barely remembered. However Mohill had a most illustrious saint, who left a literary trail and a fine artefact, the surviving mark of his legacy.

Fedaro

Going to Mohill on back roads can be fascinating, but do go slow! They take you through sleepy farm pastures and past tranquil lakes. From ancient to medieval times it was thickly wooded around here and this gave much seclusion, mystery and intrigue. There are many townlands with Derry in their name, signifying an oak wood and these would have been pastured by pigs, that feasted on the mast of the forests, gorging on acorns and the like.

From Drumsna going south down the N4, go past the Mohill turn off and turn left a little further on at Aghamore (Big Field), beside the church on the hilltop. This road will take you through the townlands of Antfield, then Fedaro, before the road connects up with the R201 road that goes to Mohill. Fedaro is an anglicised name that some translate as Fiodh Drudha - the Druids' Wood.

Fedaro was mentioned in the Annals of Lough Key in 1345. It may well have had political importance, as the Druids belonged to the elite classes and, if one was passing through their territory, it could have been pertinent to pay them a visit. And, if pursued, one might retreat to them for a place of sacred protection. This could be suggested by the following extract from the Annals of Connaught, where a fateful incident was recorded for Fedaro.

"Toirrdelbach son of Aed son of Eogan O Conchobair [O'Connor], king of Connacht for the space of twenty-one years, and a good man for the kingship of Ireland if God had vouchsafed it to him, was killed by an arrow-shot in Fedaro in Muinter Eolais. He had gone to Rinn Loch to help Tadg Mag Ragnaill against the descendants of Muirchertach Muimnech O Conchobair, and the Clann Muirchertaig Muimnig and the rest of the Muinter Eolais followed him to Fedaro and he was killed at Guirtin na Spidoige [the Redbreast's Field]." ³

Fedaro is mentioned by surveyor John O'Donovan as being a *"well cultivated townland"* with a few houses and a small bog in the north west. In the townland of Antfield, also *"a well cultivated townland"*, where it borders with Aghintaish there's a stone heap that's marked as a 'monument' on old maps. However it is only some 350 years old, having been raised over the bodies of soldiers killed in 1689. ⁴

LABBYESLIN

Labbyeslin is north of Eslinbridge, a small town on the River Eslin to the north west of Mohill. To get to Eslinbridge from the R201, take the next intersection left after passing Lough Erril. Keep going north at Eslinbridge, veer left at the Stuck Cross road, cross the Eslin River and when you get to the main road intersection at Funshinagh crossroads, keep going straight. When you go over the Labbyeslin Bridge, crossing the Eslin River soon after, you are then in the townland of Labbyeslin. (The road goes on to Rowan/Laragh Lough, where acclaimed writer John MacGahern's home overlooked the lake from a drumlin hill to the north.)

It's a tiny place with a giant story that I was told by a woman native to the area. Mrs Macnabola explained that the name of the place refers to - *"a lobby stone, oe leaba in Gaelic, which means a sleeping stone, or in modern terms a gravestone from prehistoric times. Today the stone is not visible to the eye, having being covered for thousands of years with grass and growth etc. The stone gave its name to the townland Labbyeslin or Lobbyeslin. It is mentioned in archaeological journals."* (The site is on private land of her family and is not accessible.) *"The legend tells of a giant called Eslin being killed by a huge stone thrown from Sliabh an Iarann by Fionn Mac Cumhall, another giant. Eslin is buried under that stone in a ringfort on our land. Labby stones would denote the final resting places of important people in prehistory,"* she told me.

The Eslin River that runs through this district, flowing roughly north - south, was the eastern boundary of the parish of Annaduff and before then, the boundary of the tribal lands of the Mac Shanleys, elites of Muinter Eolus. Perhaps the river dictated the choice of location for this tomb, if it is one. Or it might have been a boundary marker, or both. Around here, the Shanleys are long indigenous, indeed, the original form of the name Mac Seanlaoich means Old Hero.⁵ Shanley lands included Aghamore, where the hilltop church and graveyard are located, also Mullagh townland, plus their capital, just south of Annaduff, at Corrick (previously Corrickmacshanley), which was once a minor fording point on the Shannon. It was a fertile strip beside the river and they were often at war over it with the MacRagnaill overlords. One battle is recorded to have occurred in 1473 in the Derries (which must refer to the three townland names there with Derry/Oak Tree in the prefix). After the Plantation of Leitrim, planter family the Nesbitts were given control of these lands, but the MacShanleys co-operated, dropped the Mac from their name and received much of their lands back. ⁶

MOHILL

One of the most prestigious monastic centres in Moy Rein was based in Mohill, in the valley of the Rinn River. Mohill used to be a lively place, the third most important county town, with the biggest weekly market and fairs in south Leitrim. The bustling market town hosted fifteen annual market fairs through the year and the railway junction helped it to thrive in more recent times. But after the railway was dismantled in 1959, the town became a shadow of its former self. Which means that its streetscape has retained its old character.

Mohill had an early and prestigious abbey, but little of certainty is known of the monastery's founder, St Manchán (pronounced Mawn-e-chan), who gave his name to the town - originally Maothail-Manacháin. His life and genealogy have been widely debated. It gets confusing as there seems to be more than one St Manchan in the literature. One Manchán was born in Ireland or Wales, possibly in the year 464. He became a saint in Irish and Welsh tradition. When he lived and died is debated. The Annals of Tigernach say that the scribes of Iona Abbey recorded 538CE as the year of his death. The Book of Fenagh suggests Manchán was contemporary with Saint Caillín (464CE) and became his successor as Abbot of Fenagh. Some say he was a second cousin of St Caillin. His feast day was on February 14th. [7]

Manchán's great sanctity is recorded in various annals. They identify him as the Saint whose venerated reliquary, the Shrine of Manchán of Maothaill, was made in the monastery in Roscommon town probably in the early 12th century, some 400 years after his death. One of Ireland's greatest medieval treasures (seen depicted on the flag above), this unique and intricate piece has extraordinary craftsmanship. It's a tent-shaped book container made of Yew wood and adorned with gilded and incised bronze decorations. It was once covered with silver plates too, of which traces still remain. About the size of a suitcase, it's raised up by short legs that slot into metal shoes and it's attached to metal rings that are probably meant for carrying-poles, as the shrine was carried in procession. Patterns of beasts and serpents adorn it and inside the shrine, fragments of human bones were kept. Tradition holds them to be that of the saint himself. Or the other Manchán perhaps.

The relic was recorded at Lemanaghan church (now in ruins) around the year 1630 and it's now preserved in the nearby 19th century parish church in the tiny village of Boher in County Offaly. While it's common for people to revere a local saint associated with the district (and usually not officially recognised by the Roman Catholic Church), it isn't typical to find a 900 year old treasure on display in a local church. The shrine is also the central motif of stained glass windows made by the renowned Harry Clarke of Dublin that were installed into this church in 1930. [8]

Mohill's tradition is that Manchán was born in Mohill. For some, he was the son of Daga, for the others, of Innaoi. His mother's name was Mella and he had two sisters, Grealla and Greillseach. He went on to spend much of his life in Leamanachan, Co. Offaly, at one of several of his foundations. Firstly, Manchán founded the monastery of Mohill in the 6th century. He went to establish between four and seven more churches along a north-south corridor between Mohill and Liath Manchain, a name now corrupted to Lemanaghan, in Co. Offaly, where the early monastery bears his name. He probably travelled between them via inland waterways where possible, because the overland route was difficult, slow and uncomfortable. The key rivers serving Manchán's route were the Shannon and the Rinn.

If a legend about St Manchán is true it must have been particularly slow getting around, for the saint is said to have had a magic cow that bestowed unlimited quantities of milk to all whom he offered it to. Rich and poor alike were all benefiting from her. But when a greedy woman tried to milk her out into a sieve and it was wasting away on the ground, the poor cow eventually started to bleed and her milk dried up, permanently so. [9] As a theme common to other saints, such as St Bridget, one can imagine the tale is merely a plagiarism. Because I'd say that originally this is a generic morality tale for the teaching of environmental truths. It tells us that the resources we take from the Earth are not unlimited, we have to keep within Earth's carrying capacity and not 'over-milk' her bounty. It also gives a nod to the Indo-European origins of religion here, where the cow goddess has been revered as a bountiful being, as She still is in Hindu India (as on the left), as well as by modern Pagan folk who revere Boinn, the Irish cow goddess.[10]

In the 13th century the Augustinians took over the monastery at Mohill and it became an important priory that thrived until the time of Henry the 8th. In 1590 the monastery was destroyed by an "immense army" of British forces that were enforcing Henry's Reformation. They fought with troops of the O'Rourkes and MacRaghnaills and stole 1,000 cattle from them. The site is now occupied by a Protestant church and graveyard, and only an old school house remains at the back, while the original monastery was of considerable extent. St Mary's church was built in 1815 on the site of the monastery and priory, notes Fiona Slevin, a local historian and author from Mohill.[11]

People of prestige were no doubt buried there, as the folklore has recorded. *"It is said that the last of the Mac Raghnaill chiefs is buried in Mohill Protestant Churchyard, to the east of the entrance gate."* [12]

PLAGUE SAINT

In the mid-6th century there was huge fear and panic experienced from the Justinian Plague (bubonic plague) that arrived around year 544 and devastated the population. Inexplicably, some dropped dead from it in less than a day, some fell ill but then recovered, while others were not affected at all. These random results could have been interpreted as evidence of divine selection and no doubt it fuelled peoples' desperate pleas for help. Religion must have become more popular in those anxious times. Manchán was active around then and he came to be venerated as a protecter from plague.

I don't think he was overly successful however, because mass burial place names attest to catastrophic waves of multiple deaths that occurred in the area. The presence of the plague and the sad loss of lives is immortalised in townland names. Tamlacht signifies a mass plague burial place. Three are located near Mohill - at Tamlaght More, Tamlaght Beg and Tamlaghtavally, to the west and south-west of the town. [13] These townlands are confirmed to be the locations of mass plague burial sites. Other plagues came and went also, up until more recent times, as the following story attests. The disease that killed people was caused by mass starvation and weakness, one of the follow-on effects of famine.

"After the famine [1846+] there was a plague of Black Cholera around here and the people died like flies. There had to be a special graveyard provided to bury the dead, one convenient so that the sad journey wouldn't take long. The one provided is Bully's Acre and my grandmother told me that she herself saw as often as twelve bodies heaped on the cart going to Bully's Acre, and there were no coffins as there was no money or time to get them. Also that lime was largely used in the burying of the dead". [14] The townland name Bully's Acre sounds silly in English, because it's another sloppy anglicisation of an Irish name. It's derived from Acra an Bhulai, meaning Burial Ground.

Manchán probably had a holy well of healing waters associated with his cult. John O'Donovan, in referring to 19th century Mohill, claimed that St. Manchan's Well was still in the town somewhere, but its location is forgotten now. The Archeological Survey makes no mention of it. Memory of it is found in the Folklore Commission files, however. *"At the back of John Thomas's house as you go into Mohill there is a well and Saint Patrick is supposed to have blessed it, it cures warts. You have to go three days to the well, on Monday, Thursday and Monday, Then the person leaves a ribbon or something after them".* [15]

St Manchán may have put Mohill on the map originally, but he's hardly remembered today, although up until the late 20th century there was the renowned Manchán's Fair, a name that became corrupted to Monaghan Day. This was held in Mohill annually until the 1970s. Its date was the feast day of the Saint, the 25th of February. (Originally his feast day was on February 14th. The day change may have been enacted after the Julian Calendar was imposed, that shifted events by around ten days.) Not only did the name subtly change over time, the memories have warped and wafted along with it. One Folklore Commission school story explains the origin of the fair day name as two families of Monaghans who use to fight between themselves at fair day and gave their name to it! [16]

The plot of highly acclaimed novel 'Amongst Women', by Leitrim author John McGahern - a writer of mythic proportions! - revolves around Monaghan Day (Manchán's Fair) in Mohill. McGahern was a native of the area and during his life he was considered Ireland's greatest living writer. He once wrote: *"Mohill is our town. . . In its plain way I think it beautiful. I think of Mohill as one of the happiest towns in the world".* [17]

After penning a few controversial books, some banned, and having to leave the country to a friendlier nation (England), McGahern returned to Ireland and ended his days more peacefully, living and writing about rural life and characters he knew there (causing some ire!) around his farm in Aghaboneill townland. His home overlooked Rowan Lough, south west of Fenagh. He died in 2006 and is buried in Aghawillan, where he had his childhood.

Just after McGahern died, a local woman told me, a group of swans provided a stately

spectacle. They were seen to line up on the lake, as if performing a graceful tribute to McGahern's passing, a final 'swan song'.

Mohill was once the home of Turlough O'Carolan (1670 -1738) who spent a few years living there. He was the famous harper known for his great gift for melodic composition. A statue of him takes pride of place in the centre of town, across the road from the church and monastery site. O'Carolan became blind after catching smallpox in his youth. Fortunately he had a wealthy patron who paid for his apprenticeship with a harpist. He then toured the countryside as a guest of other wealthy patrons, entertaining them and writing songs of tribute to them (called planxties). One of his most famous compositions is the tune 'Sheemore, Sheebeg', said to be inspired by the mythic fairy hills. However, as musicians have always done, he was probably recycling an older piece, a Scottish air!

Hyde Street in Mohill is named for Douglas Hyde, first President of Ireland, whose father and grandfather lived on that street. Hyde spent some of his childhood in the town and went on to study Ireland's legendary past. He was a keen collector of folklore. The Douglas Hyde Centre, in Frenchpark, Co Roscommon, celebrates his life.

MULLAGHBRACK AND BELCARRA

Heading eastwards from Mohill, passing Broom St village on the R201, Mullaghbrack is the next townland on the right. It hides a vanished past, that took a bit of detective work to find. Here, on the south bank of the Cloone River, was once the village of Belcarra, a name that could well mean the same as the other Belcarra (Baile na Cora) in Co. Mayo, whose name translates to the Village of the Weir / River Ford. Clues are found in local folklore gathered in the 1930s by school students for the Folklore Commission. *"Belcarra, along the Cloone River about three miles from Mohill, the scene of many a skirmish between the O'Reillys of Cavan and the Reynolds of Muintur Eolais."* [18]

Cloone River is a virtual continuation of the Rinn River north of Lough Rinn and it would have been a regional boundary marker of tribal territory. Hence the mentioned skirmish in this edgy border zone. Past warfare must have been of a provincial nature, judging by another story about the mythic black pig that dug the borderline embankments and ditches of this once very fluid Ulster - Connaught divide. *"The black pig rooted his way from Ballyshannon to Athlone and the hollow is still to be seen where he rooted. People in Belcarra were known to sell their land and to buy land in Rooskey to get away from the Valley of the Black Pig."* [19]

So, where was Belcarra and why would its residents not want to be there? It wasn't on the current OS map. But poring over the 1890 map online, I did eventually find it, in the form of 'Belscarry', located beside the River Cloone at the north end of the townland of Mullaghbrack. Located beside an ancient stepping stone ford on the river, it was once an industrial landscape,

with a corn mill, corn kiln and other buildings, but it's only marked on the older maps.
"The townland of Mullaghbrack ... is 321 acres and although there are eight houses in it there is only one Catholic child in it at present. It is the only place I know of where there is a ford across the river. There are waterfalls in the river. There was a flax mill in Mullaghbrack owned by a man named Bell. There are no ruins in it now." [20]

So, it looks like Belcarra, the village at the ancient river ford, was a fertile Plantation settlement and perhaps the Catholics were being driven away with false prophecies that the Planters propagated (more on this later). The buildings are long vanished, recycled into other homes, fences and stonework. The name became redundant after the population left, long after the Black Pig was rooting around. Folklore often muddles distinctions of time and place. We'll see later where this idea of escaping from the Valley of the Black Pig may have originated.

Just west of the ghost village of Belscarry/Belcarra, in the adjacent townland of Drumkeilvy, and above the old fording point, is a possible megalithic tomb or ancient territorial marker for this strategic boundary point. The dolmen, as recorded on old maps, consists of three orthostats (standing stones some 1.2 m high) and a displaced stone that form a rough, and overgrown, possible tomb chamber. [21]

CLOONE

A short distance further east of Mohill lies another famed and possibly older monastic centre, in Cloone. An Chluain Conmhaícne / Cloone Conmaicne is the historical name that goes back to the Iron Age. The parish is also called Cluain Conmaícne, the Meadow of the Conmhaícne. The Conmaícne tribe here differentiated themselves from the clans of Magh Rein. Nearby megalithic portal tombs and a barrow grave mound attest to a long line of ancient populations. The well preserved skull of an Irish Elk was found in the Cloone River near the village in the late 19th century. An Elk skull was found at the ford at Drumsna as well, a coincidence perhaps? Or votive offerings to the river spirits?

St. Cruimhthear Fraech established an important monastery in Cloone at the beginning of the sixth century, yet the whereabouts of the site has not been confirmed. Cruhir-Ree, as the name is pronounced locally, is the patron saint of the parish of Cloone, that adjoins the parish of Fenagh. Later referred to as both St Cruihir Ree and as St Fraoch, he was famous as the founder of the highly regarded monastery in 570CE, however others give this date as his death. While the Conmaícne resisted Christian conversion, this young prince of the ruling clan was said to have been converted by St Patrick, who was passing through Cloone on his way to Maigh Sleacht, leaving in his trail a line of holy Tobar Patraig wells dedicated to him to mark his route. He must have been old when he died to have been contemporary with Patrick, or the dates are wrong. (In pseudo-myth anything can be changed to suit the dominant paradigm! Often, an older name will indicate the original dedication to the well.) Fraoch's feast day was celebrated on December 20th. The hereditary coarb clan there were the McKeahan or McKeegan family.

St Colmcille was said to be one of many important holy men to have visited Cloone. He had come looking for advice from Fraoch, who was renowned for his wisdom and piety. Nonetheless, he had a big job to convert his hostile Conmaícne tribe, who would have seen no good reason to upend their age old spiritual ways, that combined animism with polytheism (plus their well established social mores). The task was taken up more successfully by his nephew, who became the famous St Barry. Barry was born just outside of Cloone in Gortnalougher and he was trained in the monastery in Cloone. He later became a disciple of St Kevin of Glendalough and went on to establish his own monastic settlement at Kilbarry in Co. Roscommon.

The Cloone abbey site is believed to be on an eminence on top of a drumlin in Cloone village. But abbey has left little physical trace, if it was indeed here. It's unusual for an abbey to not be beside a river or stream, although Cloone Lough and Cloone River are not too far away. Active until the early 12th century, nothing much remains apart from some relics that were installed in the current graveyard when it was refurbished. A former high cross that once stood there, has been described as a *"substantial cross base known locally as the wart well."* [22]

There are also three cross slabs, a piece of headstone with animals carved on its back and a bullaun stone, although it appears to be only a portion of it. Two stone heads and part of the shaft from a high cross have been inserted into the wall around the current Church of Ireland church, that replaced earlier churches. Another part of the same cross, that could date from the 10-12th century, is displayed in the graveyard of the early 19th century St Mary's Catholic Church, on the eastern slope of the drumlin. The site of the monastery itself is believed to be where the present tower of the former St James Church (built 1822) stands today, on the summit. However the archaeological trace is virtually non-existent.[23]

Cloone is only 8.5 km from Fenagh and there was serious competition between the two saints. Cloone was a popular foundation and monks would defect from Fenagh to join it. As a result, Caillin became incensed and warned them in no uncertain terms that if they forsook Fenagh their lives would be shortened and they'd go to hell for eternity. That must have scared them off, because he won the battle for allegiance and Cloone's popularity waned.

Interpretive panels recently installed below the graveyard in the Garden of Remembrance, below St James church, give a great introduction to the local history. They mention some trouble in establishing the monastery. In local legend, they tell, there was supernatural intervention in building work at the monastery, in the form of a formidable black pig. *"It came each night to destroy construction work that had taken place during the day...the laneway directly alongside this garden became known as Torc Lane, the Lane of the Boar"*.

Fraoch had a special relic in the form of a bell that was reputedly brought from Rome and given to him by St Patrick. It was known as Clog na Fola, the Bell of Blood, because it developed some controversy over its use. The bell custodians used it for measuring gold, corn and the like, for the payment of church taxes. But they removed the tongue to greedily fit more in, keeping the excess funds. Fraoch discovered the deception and cursed them. He foretold that the bell would go on to be a source of discord. It fell into foul hands and was abused more, so the prophesy came true.

The bell was kept in a shrine that depicted a donkey's head turned backwards. It was used for the making of oaths and the determination of guilt by its guardians, the O'Rourkes. The idea being that if you told lies, your own head would also turn backwards. *"They brought it around the country, to any place there was a lawsuit. It was taken into a room by one of the O'Rourkes, taken out of the shrine and left on a table. Then the people ... came into the presence of the bell and said, "I swear by clog na fola and the full of it" They then proceeded to state their evidence and if they told a lie, the bell rang."* [24]

You can imagine the trickery that could used in such a situation. No wonder it caused dissent. *"There was a curse on this bell, and it was said that there would always be quarrelling and trouble wherever it was kept. The people that swore before it often fell out and riled each other and that was how it got its name 'The Bell of Blood'. About 200 years ago the priest in Aughavas ordered the bell to be buried and the bell and shrine was buried 9 feet deep in a garden in the townland of Aughavas."* [25]

DRUMHARKIN GLEBE

St Creigharee's Well, dedicated to St Fraech, is located in a peaceful rural setting approximately 2 km south of Cloone village, in Drumharkin Glebe. It has stones, a low mound and a 1950 concrete shrine and cross, with a niche for statues.[25] It was once a much-visited holy well. When Fraoch first joined the new faith he left his family and went to live in a little stone hut in Drumharkin, where he lived the simple life of penance and prayer. He lived near the holy well that was in a triangular field at the base of a west facing slope. [26] It was a popular site for festivities on annual Pattern Days, held on Garlic Sunday, the last Sunday in July, a date that gives a nod to Pagan traditions of the harvest festival. The Pattern Day continued there until circa 1860, after which it was transferred to the well at Kiltoghert, O'Neill reports in her round up of Lughnasa traditions.[27] The well in its current state is described as *"a shallow hole with no water."* [28]

"St. Creigharees Well...was once a famous well, but is now almost dried up. All that now remains is a little marsh covered with green moss. There are also some ancient looking trees and a few mounds....The Station was done on Garland Sunday. It used to be as throng as a 26th of May Fair in Cloone. There used to be 'standings' [food and drink stalls] and clowns and all kinds of gaiety. It was also a great place for matchmaking and when the match was made the matchmaker, and the boy and girl used to be treated to a jug of punch. Several cures were wrought at it. A man once came to do the Station riding on an ass. He was lame and he went away perfectly cured.

"The Station at St. Creigharee's Well involved the typical activities of walking round the trees (keeping to right all times) saying seven Paters seven Aves and seven Glorias in honour of St Creigharee, and when finishing the above prayers, kneeling at a heap of stones opposite the well. Then, at the face of the well, people would tie a piece of string on a small bush that grows beside the well, as well as bring a piece of clay or moss home with them. The prayers and rounds were repeated three times." [29]

You can access the site by turning down the lane on the right hand side (west) of the sports ground before the Cloone turnoff. Park at the corner where another smaller lane joins this lane on the right. Walk up the steep lane (that's not accessible by car) that crosses over what looks like an esker, a long narrow ridge. At its base on the other side you will find the triangular field. It has a sublime atmosphere and lovely trees.

Here was once the go-to place for the saint and his people, so not everyone is convinced that Creigharee's abbey's was on the hilltop at Cloone. *"I believe that St. Creigharee had his monastery or cells at Drumharkin Glebe. This tract of land is fertile and for generations has been in the possession of Protestants of the titled class. The lands are called the Grange and the Rectory. The Grange was owned by the Whites and Fitzpatricks, who were titled people in England and the parson lived in the Rectory till recent years. We generally find that the English resided on the lands of the old monasteries and that is why I claim that St Creigharee's monastery was in the Glebe and not far from the place where his holy well commemorates his name."* 30

Before the holy well was revered at Drumharkin Glebe there was a well at the nearby townland of Esker that attracted hordes to celebrate an annual Pattern Day there.

"[The] St Creigharee ... holy well was on top of John Donohue's field, townland of Esker, just at Cloone crossroads. One time a woman went to wash clothes in the well and it disappeared and came up in Drumharkin Glebe about one mile away in the lands of John Foley. There were trees growing around the well and a man went one day and cut one of the trees and he died suddenly that evening. The water if boiled for any other purpose than drinking always turned to blood. People yet do stations to the well. When it was at Esker there was a great station to it and people used to come to it from all parts. There are yet remains of stones to mark its first site."
31

"On top of this hill [in Esker] there still remain a number of round stones and a lone bush. Those stones are said to return to the spot no matter where they are placed. Once a Protestant man that lived in the Glebe took them and threw them into Keeldra lough, but in the morning they were back again on top of Donohue's hill and they have never been disturbed since." 32

On the other side of the river, on top of a drumlin in the north west corner of Drumharkin Glebe (that some say is in Annaghmacconway, the adacent townland), are the remains of a ring barrow, probably a prestigious Iron Age tomb. It's described by archeologists as a D shaped mound, 10 m by 9 m by 70 cm high, with shallow fosse 4 m wide and 30 - 40 cm deep. A north- south field boundary bank has truncated it to the west. [33]

CLOONE SURROUNDINGS

Ancient markers of habitation surround the Cloone area. *"Cloone forms the centre of a surrounding range of hills bearing the same name Sunach e.g. Sunnaghmore, Sunnaghconnor, Sunnaghhennity, Sunnahbeg, and also a smaller range bearing the name Annaugh, Annaughmacoolin, Annaughmaconway, Annaughbrennan, etc. On each of the Sunnaghs there are the remains of forts and these I believe were strongly fortified by the Con-Maicne. In Annaughmaconway there is the remains of an old burial ground. It is on a hill called Caldaragh. This is not a pagan burial ground as many suppose, because leading from Cloone across the bog to Caldragh, there is the remains of an old pass which the very old people tell me was called Bóthar na Naomh [the Saints Road]. Along this pass was carried the corpses of the dead from Cloone Monastery to be buried in Caldaragh."* [34]

This Bóthar Na Naomh path has been revived of late and is today a new walking track developed in the Cloone town area. It's a looped walk through a scenic, rural landscape with vistas of riverbank, damp meadows, woodland, bog and lakeshore. It derives its name from the old route that connects the purported monastic site in Cloone Village to the burial ground on Caldragh Hill nearby. The northern section follows this route, while other parts of the track use modern pathways to the school, church, village and bog. The total length is 5.75 km.

SUNNAGHMORE

Adjacent to Drumharkin Glebe to the east is Sunnaghmore townland. It must have an ancient lineage, because on the western boundary of the townland are two portal tombs, marked on the OS maps in a north-south alignment. It also had an important fort, according to the folklore, although there appears to be no other record of it. *"Sunach Mór - the 'great fortification', embraces one of the most commanding and imposing hills in the neighbourhood. From the top there is a perfect view of the country for 30 miles in all directions especially towards the Nth West. There are several divisions of the town-land. The top of the hill is called Barr-na-Ranna. ... Sunach Beag, the little fortification, a small hill north west from Sunnaghmore and about one mile distant. ...Also in Mount Ida* [in the south west corner of Sunnaghmore, a name not now used] *there is a castle or cave of three large stones called (Leabaidh Gráine). Graine lived there when she came to this part of the country. They say Finn MaCool built this strange house for his mother. When I was young people used to steal convenient to it of a Hallow Eve night to see sights that were very strange. "* [35]

The forts probably date from the Iron Age. However the megalithic 'cave' or chamber just described is much older. Of the two megaliths found in Sunnaghmore, one is described by archeologists as a portal tomb on a low ridge in a north-south valley, the remains of a tomb with up to four separate, overgrown stone chambers. The other portal tomb, in a low lying position in the same north - south valley, is an overgrown two chambered monument with no visible cairn or roofstone. [36] One of them is called a Diarmuid and Grainne Bed on old maps, a common name that weaves a pre-historic site with a mythic age story.

Sunnaghmore hill and fort seems to have been a fertile and prestigious location in its day.

O'Donovan noted almost 200 years ago that the townland *"contains some good farm houses."* [37] A corn kiln is marked on old maps and there was a school at Sunnaghmore, from where much folklore was collected in the 1930s. After the ring forts were abandoned, they became known as the homes of the fairies and Other world beings. Sometimes they housed the most powerful fairies, kings and queens of the Other world, as the following unique account reveals. This is the start of one such (long) story, as told by a native of Sunnaghmore, James Murphy.

"Dun Binne was the head of all the Leitrim fairies and was supposed to keep his court on Sunnaghmore Hill, parish of Cloone. ... About nightfall James McKiernan started off...[and] It was late when he was coming home, and when he was passing by the old fort on the side of the hill, he met a crowd of fairy horsemen led by Dun Binne. They surrounded him and Dun Binne said, 'James McKiernan! we are a long time waiting for you'. So the side of the hill opened and they all rode in and James in the middle of them. Inside James saw hundreds and hundreds of people that were long dead and that he knew well. The fairies put a great welcome before James and they all came up and said: - 'Arah! James McKiernan you are welcome. We are a long time waiting for you'..." [38]

Aghavas

From Cloone heading east along the R201 main road is the small village of Aghavas, just south off the road. The Archeological Survey of Leitrim describes the remains of a portal tomb here, that lie on a gentle south west slope, with two portal stones, a side stone and a back stone defining an overgrown chamber that's set into a rectangular cairn, now altered, with its north west corner becoming incorporated into a field boundary. A large slab close by could well be the original roof stone, they suggest.[39]

To get there, take the turnoff to Aghavas on the right, go another kilometre. Pull over where there's a lane running down to a house and the access to the site is a little way down this lane, on the right side through a gate. The site is on the far side of the field from where you enter. Investigators have reported that - *"The undergrowth has completely reclaimed this site. It was difficult to get any measurements or to see how many stones were involved in this site."* [40]

Miltron Glebe

Continuing north east from Aghavas on the R201, when you approach the townland of Miltron Glebe and pass a school on the left, take the next turn left into these old church lands. They must have been fertile, to be selected as such. Soon after, take a small road off to the left and close to the road are what may be a megalithic monument of standing stones, that could be confirming the past importance of the place. They are located on an east facing drumlin slope. The line of six conglomerate boulders up to 60 cm high are in a linear alignment that goes for 5.6 m. Two have been displaced. [41]

Carrigallen

Continuing along the R201 you get to Carrigallen, a town that's close to the borders of Leitrim as well as Longford and Cavan. It is a pleasant town overlooking a tranquil lake. The surrounding area has some reasonably good soils that have long favoured mixed farming. The town developed in medieval times and seems to have been referred to in the Annals in the

13th century as Tulaigh or Tulach Aliann, the ancient name for a Beautiful Hill. But little is known of its earliest origins.[42] Carrigallen means Beautiful Rock and the first church in town was built on a rocky eminence overlooking it. Today, a Gothic style Church of Ireland church, completed in 1816, is located on this rock, the namesake of the town. It's beside the remains of a 15th century Catholic Church in the grounds, that was destroyed by Cromwell's soldiers.[43]

It's possible that the rocky site was a sacred place in Pagan times with a continuum of spiritual power. Or, it may have been a defended hilltop site, the past castle of a chieftain. Or it may have been both, having been granted to the missionaries from the elites who owned the strategic site. Little of the ancient past is known here, Carrigallen has yielded few archeological finds. However a wonderful, well preserved medieval leather shoe (above), from the 10-11th century, was dug up from Carrigallen Bog around 1840. It was beautifully preserved in the acidic conditions. One of the finest examples of its kind, it's now in the National Museum in Dublin.

Another national treasure from near Carrigallen is the Ballyvalley Axe - a 4000-year-old Bronze Age axe found in the townland of Augharan, in the parish of Aughavas, in 1995 and these days displayed in the National Museum of Ireland, far from Leitrim eyes, in Dublin. [44]

CLOONCORICK

Close to Carrigallen to the north was a place of far greater importance in past times. The adjacent townland of Clooncorick has been documented in the Annals as the local centre of royal power and occasional battle ground. The name Clooncorick translates as the Meadow Land of Combat. Nearby are two standing stones, according to archeologists, but locally called the Kings Grave. Described by others as a portal dolmen missing its capstone, these are located near the bottom of a north east facing slope, closely set at 35 cm apart. They are in a roughly north-south alignment and stand at 1.35 m and 1.5 m in height.[45] The drumlin hill above them is Mullindaree, the Hill of the Two Kings. These kings fought together and died at this place, the folklore and O'Donovan say. (But the story could have been fabricated to explain the stones.)

The site of Clooncorick Castle, on a rocky outcrop in Clooncorick townland, was one of the power centres of the O'Rourkes for many a year. A village probably existed there long before Carrigallen was established. Shane Oge O'Rourke was granted 1800 acres here for the Manor of Clooncorick in 1629, but the family had already been established there for generations, perhaps using the crannog. The O'Rourke castle was in use up until the Williamite wars of the 1690s. A big house was later built there and more buildings added in the 18th century, but nothing is left to be seen now.[46] However, part of the castle courtyard and stables are still standing, according to a local history website.[47]

Nearby, in Clooncorick Lough can be seen a steep sided crannog made with many interlocking timbers that are still visible. The crannog is now connected to the shore, via the modern addition of fishing jetties.⁴⁸ It was probably the original safe haven for the O'Rourke chiefs, who, upon the crannog would have stayed in buildings of woven wattle (branches) and daub (clay), that were thatched over cosily with lake reeds.

Carrigallen's most famous daughter was Margaret of New Orleans (USA), a charitable woman of great acclaim who was born in the area in 1813. You can go back in time and see a copy of her family home, a little thatched cottage that was built to commemorate her in 2008. It has been opened to the public every Sunday in August from 2-5pm, with free entry. The location is in the townland of Tully South, eircode HI2X003.

KILLEGAR

East, north-east of Clooncorick, Kilnamar and Laheen Loughs lie near the Cavan/Leitrim border and these have several crannoga between them. Laheen townland is adjacent to Killegar village. A Protestant plantation, therefore presumably a highly arable area, it's nowadays much covered with forestry plantations. John O'Donovan described Killegar as *"greatly composed of wood and ornamental ground...It also includes the seat of John Godley Esq., Killegar village and Mr Godfrey's church."* It must have also been fertile in the adjacent Laheen townland, a name he translates as the Beautiful Half, as *"there is a good corn mill near the northern boundary...Nearly all under cultivation"*. ⁴⁹

In 1957 an ancient log boat was found under the waters of Kilnamar Lough. It disintegrated upon exposure to the surface air. Evidence of an elite bolthole in a prosperous area, two crannogs are located there, only 17 m apart. They aren't visible on the water surface, but evident by the pile of round stones piled up to about one metre in height, as the base for these artificial islands. What convinced the discoverers that these were crannoga (that are not marked on OS maps) was the finding of some "fine saddle querns" also a few "probable hearth stones", lying 75 cm or so under the lake water and visible from above in a boat. (Water levels must have risen over them.) The discoverer, John Kilbracken, noted that saddle querns were superseded when Celtic tribes arrived bringing more efficient rotary querns with them. (Rotary quern stones were first introduced into Ireland circa 150 BC.) So these are ancient places of habitation. The crannog sites are 150 m from Killegar House, a later manifestation of a regional power centre and seat of Lord Kilbracken. ⁵⁰

Saintly Envy

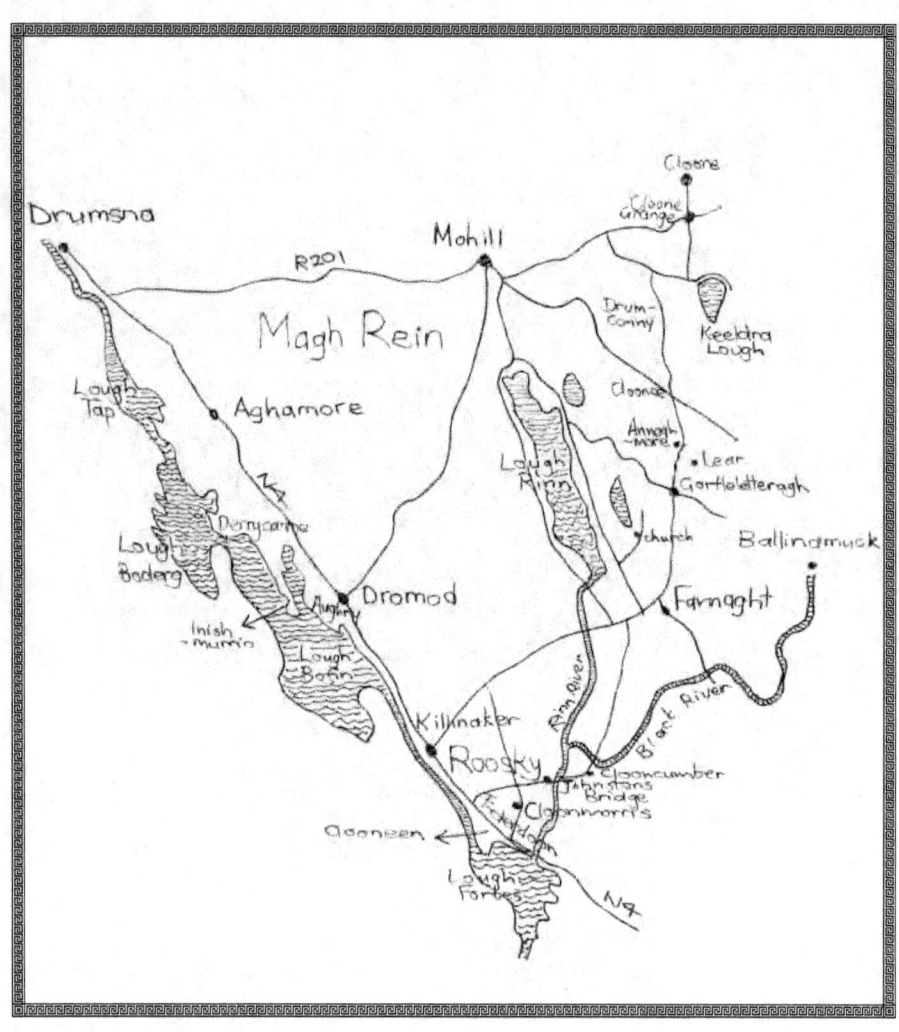

CHAPTER 6
LAKES OF THE HOLY COW

RIVER MERMAIDS AND COW LAKES

Heading down the N4 road to southernmost Leitrim there are wide vistas of river lands along the mighty River Shannon. This was once an Ulster - Connaught borderland area with several seats of political power attested to by mouldering stone ruins. Ancient river mythos also lingers. You have come to a liminal realm and need to take care, the waters are alluring and fickle. A healthy sense of awe and fear, underlying adventure, is reflected in the folklore of Ireland's watery realms. Serious respect was required when venturing near its edges, as the following tale from the locality warns.

"Stories are told about mermaids in this district. People say she has a girls head with long hair and a tail like a fish. People say when she sees anyone walking near water at 12 o'clock at night she pulls them in and turns them into a mermaid, or if a person goes near water on a Whit Sunday the mermaid will pull him in and turn him into a mermaid."[1]

The MacShanley clan was dominant here in the riverside townlands between Annaghduff and Derrycarne. There was constant warfare with the MacRaghnaills, their over-lords, who wanted to take over their stronghold at Corrickmacshanley (now the townland of Corrick). But several of their townlands were later given by the English to Viscount Grandison, who liked the strategic location between Ulster and Connaught. In the early 1600s the MacShanleys decided to co-operate with the Nesbitts and they were then re-granted back most of their ancestral lands. (They dropped the Mac in their name in the process.)

Heading south on the N4 after Drumsna, if you turn right after passing Gortintee Lough you'll be passing through their ancient territory. Or turn right a bit later on and go down the tiny road beside the ex-pub on the hilltop at Aghamore, heading towards Derrycarne. These are tranquil rural landscapes now, but there was much human activity here in the past. Near the boundary of Mullagh (once called Mullagh MacShanley) and Gortintee townlands there were once two iron mines, as marked on the 1890 OS map, as well as a school in between them, all now vanished. In its day it was a centre of industry with a much higher population. The Gortinee quarries were worked from the 16th or 17th century. At the start of the 19th century Major Francis Nesbitt of Derrrycarne was sending the iron stone to Dublin for export, as the local furnaces were closed. Then the railway line was cut right through the quarry, exposing veins of limonite [2]

This part of the Shannon has two large lakes, Lough Boderg and Bofin, the Lakes of the Holy Red and White Cows. Drenched in deep lore, the holy cow no doubt comes from an ancient Vedic Indian origin. The Leitrim legend goes that a mermaid in one of these lakes was captured by a local family, who treated her kindly. In return, the grateful mermaid started to tell oracles all around the place. She also told the people that if they put her back in the lake on May Eve and then gathered on the same spot a year afterwards, she'd give them a hearty blessing in return for their kindness. So they did as she asked. Sure enough, on the following May Eve, out of the lake waters emerged a splendid pair of cows, a red and a white one. And as the two cows went their way over the land, they left behind them a fine broad road each, one to the west and one to the east.[3]

DERRYCARNE

You can appreciate the lake and walk picturesque woodland trails near the Shannon shore at Derrycarne, in the old Plantation demesne. The fastest route to get there from Drumsna is from Aghamore on the N4. Aghamore (Achadh Mor, the Big Field) is the highest point around, so the views are wide as you go down the tiny lane beside the old pub on the hilltop on the right, heading down towards the river. Derrycarne is signposted.

Lands around Derrycarne were acquired by the Nesbitt family in the early 1800s and later passed to Edward Willis and William Ormsby Gore MP. For a while, it was elite central here, but when the place went into decline it was sold in 1924 to the Irish Land Commission, who divided up the estate and sold land to the tenants (whose ancestors may have had it stolen from them). When it failed to sell in 1954, the lavish Derrycarne House was then completely demolished. Now the only thing remaining is an ice house, a stone domed structure that can be seen along the shore. The pleasant walking trail goes through a mixed woodland of Beech, Oak, Holly, Sitka Spruce and Lawson Cypress trees. There are a few large specimen trees over 200 years old, including Douglas Fir, but most of them were planted in the 1960s.[4]

A peninsula to the south of the old demesne lands was once an island, variously called Inchmurrin, Rabbit Island, or The Island. No doubt rabbits would enjoy burrowing in the sandy soil there, as they don't make inroads in clay. Since drainage schemes have lowered river levels, it's now connected to the mainland at the north. Otter Island is beside Inchmurrin and it's attached to the mainland on the western side. On the pre-drainage 1890 map it shows them as two distinct islands with two sets of stepping stone fords marked that lead across the river to Otter Island, one from Inchmurrin and the other from the mainland to the north.

On the summit of Inchmurrin sits a mystery cairn, a circular stone mound of large boulders, 11.5 m wide by 1.25 m high. The Archeological Inventory notes it, but reports *"no structural features* [are] *visible."*[5] I wonder if it might be another estate ornament, a fake ancient cairn? However this strategic location was noted in the Annals as being an elite centre in the 16th century, as MacLochlainn points out - *"Mag Raghanill of Magh Nissi relocated here after O'Ruaric occupied Liatroim (AD1540). The Taoiseach of Muintir Eolais lived on the hill of Inis Murrin in 1556".*[6]

FURNACE

Travelling from Derrycarne towards Dromod, when you get to the intersection near the railway line, turn right and a short distance along, between the road and the railway line on your left, on an eastern slope, is the site of a ringfort. One of the few that have a name, it's called Liscromaun Fort on the 1890 map. The sub-circular fort is fairly large at 42 m by 37 m internal diameter and with a 4 m wide bank around it up to 3 m high at the exterior.[7]

Until the 1600s it was a dense woodland here. In 1695 an ironworks was established in the townland of Blenkellue. Nowadays this townland is called Furnace. Perhaps it was associated with this fort? After the woods were all reduced to charcoal, the iron works closed in 1798. After then, the iron was exported to Britain.

FEARNAGHT

A short distance north from Furnace on the N4 and still close to the Shannon, you pass through the townland of Fearnaght. The name means Place of the Alder Trees. It was once much more heavily populated, with 261 people living there in 1841, compared to Drumsna that had only 19.[8] William of Dromod, the last chief of the Shanley clan, in the early 1600s was re-granted a large estate at Fearnaught and had a big house overlooking the river there. [9]

In a field on a western slope just west of the N4, there is a small well, a hole defined by boulders around it. It's close to a bullaun stone, an oval boulder 40 cm by 20 cm, that has a small basin on it.[10] It was obviously a busy area once and it's possible the site was used for secret Catholic rituals during the Penal Times, and equally, it could be an ancient Pagan festival site, where harvest celebrations involved the grinding of grain in the basin of the bullaun, to make the sacred cakes. (Leitrim is the home of the Cake Dance, after all!)

AUGHRY

Opposite Inchmurrin, on a peninsula that juts out into Lough Bofin, is the townland of Aughry. Strategicaly located on the shore of Lough Bofin, it has a small bay and landing place. Scottish Planters the Nesbitts built their three storey castle at Aughry in 1668, but it may not have been the first one on the site. *"It was one of the biggest Castles for miles around. In one of the ends of the house was a turret which was an enormous height."* [11]

The Castle of Aughry was burned down by rebels in 1689 during the Williamite war and Lady Nisbett cruelly murdered there, after which it was not inhabited afterwards, according to Nisbett family lore that was told to OS mapping researcher John O'Donovan around 1836. [12]

DROMOD

Near Aughry and beside Lough Boderg, this charming town with its old world streetscape, was originally called Dromode Mac Shanley. It grew out of the nearby iron works at Furnace. There were also iron mines in the area (including in Gortintee townland) plus dense woodland to fuel the furnace with wood-charcoal, which continued until the area was totally deforested and the land then was divided up into farms.

Dromod train station and a large part of Dromod town is located in Clooncolry townland. Cluain Calraí is Irish for its early Conmacnee inhabitants - the Fields of the Calraighe Tribe. Being located on the edgy borderland between Ulster and Connaught, the area was important before the Industrial Age and it was remembered in folklore for battles fought over it.

"1473: A great war broke out in Muintir-Eolais; and much was destroyed, both by burning and slaying. An attack was made by Mac Rannall on the town of Mac Shanly, and the town was burned, and Donough, the son of Donough Mac Shanly, and many others, were slain by him". [13]

The railway brought renewed prosperity when it opened in Dromod in 1862. It was a junction between lines of different gauges and there was plenty of work for people transferring coal by shovel from the narrow gauge trains coming from Arigna onto the wider Dublin line carriages.[14]

Lough Rinn

From Dromod you can head north east on the R202, then turn off to Lough Rinn. It's a lovely lake some 2.3 km long running north to south and 200 m - 400 m wide. Turn left at the crossroads and as you reach the shore, you are passing the site of a holy well, long dried up now, in the townland of Clooncahir. Located in pastureland on the north shore of the lake, the once popular pilgrimage place is not now visible. *"In Lough Rynn there is a holy well and from this well it is said that one can obtain the cure of a wart by taking a rusty pin which is left under a stone and by rubbing some of the water from the well on the wart. On trees that are near this well, there are pieces of cloth hanging up."*[15]

Clooncahir is also the location of a crannog that's close to the north shore and not far from the old holy well. Now joined to the mainland, the oval gravel and stone overgrown peninsula has a circular stony centre 50 m by 33 m, with a height of 1 m. This peninsula is surrounded by structural timbers beneath the water and a stone causeway is visible under the water at the south end. Quern stones were found on it in the past.[16]

Keep going north until the turnoff to Rinn Castle, where the Mac Ragnaills had their second power centre. When factions in the growing Mac Raghnaills family split up, one faction hived off from Lough Scur to set up camp at the next best location in their territory- at Lough Rinn. The two branches of Mac Ragnaills went on to battle each other on occasion. The Annals record the presence of crannogs on the lake in the year 1247, when it was called Claenloch (the same old name that Belhavel Lough had). These were probably the original royal strongholds or boltholes to retreat to in times of danger. Crannogs were for those who could afford the great expense of making artificial islands, with piles of stones and interwoven timbers. Causeways of underwater stepping stones would allow them exclusive access. You had to know the combination of steps, or risk drowning (most people didn't know how to swim). A crannog located close to the eastern shore of Lough Rinn, the one closest to the ruins of the Mac Ragnaill castle, may well have been the earliest one. Occupation traces turned up when lake levels were lowered and two dug out canoes and a manacle were found, also a bronze arrow and spearhead nearby.[17]

The Mac Raghnaills medieval castle, now in ruins, is near the lake shore and about 500 m south west of Rinn House. Mentioned in the Annals in 1474, the castle is unusual in design in having rounded corners, to resist artillery attack. By the look of it, the ruin may have been augmented as an 'improved' estate ornament in the 19th century.[18]

The Mac Raghnaills were tenacious at resisting English invasion, so it's unsurprising they paid a high price for this, losing their properties in the Plantation of 1621. Their confiscated sovereign lands were granted to the Crofton family, who brought in Protestant settlers to replace the native Irish, ethnically cleansing them from their ancestral homelands. Later, in 1749, wealthy squire Nathaniel Clements purchased around 10,000 acres in the Mohill area and his son Robert became the 1st Earl of Leitrim, establishing themselves in a grand castle here. The current Tudor style mansion Rinn House/Castle that overlooks the eastern shore of the lough dates from sometime in the late 19th century.

A later resident, the third Lord Leitrim was much hated as a brutal, feudal style landlord. He tyrannised the population and regularly evicted any dissenters. As a result of his evil-doings, he was assassinated, following which there was much rejoicing in the land and the perpetrators were never sought, nor caught. [19]

"Lord Leitrim was the local landlord. He was a rack-renting tyrant and lived at Rinn. To those who acknowledged him as their lord and master with a good grace, he is said to have been considerate. He cleared out Rinn, Clooncoe, Errew, parts of Farnaught and Tulcon. Some of the tenants got holdings elsewhere." [20]

This criminal act would have stripped away much local lore of the land. The new lords then overlaid their own sense of pseudo-mythos in the absence of tradition. An example are the stones on a nearby hilltop that are marked as a 'cromlech' on the 1907 OS map. The two large stones are due east of the old MacRaghnaill castle. One is prone, the other upright. They look more like a chair. But local tradition has a few suggestions. *"The Druid's Altar is on top of a big hill called the Druid's Hill... and it is supposed to be a giant's grave."* [21]

It's likely that this so-called monument is actually just another estate ornament, created for amusement by the idle rich. I'm also suspicious of the name of the townland that's adjacent to the north of Lough Rinn - Lisdadanaan. It may have been created for romantic effect by an antiquarian. The name of the so-called Tuatha Da Danaan tribe was no doubt a medieval creation of the scribe monks.

However the name of Lough Rinn and the River Rinn that flows through it, I do find intriguingly archaic. The river was important as it was navigable when the lowlands were not, and it once formed a territorial boundary. I discovered that the name is a hydronym from deep in the mists of time. It takes us back to when Celtic tribes flooded into Ireland in the centuries before the current era. They were nostalgic for home and it was their habit to name features of new territories after the homelands.

The name Rinn suggests that it stems from the Rhine River valley, an ancient Celtic homeland. It is essentially the same name. Also in northern Italy, the invading Celtic Boii tribe named an important river the Reno, in Latin Rhenus, that marked the southern boundary of Cisalpine Gaul. (The Reno now passes through Bologna, but was once a tributary of the River Po.) Markale says that the old Celtic word renos meant a rushing stream, and it's related to the Irish word rian for waves. In France, where the bulk of French river names have Celtic origins, there's a Reins River [22]; while my dictionary says that the French name for the Rhine is Rhin.

We see this naming habit also to the south east of Lough Rinn, in the old tribal region of Annaly. This is the old name for Longford, originally Muintir-Anghaile of the O'Farrell tribe, who were leading sub-septs of a branch of the Conmaicne. At the headwaters of the Camlin River in Longford, the first section of the river is actually called the Rhine. *"Is it possible that this represents the original Ren, Rian, from which Magh Rein, etc, is derived?"*, Ó Duígeannáin mused in 1934. [23]

When the Norman knight Miles Costello invaded Feda Conmaicne, he seized the crannog of Claenloch on Lough Rynn and left a garrison of men there, the Annals of Connaught record for the year 1247.[24] The royal crannog is still there. But later O'Connor and MacRaghnaill raided the garrison and recaptured it for the Conmaicne. In the Annals of Connaught, it's written that they also *"broke down the castle of Lecc Derg* [a Norman castle at Lough Rynn]. *The Galls* [foreigners] *had refused to come out of the castle unless the Archdeacon would escort them westwards across the Shannon to Tumna. So they came away with him and the Clann Costello were expelled from the whole territory."*[25] However the English extracted revenge by afterwards torching parts of Roscommon and probably the castle at Port was destroyed at that time too.

FARNAUGHT

South of Lough Rinn is the townland of Farnaught, once the territory of the MacShanley clan. When the Plantation of Leitrim came about, half of the clan went over to the invader's side, dropped the Mac from their name and became known as the Queen's Shanleys. William of Dromod was their last chief, back in the early 1600s.[26] Being close to the Lough Rinn estate, Farnaught became an economic hub in the 19th century, boasting two schools, doctor and dispensary, dance hall, police barracks, post office, bakery, staging post, lime kiln and shops etc. [27] It must have been a fertile region, judging by the following local myth.

"The Wandering Cow was supposed to go about the countryside providing milk for poor people. A field of Tom Reynolds in Farnaught was supposed to be a favourite resort of hers. People when speaking about this field, always said it was great land and that the Wandering Cow used to be there".[28]

It was a place to fight for. According to the Annals of Lough Ce, Farnaught was the scene of a skirmish in 1256 between the O'Rourkes and O'Reillys. Farnaught is also a place of magical standing stones with the following story to account for one of them. *"There is a stone ... in the townland of Farnaught. This stone is said to be pegged from Sliab an Iarainn Mountain by a Giant. This stone should have been thrown at Rooskey bridge to stop the English from going across but it slipped out of the Giant's hand and fell in Farnaught. On this stone are marks of fingers and other little holes which is said to be put there by the Giant."*[29]

In the grounds of Lough Rinn Estate, near the the south east corner of Clooncoe Lough, the Farnaught lime kiln has been carefully restored by local craftsmen and is one of the finest examples in Ireland of its kind. To get there from Lough Rinn House, take the small road south, taking the right road at the Y junction just after the house. The lime kiln was built mid 19th century and was one of the last, operating for around a century before closing in the 1950s. Limestone was heated in it to a high temperature to make quicklime. This was used to break up the local heavy clay soil, neutralise soil acidity and sweeten grass for livestock, as well for mortar, whitewash, disinfectant and pest repellent.

Continue down the road and turn left at the next junction. You'll soon pass the Church of Ireland church and an old burial ground in a sub-circular stone and earth bank enclosure, with headstones from the 18th century. You can park at the main gate to the cemetery. There's a lots of history and mystery interred in this place. This includes a holy well in the graveyard. *"It is in a hollow in a small stone and would hold, if filled, about two quarts of water. It is supposed never to go dry, and to be a cure for warts."* [30]

Many were interred here during the Great Famine. *"A woman died of hunger on the roadside at Farnaught, near where the lime kiln stands today. Others died about the graveyard gate. An old woman, called Harrac, actually left her home when she found death approaching and travelled to Farnaught, so that she would be buried in consecrated ground. All these people were buried in Farnaught."*[31]

Heading to the left around the back of the church, there is a tangled tree grove with interesting ruins. Take one of the tiny tracks going into it and you enter another world. Amidst a tiny circle of woodland mantle, the remains of a medieval tower house. The atmospheric ruin has a pointed doorway that leads to a passage inside the thickness of the wall that gives access to the ground floor, of which only the base of the walls remain. Spiral stairs go off to the west side. Multiple accounts in the Folklore Commission records suggest that there was an early monastery here and it's marked as an Oratory on old maps, but archeologists consider this a misinterpretation. The loss of the true place story is probably because local folk here did not have a long connection to the place, after the ethnic cleansing of the Plantation.

GORTLELETTERAGH

Heading north from Farnaught you pass through the district of Gortletteragh, the heart of the parish of Gortletteragh, with a sizeable population in the civil census of 1841 of almost 9,000. This dropped to 5,110 in 1860, after the famine. In 2000 it was just 1,083. Much of this depopulation was a result of the emigration of Leitrim's 'economic refugees'. (People are said to be Leitrim's greatest export!)

Yet the Gortleletteragh area, a name meaning Hillside Field, has nurtured farming communities for millennia. Such is evidenced by artefacts occasionally found in the bogs. A stone axe was dug up in the area in 1980.[32] Around here it's a maze of unsignposted roads, so - good luck in finding your way around. Or, you might get lost and discover something you weren't looking for!

LEAR

Continue going northwards from Gortleletteragh and before the next intersection, in a field on your left, on the crest of a north facing slope, are the remains of a portal tomb. A large flagstone 3 m by 2.6 m rests on a lone one metre high orthostat (pillar) now lying on the ground at the back, near a field boundary bank. Another orthostat (pillar) is adjacent. An overgrown cairn surrounds it, where it has survived, to the west.[33]

CLOONEE

Crossing the next intersection in a dog legged route to the north, you pass through the townland of Cloonee, where, on top of a low hill near the road, is the site of what used to be a 9 m diameter cairn. Workmen were removing the cairn when they discovered an undisturbed tomb within it. Inside the cairn, within a stone lined cist, a food vessel bowl with cremated human remains inside of it was removed, as seen on the right.

Nothing is now visible at ground level and the beautifully decorated bowl is now in the National Museum, far from Leitrim eyes. The Cloonee Bowl was locally manufactured around 1600BC, it has been estimated.[34]

The site developed supernatural associations, too. *"Burial urn found at Cloonee, near Duimmin NS 1934. Removed to National Museum. Lights are seen there late at night now. The father to the man on whose land the urn was found dreamt one night that if he slept on a ridge in his land he would get a pot of gold* [long-story-short:]*... and he got the pot of gold which he put in a drawer when he reached home. Next morning he went to look at the pot of gold but instead of a pot of gold he found a pot of ashes. The urn was got at the place where he slept. Said to be True"*.[35]

DRUMCONNY

Drumconny townland is adjacent to Cloonee and part of a megalithic hot spot, but to get to the parallel road you'll have to go north to the intersection, take a right, then the next small road on the right. When you are near the end of this road, on your right are some interesting standing stones. They are described as being located on a low hill in a north-south valley. There is one stone still standing at a height of 1.2 m. Nearby, about 10 m to the south, are five stones lying down and locally called Finn Mc Cool's Fingers.[36] It was probably part of a ritual landscape.

Because if you continue a short way down the road and take the second and last side road on the left, in the road junction area, on a west facing drumlin slope, there is a possible megalithic tomb. It has three stone slabs that form a triangle 7 m by 6 m.[37] On the 1907 map this is marked as a Giants Grave, although the standing stones are not marked on it.

KEELDRA

Heading back northwards, turn right at the next intersection onto the road going to Keeldra Lough and the old village of Keeldra. *"About seventy years ago* [circa 1860s] *the people were more numerous in* [Keeldra] *than now. There lived nine or ten families around the cruckan* [old village] *and their houses are not to be seen now. There is the ruin of an old corn-mill to be seen in Keeldra yet. There was a bleach-mill a short distance from the corn-mill, at the end of a lane, and it is called the Bleach Avenue. There is a lake situated in the townland of Keeldra and it is said that water horses were often seen coming up and eating on the green fields. There is a river running from the Lough through the mill and the part beside the lake is called the Plug."* [38]

"The battle of Ballinamuck was the finishing up of the fight in 1798. The French marched from Castlebar to Ballinamuck passing by the village of Cloone. The French camped in Cloone that night and the old people say that is why the field is called the Camp Field. A man called West had a feast for the French. He killed bullocks and roasted them on gates. Those gates are said to be on the graveyard in Cloone now. The French caroused all the night and the drinks which they got were drugged. West and his men stole some of their ammunition and chains [for hauling the canon with] *while they slept. Early in the morning they started for Granard without delay. They passed the old Cruckáin and up by Keeldra Lough. When they reached Rosses Bray they were not able to go over it* [with the canon] *for want of chains. They flung the chains they had into Keeldra Lough. It is said that these chains can be seen on a bright sunny day in the Lough"*.[39]

Other folklore suggests another explanation, in that Humbolt's men were too drunk from their host's generous hospitality to remember the next morning where the chains had been hidden overnight! It wasn't a theft at all then, it was the drink that did them in, you might say.

Around Keeldra Lough today a picturesque walking trail wraps around the lake, going up to the bog field at the top of the lake, then through a rocky area and on to the elevated bog pass. Here walkers can view the lake in its entirety, as well as wide views of the adjoining five counties. The 2.7 km trail starts and ends at the Keeldra Lake amenity, across from the pier, and has an off-road car park. At the amenity area there's places for swimming, fishing, water sports and relaxation, as well as toilet and changing facilities.

"Long ago strange animals were often seen in Keeldra lough. A man named Michael Heatherton was up very early one morning and he looked down towards Keeldra Lough and he saw a strange animal eating grass at the brink of it. He knew it was a young horse. He started down towards him and tried to catch him but when he was about to catch him he ran into the Lough." [40]

South east of Keeldra lies a chain of lakes through which the border with Longford weaves its way. Clooncose is in this edgey area. Border tensions could have got high here. Fear of invasion was felt keenly in the following story, where memories, mythos and paranoia blur together. *"Long ago the people of this district were afraid that the Orangemen of the North would come down and take the lands from the Catholics. The people East of the Valley of the Black Pig sold their lands, and went to live west of it. Mrs Higgins, Clooncose, came to John Higgins a few times and told him to have the horse and car ready to bring herself, Catherine and the children west of the Valley of the Black Pig when the Orangemen would come".* [41]

This extreme fear may well have been fuelled by colonial propaganda. Kane heard of one folk tradition, in the west of Co. Monaghan where he lived, where the locals believed that *"when the great war arises they must escape west of the Cuilcagh mountain beyond the source of the Shannon."* Kane related a prophecy, supposedly made by St. Colmcille and cited in the 1189 invasion propaganda book Expugnatio Hibernica (Conquest of Ireland) by Giraldus Cambrensis (Gerald of Wales, a relation of the Anglo-Norman invaders). Colmcille's so-called prophecies only appear in the literature centuries after his death and are nowadays considered to have no merit. In the 'prophecy', all the Catholics have to flee south from Ulster to avoid a massacre. Kane thought that *"it may be that the Prophecy of St. Colm Cille, was nothing more—or less—than a diabolical politically inspired rumour originally set in motion by Giraldus to inform the native population of Ireland that the violent colonisation of their land was foretold by Colmcille, one of their most revered saints".* [42]

This explains why people were so scared that they'd be forced to flee from the Valley of the Black Pig, i.e. from Ulster, to avoid a coming war and violent death. From his OS related research in 1837, John O'Donovan noted of the pseudo-prophecies of Columbkille, that - *"people believed in them with the most implicit faith."* [43]

ANNAGHMORE

To see an impressive portal tomb, turn right at the intersection before the Keeldra Lough, go south to the first intersection, the Cornageeha Crossroad, then turn right. Your destination is just past the first side road on the left. Or, if you are coming from Mohill, head towards Gortletteragh and follow signs for the Gortleletteragh Social Club. Then continue past the club, go up the hill a short distance and it's there beside the road on the right. You can park right beside this remarkable megalith in the townland of Annaghmore.

The portal tomb that graces the summit of the low drumlin is in remarkably good condition. Such a relatively intact portal tomb is a rare thing. To be able to just drive or ride right up to it is a bonus. It's sad that it wasn't given more space and it seems greatly undervalued. But it turns out that it was once incorporated into the junction of two field banks that have since been cleared away, so it has been in a worse state. To the south of it are the possible earthen remains of a cairn that would have have once covered the tomb, although this could just be waste from clearing around the stones.

"There is a cromlech in the townland of Annaghmore...[with] a tract of five fingers on one of these stones and in another there is the tract of an elbow and in a third one there is the tract of a foot. It is said that the stones were pegged by a giant on Corn Hill [Longford].... There's a fairly big ringfort with a high wall in the same townland. There's an old ruin in the middle. Fairies are associated with it." [44]

"It is the local belief that it was used as a Druid's Altar or Gráinne's Bed... The imprint of the [giant's] five fingers is there for anyone to see." [45]

CLOONCUMBER

Continuing west-south-west on this road will bring you through Gorteletteragh and Farnaught, then there's a crossroads where you take a right and next left. This will bring you to the Black River and Clooncumber townland. The Black River was once a tribal boundary, a continuation of the Rinn River border. Rivers were historically associated with boundaries and local school children well knew this, stating that - *"Black River was once the border between Longford and Leitrim."* [46]

"There was a fight at a small hill in Cloncomber called Cnoc na Muck [Hill of the Pig], between the Reynolds of Leitrim and the Farrells of Longford. The Reynolds of Leitrim won." [47]

Across the county border in Longford, Ballinamuck is just south of the Black River and it's obviously associated with the mythic Black Pig, as the name Town of the Pig alludes. It was the scene of borderland battles.

Des Guckian, who was an independent councillor with Leitrim Council for ten years, had a keen interest in local history. (Sadly, Des passed away in May 2025). To help preserve the memory of his local heritage, in March 2024 he showed me some of the last remaining traces of the Black Pig's Dyke in south Leitrim. Des, who grew up in the area, told the classic story in his book the Annals of Annaghduff. After rooting up a provincial boundary, the black pig met its match with a feisty washer woman, as the story goes.

"The Black Pig was killed, by a woman wielding a large clothes beetle, at Cruck na Muck / Cnoc na Muice. There is a place still called Cruck na Muck a short distance back behind the Clooncumber Church of Ireland chapel-of-ease. The remnant of one embankment of the dyke is very visible where it crosses the road from Clooncumber Cross to Fearglass. A second bank is visible, a short distance away, suggesting a defensive fort lying in between.

"To the right, as you cross the first mound, is a field known for years by my ancestors and others, as 'Thum Doo'...tuaim means burial place...I believe [it to be]... *the burial place of the Black Pig. In the far corner of this field is a very dry* [now vanished] *mound which has the appearance of a very old burial area...A short distance westwards from Cruck na Muck, there is a definite ridge along the edge of the bog. Less than half a mile away, there is a site between some meadows on Cyril Notleys land, in Clooncumber, where people died during the Great Famine. Because of this, the surrounding area was not much disturbed and it is possible to make out the track of the dyke"*, he wrote. From there, the line of the dyke coincided with the boundary between Leitrim and Longford. [48]

JOHNSON'S BRIDGE

The road continues west from Clooncumber to the Rinn River border with Longford at Johnston's Bridge. It's ancient importance is remembered in previous names.

"Johnston's Bridge was called 'Shancla'."[49] Shancla means the Old Dyke.

"I think the dyke passed close behind the large statue of Lady Baltimore and then downhill to an ancient ford that was on the Rinn River, 400 m downstream from the present Johnston's Bridge. The old name of that ford was Atha na Claidhe (Ford of the Dyke)," Guckian wrote. [50]

From Johnston's Bridge continue on the road towards Rooskey and turn left at the next intersection to get to the ancient ecclesiastical centre at Cloonmorris.

CLOONMORRIS

Close to the county border and located on a small hill, Cloonmorris Church was a point of spiritual power that remains a good looking ruin. It was established in the 12th century and displays a fine east window and carvings. The Gothic style window is a *"slender lancet with external embrasure and hood moulding,"* wrote Siobhan Scully.[51] Described as an abbey in the folklore, it was affiliated with the Augustinian Priory of Mohill.[52] Probably the site was already significant and earlier churches existed here. The site is located beside the path of the Black Pig, so it was on the frontier edge. *"The dyke was not confined to the line of any river but climbed up onto Cloonmorris Hill"*, Guckian explained. An old woman who lived there had confirmed its path in the 1950s.[53]

To get to Cloonmorris from Dromod on the N4 head south, go past the Roosky turn-off and the end of dual carriage-way. After the last roundabout turn first left (signed to Bornacoola Community Centre). A short distance along and you'll see the ruined church on your right, just before the railway lines. Inside the gate on your right in the churchyard is a rare ogham (pronounced o-am) stone grave marker.

The rectangular church building, some 14 m by 8 m, has it walls relatively intact, apart from the missing west wall. As you enter through the pointed doorway in the north wall and step back in time, you'll see an unusual bullaun like stone inside, said to have been used as a piscina, for washing communion vessels in. It may have been previously located elsewhere (such as, typically, near the altar).[54] The stone seems to have a more ancient vintage than the church, perhaps it was used in Pagan times for grinding the sacred grain during rituals? This unusual specimen gives that impression, as its basins are on both the upper and lower surface of the stone and they almost break through from a huge amount of grinding done on both sides. I detected strong energies at this stone by dowsing, while a big landscape spirit presides over the church and graveyard, I also found. The atmosphere is delightful to experience.

The church was believed to have had a magical beginning, but who knows which version of folk tale to believe? *"There is a church in Cloonmorris which was built by St. Morris in one night. There was never a sound of hammer nor chisel heard during the night of its erection. It is an old ruin now. Cloonmorris is called after St. Morris."*[55]

"It is said that it was St. Morris who built the abbey in Cloonmorris graveyard, and he built it in one night. It is believed that when he was building it, a man passed by and did not say, "God bless the work." St. Morris never came back there again and the abbey remained unfinished...

"Another version of this is, St. Morris built the abbey in one night; and one day when he was saying mass and there was a large congregation attending the walls were heard cracking. The people ran out and never went near it again".[56]

Just outside the church and beside the roadside wall, the Ogham stone (seen on the previous page) has been re-located and cemented into place upside down. Ogham is believed to have been a system of writing used between the 4th and 8th centuries CE. So the stone suggests a greater antiquity to this site than meets the eye. It has the primitive writing down two of its sides, that spell out someone's name, but it's badly damaged. It was once a grave stone in the adjacent rectangular burial ground. Most of these carved commemorative Ogham stones are found in Munster province to the south. This is the only known example from Leitrim.

EDERCLOON

Edercloon, south west of Cloonmorris, was once known as Cnoc na Peiste, (the Hill of the Beast). This clue made Des Guckian think that this was where the Black Pig left its track. It's also the townland where, in 2006, archeologists found numerous woven brushwood trackways and platforms in the bog, and recorded them in detail (after which they were consumed by roadworks).[57] There used to be much traffic here on the water margins, the numerous findings reveal. A quiet landscape now, it was previously more populated.

"In olden times there were thirty two families living in Edercloon, as the old coach road ran through it." [58]

CLOONEEN

This is a group of townlands bounded by the River Shannon and south west of Edercloon, in Co. Longford, just south of the border with Leitrim. In Clooneen Beirne (that was once the province of the Beirne clan) it's recorded as having a collection of large standing stones, known locally as the Druids Altar. [59]

More is learned from Cloonmorris folklore collected for the Folklore Commission in the 1930s. *"There is a druids altar in John O'Beirnes field in Clooneen. Some of the stones are tons in weight and are built like a wall and a couple of big stones for the altar. It is surrounded by a great many trees. There are words and letters carved on it."* [60]

ROOSKY

Roosky is a river town on the Shannon that straddles Leitrim and Roscommon, once the provincial Ulster - Connaught divide. It didn't always have a bridge, nor look the way it does today. But it was long a minor fording point on the river. A student from Gortermone school recorded the remembered significance of this ford in the 1930s. *"The people still imagine in this district that a Black Pig ran from Armagh to Rooskey Bridge and made a ditch as he went along. The territory of land inside that line was called The Valley of the Black Pig."* [61]

A Ballinamore school student reported that - *"According to [legend] the Black Pig was a schoolmaster in Co. Armagh. He had the 'black art' and...he changed himself into the Black Pig... On his journey southward he cut a valley in Armagh. He cut other valleys on his course, including the one between Annally and Breifne. He crossed the Shannon and rooted another valley in Co. Roscommon. The Valley of the Black Pig was the name given to a natural hollow between Annally [now Longford] and Breifne."* [62]

One thing was sure and fixed about Roosky's location - the river. The town and its bridge is centred around a part of the Shannon that was once narrow and a minor fording point, long before the bridge was built. It has since been deepened and made more navigable, while the tracks of the mythic pig have long since been erased. So there's little physical proof of it left.

With no official archeological record, the record of the dyke is so-far mute, only for what can be gleaned from folklore and memories, and suggestive place names. The Black Pig's Dyke here is virtually forgotten and any remnants there may be have no heritage protection status. Yet even the name Roosky could be signalling to us. Roo being one of several Old Irish words for such a dyke, rather than 'marshland', the usual interpretation of the name. [63] Clee-roo is the usual name for dykes further south of here, Mary Butler pointed out in a talk for the Historical Society of Carrick on Shannon in 2024.

KILLINAKER

Stopping at the northern edge of Roosky, Des Guckian pointed out the site of a ring fort near the banks of the Eslin River, in the townland of Killinaker. It could well indicate a past terminus of the Black Pig's Dyke. Here in the watery zone, the fort was on a low eminence close to the bridge over the Eslin. This flows into the Shannon and it was an obvious point of defence, where a dyke could connect up to the flood zone of the river. Linear boundary embankments often incorporate forts and connect up to water bodies. Though the banks of the rath are now razed low, the lie of the land still delineates something of its form. Oral history completes the concept.

"The late Jim Crowe, of the Dromod garage, recalled his father telling him that the area across from Killianker was known as The Valley of the Black Pig." Des Guckian wrote in his Annals of Annaduff. [64]

"Jim Crowe said to me he was told by his people that it [the Black Pig's Dyke] *came as far as Roosky,"* he elaborated.

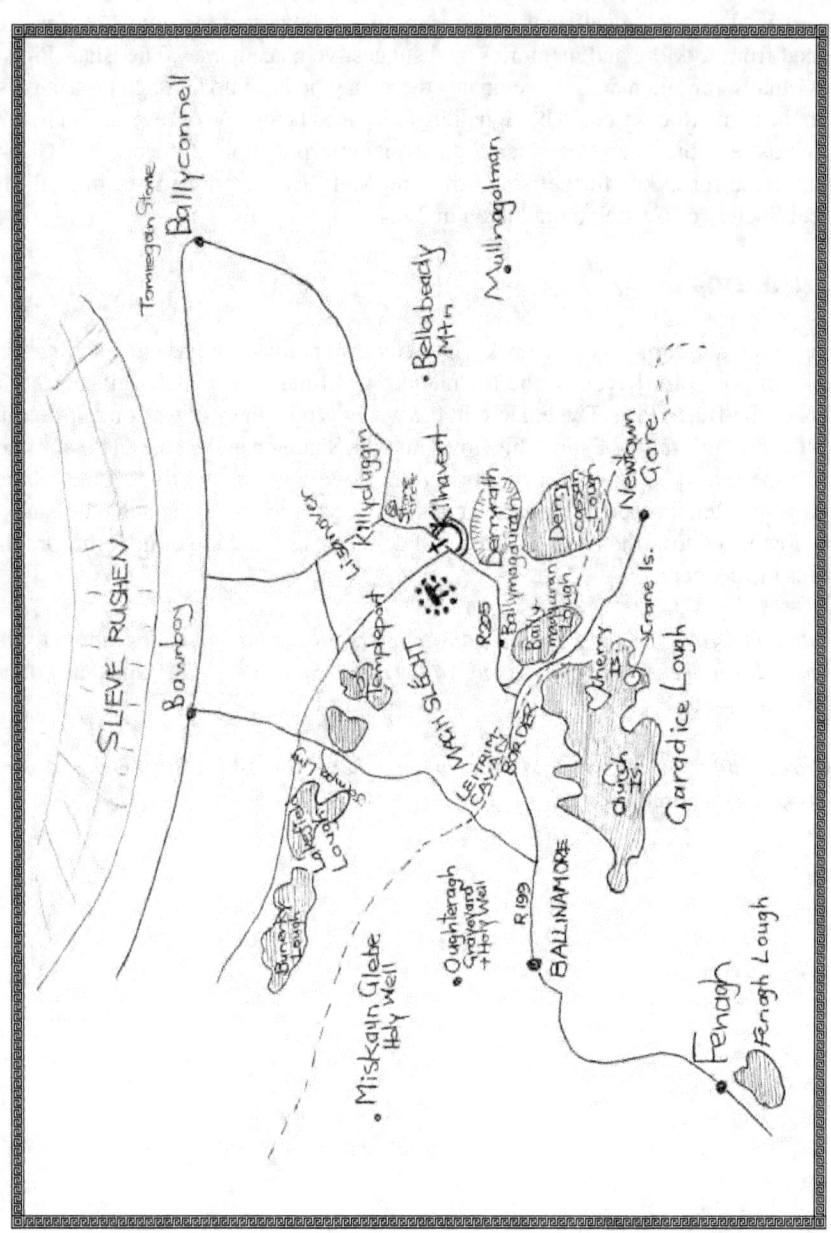

Chapter 7
Land of the Dagda

Pagan Fenagh

The sleepy village of Fenagh was once thronged with people visiting its famous monastery from far and wide. In the 13th - 15th centuries Fenagh was one of the most celebrated places in Ireland, drawing pilgrims from across the country and Europe. The choice and appeal of the location of this spiritual mecca goes back much earlier, to Neolithic times, when people first moved into the area and found good soils for farming. They created an oasis of lush pastureland amidst the bog and clay lowlands of south Leitrim. As their prosperity and population increased, so they flexed collective muscle to memorialise cherished ancestors with monumental stone structures.

Tombs, megalithic ritual structures from different eras, can still be seen in the Fenagh landscape and they remind us of the past importance of this area.

Around Fenagh there are two (or possibly three) passage tombs, a portal tomb and a court tomb dating back to 3,500 - 4,000 BCE, making it quite special. *"What distinguishes Fenagh and its abbeys from other sites is the continuation of it being a sacred site from the Neolithic to the Middle Ages,"* notes local tour guide Karin Holzschneider.[1] It was also the place-to-be for the dead in the medieval era, with as many as nineteen Irish kings buried (or just baptised) there in tradition. Ancient burial sites were often re-used for newer internments. *"In the case of the portal tomb, they used it to bury Irish king Conall Gulban in,"* notes Holzschneider. Well, that's the story, but other places claim his body also!

An illustrious monastic centre was based here for the same reasons that brought the Neolithic farmers. The land was productive and Fenagh Lake provided water. Extensive monastery farmlands supported hordes of pilgrims and students who flocked here to attend Fenagh's acclaimed divinity school. The monastic settlement began in the 6th century and continued for around one thousand years. Unusually, the community was pretty much unchanged by monastic reforms that were the norm elsewhere. But it was doomed after the Plantation. In 1652 Cromwellian soldiers destroyed much of it.[2] You can see the huge holes in the walls blasted by canon fire.

To introduce Christianity, St Caillin had to be persuasive in his political manoeuvring. He succeeded and became the patron saint of Fenagh and the Conmaicne tribe of Magh Rein. His distinguished position was facilitated in that he was already a member of the most elite clan, *"claimed by the family of the Reynolds as being akin to them."*[3]

The Reynolds were the ruling Gaelic lords here, the O'Rourkes their overlords in medieval times. Such was the might of these tribes in their day, their protective influence must have been strong enough to keep the status quo at the abbey.

Church legend has it that an angel came to Caillin to show him the site for the abbey at Fenagh. It must have been an influential one, as the land was gifted by Fenagh's King Feargna after his son Aodh Finn was converted and Caillin was given his royal stone cashel to build a monastery and school within.[4] This gave a powerful message to the people, demonstrating that Feargna was handing over a large degree of social control over them to the incoming church. (Or perhaps it represented a political coup between factions of the chiefly clan?) The angelic embellishment to the tale gives it a divine tick of approval.

Subsequent mythos shows there was resentment of the abbey being built and attempts to block the process were strong, represented as the wrath of supernatural beasts. One would imagine that those 'beastly' peasants had no need for the church, no reason to change their lives and give up their spiritual sovereignty. They were happy enough the way things were and were ruled by a wise set of Brehon Laws, with clan leaders who protected them. It was nothing like the hysterical accounts of medieval spin-doctors who would falsely characterise their "barbaric ways". Gaelic society was more egalitarian in terms of women's rights, for one. Suddenly a misogynist, browbeating, middle eastern tradition claiming the higher moral ground was trying to control their lives. They surely weren't going to take that lying down!

How to deal with the outraged, aristocratic Druids who were the spiritual elite of the clan? In legend Feargus at first sent his son Aed Dubh and his warriors to stop Caillin, but instead they were converted and Caillin then turned the Druids into standing stones! Perhaps they were violently silenced. The pillar stones were already there, possibly from Neolithic times and acting as territorial boundary markers. They remain to this day in the village, as stark signposts - resist conversion or die!

In some medieval Annals Fenagh and nearby Longstones are given as the locations of St Patrick's most graphic attack on Paganism, the alleged dismissal of underworld god Crom Dubh's stone 'idols'. But there is a better candidate for this - at Magh Sleact, which will be discussed later on. Along with the 'petrified Druids', these literary mentions give the impression that this area remained a Pagan hot spot well into the early Christian era.

FENAGH LOUGH

At Fenagh Lough, a lake 800 m by 550 m in size, the ancient Pagan world was lurking dangerously near, beneath the surface of its waters. Supernatural influences could be overwhelming. *"When the High King lived at Fenagh, a number of his soldiers went to bathe in a small lake nearby. A serpent that dwelt in the lake devoured them all, and the lake is since called Loch na Peiste* [Lake of the Serpent/Great Pest]. *Nobody ever bathed in that lake since. Lough na Peiste lies south of the Village of Fenagh."* [5]

Fenagh Lough must have been sacred before Christian times. Already a prestigious location, there's a crannog in the lake's north east end, in the townland of Glebe (church land where the abbeys and pre-historic monuments are). The crannog possibly dates back to the Bronze Age and two bronze swords were recently found on it.[6] It's described as an overgrown circular, stony island with a one metre wide underwater stone causeway curving towards the mainland at the north.[7]

THE ABBEY AND THE SERPENT

So how easy was it to build Fenagh Abbey in such a staunchly Pagan community? It was not! There are stories of powerful hindrances encountered, in folklore archives from the 1930's.

"A party of monks of the Franciscan order resided there long ago. At first the monastery was only a little hut, and because of that the monks decided to build a new abbey. On the first night the building was two feet high. When the monks rose the following morning they found the building knocked. The masons rebuilt it but it was knocked again. The monks then became very angry and one of them decided to stay up and guard the place. There was a lake convenient to the place and a half-human serpent was supposed to dwell on it. At twelve o' clock that night the monk heard a horrid noise. He lifted his head off his prayer book and then he saw the horrid serpent endeavouring to throw the building. The monk almost fainted but he prayed to God for help and then by the power of the Almighty he changed it into a wire rope. This strange object is to be seen to the present day. The monastery was then built without any hindrance."[8]

Or, in another version - *"To commemorate his victory over Satan, [Caillin] caused an image of the Serpent's Head, tied by a rope made of stone to be placed on the Eastern gable. This rope and serpent's head are still there."* [9] Indeed, the carved wire rope and head on the exterior east wall of the old abbey is still to be seen, a curious and finely carved feature that, but for the folklore recorded of it, would be otherwise mute. The serpent legend sprang from original, archaic Pagan mythos and it's not mentioned in official spiel for visitors.

FENAGH GRAVEYARD

The great prestige of Fenagh Abbey in its medieval hey day made its graveyard the top place to be buried, a privilege that came with a price! St Caillin had to fund his establishment somehow. He also had something of a 'turf war' with the nearby monastery, where St Fraoch was stationed only 8.5 km away in Cloone. His economic base under threat, Caillin strongly asserted that any true believer who was buried at Fenagh would take a short cut to heaven! On the other hand, if people chose to be buried elsewhere, and especially in Mohill or Cloone (which may well have been the cheaper option), he'd threaten that they'd go straight to hell! [10] "Location, location", as they say, even in death.

The remains of St Caillin are said to be buried in a vault on the south side of the abbey (possibly in the vault seen on the right). As mentioned, nineteen kings are traditionally interred in this exclusive graveyard and the prestige continued, as the following attests.

"Under the arch in the abbey [seen below] *there are graves belonging to the Lawders and they kept gates on them and nobody was allowed in. The Lawders were landlords and lived near Ballinamore. Seán na gCeanns* [Reynolds] *grave is in the south eastern corner of the abbey, and beside is a new grave stone to the memory of the Peytons* [another landlord family]." [11]

I hope that Sean of the Heads paid a suitably high price for his after-death salvation!

THE BELL OF THE KINGS

St Caillin had a famous bell, the Clog na Riogh, that was used as a font for the baptism of nobles and kings, and also for making treaties between warring parties and the collection of fines. When he went around collecting taxes and money for fines, Caillin paraded around the district carrying the bell and its shrine. [12]

"St Caillin collected his annual dues for the upkeep of the Monastery in this bell. The full of it was sufficient for the year. His greedy servant, to make it hold more, had the tongue pulled out of the bell, but it held no more. St Caillin cursed him and said none of his name would ever prosper in the parish of Fenagh. St Caillin's Bell is a small, oval shaped Bronze Bell, tongue missing, to be seen in the Parochial House Foxfield." [13]

TWO ABBEYS AND A BOOK

St Caillin's Abbey burned down in the 14th century, after which two new abbeys were built consecutively on the site, not far apart.[14] The larger one on the elevated position is known as the Abbey Church. It's the one with the carved rope and serpent head, plus the fine and elaborate Gothic east window. The abbey walls are known to be very strong for the mortar being mixed with bullocks blood. (Unfortunate for the poor live animals that had to donate it!)

Cromwellian troops in 1652 tried to destroy the abbey with canon fire, which did much damage; and later it was attacked during the Williamite wars of the 1690s. Yet still a few monks hung on there and the last abbey service was held in 1729.

The shell of the two 14th century abbey churches, on a low rise 100 m apart, are all that remains of the monastery, but much history is layered beneath them. Legends speak of a tunnel that once connected the two abbeys together and was the hiding place of treasures. It hasn't been found yet and a story explains why it's not a popular place to seek out. *"There is also an underground tunnel about a half mile long but people never go there since a man went in and came out with two heads on him"*.[15]

Archeological studies include geo-physical, non-invasive imaging that have revealed a large complex of now disappeared buildings, with circular stone walls enclosing the ecclesiastical compound. With the old abbey being centre stage, the protective cashel wall enclosed an area of 100 m diameter and a large community of monks was able to live there in a sacred, inviolable precinct. Later the population swelled enough to make a second grand ring of enclosure, that spanned a diameter of 200 m.

The Book of Fenagh was written about Fenagh's history in 1550 and much can be learned in there. But its purpose was to promote Fenagh after its popularity had already waned, so it was an embellishment of reality. The Shrine of St Caillin, a decorated book cover made to hold it, is thought to date from 1536. It had an inscription on it from Brian O'Rourke, the King of Breifni. However it was badly damaged in the fire at St Mels Cathedral in Longford town in 2010 and is undergoing restoration. The Bell of Fenagh was in the possession of coarbs until the 1700s until it ended up at St Mels. But it was totally lost in the fire. Perhaps it had accrued too much 'bad karma' from being abused as a 'holy' relic?

BALLINAMORE

Ballinamore (Beal an Atha Moir, the Approach to the Big Ford) is a town of about 1,200 people that developed around a fording point on the Yellow River. It had its hey day when iron works operated there (located where the convent now stands), using iron mined from around Sliabh an Iarainn and charcoal from the local woods. There were also associated forges, an engineering works, a thriving flax and linen industry, and later a busy canal, plus the headquarters of the local narrow-gauge railway that ran for almost 100 years. The resources ran out by 1750 and the iron works had to close. Later the railway was shut down. So it's more tranquil these days and, surrounded by lush rolling hills, the town provides the perfect base for visitors to explore natural landscapes, with numerous local walking and cycling trails. Ballinamore is also a legend as an angler's paradise, with 28 lakes in the vicinity.

Many an ancient folk tale have placed Ballinamore within the Valley of the Black Pig, although the Iron Age border embankments are rarely evident, many having been removed by Plantation landlords. The province of the Ulaid kept shrinking to the north east. At some point in time the Ulster border coincided with the current Leitrim - Cavan county boundary, or near it. One of many trackways of the Black Pig is recorded in the following tale, as told by Peter Dolan (age 75) in Ballinamore to local school children in the 1930s.

"In the northern part of Ireland there was a school-master who was very fond of treating his pupils very cruelly. It is said that a Catholic priest on hearing of his wicked deeds got him banished from the school, and tradition tells us that he was changed into a a pig, and was a black colour. It is said that the pig travelled three miles [4.8km] east of Ballinamore, always keeping to the valley of the country; and went past Carrigallen in County Leitrim, but when he went some distance below Fenagh a woman, who was washing clothes on the bank of a river, was surprised when she saw him approaching, and killed him with a stroke of a beetle she had in her hand." [16]

During the tragic Great Famine, relief jobs came in the form of digging the Ballinamore - Ballyconnell Canal between 1845 and 1860. The great exertions of starving workers no doubt killed many in the process. It did result in much drained land being made available for farming, while navigation was made possible too. But after the huge and expensive project was finished, it turned out to be rather flawed and only eight boats were able to sail it before it was moth balled. A new railway line also made it redundant as a transport corridor.

It seems that folklore sometimes kept abreast of the technological changes, bridging millennia breathlessly in its assertions. The author of a 1957 article was collecting stories in the countryside when she was told in two different villages (Redhills and Ballinamore) that it was the Black Pig making its tracks throughout the land that was responsible for the railways. [17]

Ballinamore is an edgy borderland area close to the border with Northern Ireland. It's been a hotbed for radicals and rebels, and an IRA stronghold in the past. When peace was restored in 1998, the EU responded with funding for peaceful projects around the border regions. As a result of this, the canal was brilliantly restored, improved and revitalised over several years.

OUGHTERAGH

In early Christian legend, St Brigit visited this area with her holy cow in tow (an attractive selling point for the new religion!). She came to Oughteragh (Uachtar Achaidh, the Upper Level Field)[18], near Ballinamore, where she founded a church and a holy well that still has an annual Pattern Day dedicated to her, the patron saint of the Parish of Oughteragh.[19] Here, it's believed, was once the parish church of Oughteragh. No church remains, but in the graveyard are relics of earlier buildings, including a medieval window mullion and window head fragment, repurposed and utilised as grave markers. St Brigit's Holy Well is about 550 m to the north, north-east, on private farm land.[20]

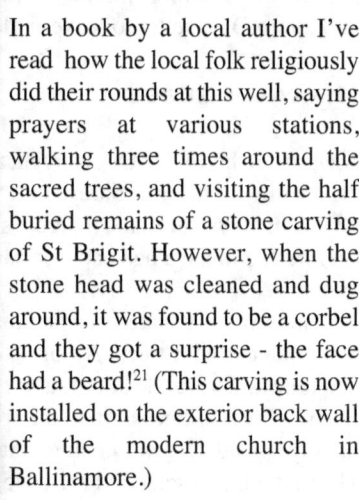

In a book by a local author I've read how the local folk religiously did their rounds at this well, saying prayers at various stations, walking three times around the sacred trees, and visiting the half buried remains of a stone carving of St Brigit. However, when the stone head was cleaned and dug around, it was found to be a corbel and they got a surprise - the face had a beard![21] (This carving is now installed on the exterior back wall of the modern church in Ballinamore.)

The well is often mentioned in local folklore, from the time that its tree stumps were living, sacred trees. The local Pagans, who also venerated trees, weren't exactly welcoming to the new Christian faith, as we see in the following tales. No wonder the church had to emulate or incorporate some of their old spiritual ways, such as tree reverence, to gain converts. Such were the socio-political machinations!

"At Uachtar Áth[a] near Ballinamore the people prepared to build a church. But the wall built each day was knocked down at night. They built it several times and in the end decided to stay and watch. At midnight they saw an animal like a hare running in and out and knocking the wall so they decided not to build any more. The Church was afterwards built in the town

of Ballinamore...At the same place there was a a Holy Well and it was once interfered with and the Spring dried up and opened in another field about 4 mile distant. It is at that Holy Well that the Station is now made on St. Brigid's Day." [22]*..."It is customary to bring some water from the well or a piece of a branch from one of the trees growing at the place. These emblems are hung in the house until the following year."* [23]

Oughteragh holy well experience

Oughteragh's holy well remains the focus of a *"very conservative tradition"* for local Catholics, I was told in no-uncertain terms, when attending the annual pilgrimage to the well. It was February 1st, St Brigid's Day, the traditional first day of spring and now a public holiday in Ireland. It's also the only day of the year when public access to the holy well through private property is granted. As a curious outsider, I watched as groups of attendees said their prayers as they visited the sites of the ruined church, sacred tree stumps and well. A cold, grey, wet, dismal day it was and the joyful shaking of our rattles to usher in springtime was perceived as a threat to the proceedings and attracted some negative attention. The locals tried vainly to contain their amusement at the ensuing tense confrontation, where we were asked if we were trying to conjure up bad spirits with the rattles. That had not been our intention, but perhaps the innocent rattling had in effect done so, the angry local woman being the inadvertent product of its calling? So, the moral bit of the tale is this - if you go to Oughteragh Holy Well on Pattern Day, better to leave rattles at home.

Miskaun Glebe

Apart from the well at Oughteragh, there are at least four holy wells in this parish that was once the territory of the MacDarcy clan.[24] The most well known one is St. Patrick's Well at Miskaun Glebe, in the Aughnasheelin area, some 6.5km from Ballinamore.[25] The townland must have been fertile to have been appropriated by the church, as the name Glebe attests.

The holy well is situated in a natural amphitheatre around 30 m across and defined by an earth bank planted with trees. An ugly, one metre wide concrete well housing replaces an older drystone structure. Beside it, a rag tree is festooned with strips of cloth.[26] There were once five mighty Ash trees around the well and perhaps just two remain (Ash Dieback disease has rapidly spread here this century, claiming many trees). Its a charming and sheltered location. The mounds and scattered rock suggest previous structures existed here. It's quiet these days, but it once hosted a lively annual Pattern Day, held on St Patrick's Day.

Traditionally, the well provides a cure for warts and sore eyes, for both people and animals, the water being applied to the affected part. A rag of your own clothes was left behind on a Blackthorn tree and the cure was deemed to be effective by such time as the rag had rotted. You washed your hands in the well water and said three Hail Mary's, before tying your rag to the bush.[27]

Lough Garadice

As you go along the R199 towards Newtowngore east of Ballinamore, there are views of this picturesque lake, one of the largest in Leitrim. Once called Lough Fenvoy (Finnmhaighe, the Lake of the Fair Plain), it gives a beautiful vista of water, trees, islands and cattle grazing peacefully.

It was a coveted location and, on its eastern end, was once part of a tribal boundary and the edge of Ulster, with a Black Pig connection. At some point in time, Dan Gallogly wrote, a boundary line went from Newry through Monaghan, entering Leitrim at Garadice Lough, going past Ballinamore south west to Muckross (named for the Black Pig?), where it divided, one section going to Fenagh, the other to Adoon and on to the Shannon at Roosky.[28] Some of this route also seems to roughly coincide with the path of the old Mohill to Ballinamore railway line. It's not surprising that the O'Rourke elites should gravitate to here also. The O'Rourkes reached their peak dominance in the 12th century under Tiernan O'Rourke, who, reigning from 1124 to 1172, spent much of his time battling. He had his main stronghold on Garadice Lough.

There were three important islands on this lough that were used strategically. Amongst various abodes, Tiernan O'Rourke kept a fortress/castle on Cherry Island, then called Cloch Inish na d'Torc, the Isle of the Boar. It served the family well between the 12th and 15th centuries, as they guarded the borders of the eastern frontier from attacks from the O'Reillys of East Breifni. The island has the remains of a rectangular structure about 20 m by 8 m has the west gable surviving the best. It's set within a D shaped enclosure with a cairn containing a kiln.[29] John O'Donovan noted in the 1830s that Cherry Island: *"Belongs to Lord Leitrim. It has the ruins of an old fortification. It was frequented by the United Irishmen in 1798 as a place of refuge from the English Army."*

Church Island has the ruins of a church said to be have been built by Tiernan O'Rourke (although the current one may be more recent), as well as an exclusive O'Rourke-only burying ground, according to the parish history book. The ruins are quite intact, but archeologists reported no evidence of an enclosure or burials. They only noted a bullaun stone, 80 cm by 90 cm by 30 cm in size, and having a single basin, located 120 m north of the church.[30]

Crane Island, the smallest of the three in Garadice, is close to the shore and, according to

O'Donovan, it is *"said to be linked to the mainland by a subterranean passage and was used by the United Irishmen"*.[31] It's also another possible castle site of the O'Rourkes. A large rectangular wall in the centre and circular tower could indicate the remains of a 15-16th century tower house or a bawn (defended courtyard).[32] The name suggests a magical, Druidic connection, the crane being associated with rituals of death.

Tiernan O'Rourke was killed on the Hill of Ward while negotiating with the new Norman Lord of Meath in 1172. O'Rourke chieftains continued to reside there for the following 200 years, alternating between their fortified homes in Woodford (in times of peace) and on Cherry Island (for safety, during war). The importance of these locations waned after then. In 1257 Tiernan's son Con made a peace deal with the O'Connors that gave them Cherry Island and they sent a garrison to be stationed there. But in the same year the Annals state that O'Rourke returned and burnt Cherry Island and allowed the garrison to leave. There are other mentions too, but, after the last one in 1418, Breifni shifted its focus from Lough Garadice to Dromahaire, as well as to Clooncorick Castle to the south.

WOODFORD

On the border of Counties Cavan and Leitrim, Tiernan O'Rourke also ruled his vast kingdom from Tuam Shanshadha, now called Woodford, near the eastern shore of Lough Garadice. His great fortress at Tuam Shanshadha is said to have covered over 500 m² in area. Here also is the site of Woodford Castle, a 17th mansion on the south bank of the Woodford/Grainne River. It's thought to have been sited over the earlier Tuam Seanachaine/Shanshadha in the 14-15th centuries.

O'Donovan reported of this townland in the 1830s - *"in the northern part is a place called Toomonaghan, the seat of the Gore family, formerly a genteel residence, but now in a ruinous state."* [33] Usually when Toom / Tuam / Tom is in a name it refers to an ancient burial mound or stone monument. So, this must be a site of ancient significance. Indeed, O'Donovan noted in the 1830s that here was located Monaghan's Mound.

The Gores, who gave their name to the nearby town of Newtowngore, were a Norman family who acquired land in Ireland in the 13th century. Their main seat was at Woodford and they were its majority landholders. But in the mid 19th century their seat was moved to Derrycarne, beside the River Shannon. Another branch of the family went to live at Lissadell, near Sligo town and the famous freedom fighter Countess Markievicz was a descendent of theirs.

TULLYHAW AND MAGH SLÉCT

Breifni O'Rourke once included north Leitrim, plus the Baronies of Tullyhaw in modern north-west Cavan (the pan-handle part at the top) and Tullyhunco, below it. (It was common in Plantation times that confiscated indigenous territories were re-invented as baronies.) Tullyhaw's earliest inhabitants in historical records are the Masraighe, a clan traditionally hostile to the tribes of Magh Rein. Tullyhaw retained its ancient character longer than most areas. *"It was also known as the kingdom of Glangevlin and is about sixteen miles in length and seven in width (Irish measure). It included the present parishes of Killinagh and Templeport and parts of the parishes of Drumreilly, Kinawley and Tomregan.... In the historical tracts of Sir John Davies it is said that when Sir John Perrot converted 'O'Riellie's*

Country¹ into the present County Cavan in 1584, he left the wild and barren tract of land owned by the sept McGovern untouched and subject, as before, to the exactions of the chief. It has been maintained, however, that Perrot was afraid to interfere with Tullyhaw as the place was so well suited to native warfare." [34]

Tullyhaw, a corruption of Teallach Eochdaich, was previously the tribal Land of the Eochaidh, an old Conmaicne family and ancestors of the ruling Magauran/McGovern family. One of the names of the Dagda, Ireland's Good God of Pagan times, include Eochu or Eochaid Ollathair, meaning horseman or great father horseman. He lived in the underworld and was believed to influence life, death and the weather. Dagda's fabulous horse transports him anywhere, often sky flying. Several ancient tribes considered the Dagda to be their ancestor too and it was popular to take his name. Perhaps the monks should have called the supernatural tribe Tuatha da Danaan - the Tuatha da Dagda? But they were obviously hell-bent on obscuring His memory, as well as that of Crom Dubh, who appears to be a later, synonymous deity.

Medieval literature described this Land of the Dagda as a place of ancient pilgrimage, for reverencing the dark, underworld gods. In typical propaganda of its day they were re-cast in the literature with cruel terrorist tendencies. Crom Dubh, or Crom Cruach, is the dark one, bent from carrying sheaths of golden grain on his back. A cruach is a hay stack, because he was an agricultural god. Medieval spin linked him to human sacrifice, however there is no evidence at all for this. Ritual animal sacrifice may well have been involved, but his spiritual lineage was basically a "legacy of joy". [35]

Of great interest to the antiquarian, Magh Sléct is a legendary portion of Tullyhaw, once a border area where the mythic Black Pig rooted its territorial defences. Located around 13 km east of Ballinamore around the road to Ballyconnell in Co. Cavan, it's an area of huge significance in the past, with many megalithic monuments from Neolithic times, plus significant features from the Iron Age to medieval eras. A well described battle ground for early Christian missionising, Magh Sléct remained a stronghold of Pagan Gaelic culture until relatively recent times and was thus a particularly strong focus of conquest mythos. They even misinterpreted or changed its name to 'Plain of Prostrations' or 'Plain of Adoration', in a derogatory reference to Pagan worship.[36] (So many Irish names were corrupted over time that their original meanings often came to be obscured or forgotten, so they could get away with this.)

Magh Sléct, with its extraordinarily large concentration of monuments, is better translated as the Plain of the Monuments. (It's more of an undulating landscape, but when compared to nearby mountains, it's a relative plain.) There are said to be over 80 monuments of different types here, showing evidence of occupation lasting over 6,000 years, with many others bound to be discovered in future. There are known remains of no less than nine megalithic tombs, seven ring barrows, three stone circles, nine standing tones, two stone rows, five enclosures, six crannogs, 33 raths, three early Christian churches plus their associated holy wells, two bullauns and two medieval castles.[37]

The ancient ritual landscape of Magh Sléct is mostly focussed in two adjacent townlands of Killycluggin and Kilnavart, with some 33 recorded monuments, including several important early medieval sites, within an area measuring 5km by 5km, says White. This must have been Pagan Central and the probable location of 'Crom Cruach's idols' in the famous St Patrick legend that we are soon to consider.

"Nowhere else in Co. Cavan and very few places in Ireland contain this sort of density of archaeological monuments in such a small area. This makes the area of Magh Slécht further significant as a monumental landscape".[38] Artefacts, such as axes, both stone and bronze, and swords have also been found within Magh Slécht, as more evidence of the deep past.

BALLYMAGAURAN

The village of Ballymagauran is picturesquely located on the banks of the Woodford (previously Grainne) River, now canalised as part of the Ballinamore - Ballyconnell navigation scheme. In medieval times, it was the chief seat of the Magauran tribe. The lords of Tullyhaw ruled from various castles, at Ballymagauran, Bawnboy, Lissanover and Derrycassan. Ballymagauran was also the site of an ancient fair each August 12th, a Lughnasa date. The castle at Ballymagauran, built in the late 16th century (another account says 15th century), was a two storey tower house, of which only the base survives.

The ruin can be easily visited, as it's located beside a road. Turn right just past the village, down the tiny lane that goes around the lough. The overgrown, atmospheric site is on a rise on your left. I imagine it could have once been right on the shore of the lough, because in the past the loughs here were much deeper, they were connected up together and had different names, as shown in the Down Survey (conducted between 1656 -1658).[39] Before drainage, the lake must have gone past the castle and up to the base of Derryrath, to where we travel next.

Significant artefacts have been unearthed in this area, some of which are still around, others only surviving in folklore. Some are mentioned here. *"A man in Derrycasson [an adjacent townland to the east] named Mr J. Martin found two stone axes in a bog while cutting turf in Derrycasson. ...and* [in the] *townland of Ballymagovern a sword was found...near the walls of an old castle, by Mrs. William Kells, the owner of the land. In olden times the castle was owned by the Mac Govern clan of West Cavan. The castle walls are supposed to have been wet with bullock's blood."* [40] [Blood being a strengthening agent in the mortar.]

Being situated on a boundary between enemy tribes, the Masraige and Conmaicne, this castle saw a lot of territorial defensive action.

"Ballymagovern was besieged three times, first in 1354, secondly in 1545 and thirdly in 1549. In 1485 it was burned to the ground by the O'Reilly's. Mac Gaurans ruled it as a kind of kingdom in itself. The McGuires and McGoverns were constantly fighting. In the fifteenth century John McGuire Lord of Fermanagh was killed near Templeport church. In 1485 a fierce conquest took place between the O'Reilly's and the McGoverns, the Mc Governs won the battle... In the seventeenth century the O'Reilly and the McGoverns united. From that they fought side by side against the English." [41]

The Magauran name was originally Samhradhain, pronounced Sauran, that became Mag-Sauran, then MacGauran and Magauran, and was finally anglicised to MacGovern. In 1256 the Magaurans joined forces with the O'Rourkes to defeat the O'Reillys, in the Great Battle of Magh Sléct (this occurred further north, at Bellavally Gap, according to the Annals).[42] Eventually they bent to English control to some degree, changing their name to MacGovern. Their ancestral lands were then re-granted back to them and they were able to continue a high level of autonomy in the region.

Tullyhaw's chief Druids also belonged to the Magauran clan. An associated family, the O'Cianains, provided the bards (historian poets) to their highly cultured society, while the Macgaurans were themselves renowned as a most literate clan. A medieval Duanaire or Poembook of theirs, the oldest such surviving poem book in Ireland, describes various incidents at Ballymagauran. The Macgauran Druids were also famous for having the hereditary cure for hydrophobia, a symptom of rabies.[43]

This cure was described in the Freemans Journal of 6/4/1815, in an article that including a testimonial letter from a land surveyor who confirmed its efficacy. *"It has …. never failed… even just after the first symptoms have begun to appear. What medicine they give is concealed in three small barley cakes which, with a little water, is the only sustenance allowed the patient for three days, when the cure is complete. The secret is transferred from father to son."* [44]

Another prominent Tullyhaw family were the O'Dolans. *"In ancient times the O'Dolans were eminent among the poets and historians of Tullyhaw and Leitrim. Their coat of arms, like that of the McGovern clan, bears a tree in full foliage."* [45]

DERRYRATH

Because of its entrenched Pagan culture, the region attracted the wrath of the church in a big way. So much so, that on a hill called Derryrath (locally called Darragh), the next townland along from Ballymagauran, the most graphic literary example of St Patrick's spiritual one-upmanship was set. A tiny country lane off the R205 to the right takes you up to the base of the drumlin hill. From the top of the 100 m high hill, the highest point in Magh Sléct, there are extensive views all around and, conversely, nearly every hilltop monument around has a view of Derryrath, including the enclosure on its summit.

"There is one fort which I know about called Darragh… near Ballymagovern Co. Cavan. It is just a small plot and it is round in shape. There is a thick ditch and trees round it also. There is one lone tree in the centre of the fort and it is believed that fairies are dancing round it every night. People dug away the ditch that is round it and they had very bad luck. People often hear cats and dogs in it and they often see lights also. Some people say that there is a pot of gold hid there. There are mountains or hills beside it and people often go there and view the country." [46]

Originally, the hill was surrounded on three sides by water, because, prior to various drainage works, the lakes seem to have been one large continuous lake, with Ballymagauran lake joined to present day Garadice Lough, with the mega lake called Guth-Ard in the Annals. This explains why Patrick was said to have arrived to the pilgrimage hill by boat, scholars have deduced.

Derryrath's hilltop enclosure is a circular low bank of earth some 100 m by 60 m across, its banks topped by a hedgerow of small trees. On the west, north and north east sides are the possible remains of a wide internal fosse (ditch), however it's unclear whether this is natural or a man-made feature, says White.[47] It was definitely not configured as a defensive enclosure, otherwise a fosse would have been on the outside. Nor is there evidence that it was lived in. It's rather more suggestive of a ritual site, say archeologists. This must explain why it was seized upon by Armagh as a fitting setting for their tale of violent overthrow of the Pagans.

"No other event in Patrick's mission in Ireland is as vividly recorded as his destruction of Crom's idols," White notes. The story describes how Patrick confronted the 'Crom Dubh idol' at Derryrath and threw it and twelve other 'idol' stones down into the ground, before converting the locals to Christianity. There's no archeological evidence for any standing stones. Folklore also preserves the memory of a Fairy Line/Pass/Path that ends here.[48] So, ample hallmarks of a centre of spiritual and political significance.

"In this district there are some ancient forts, the principal being Darraugh fort. On this fort pagans in Ireland erected a false god which they named Crom Cruagh. They also had twelve idols spread round the district. Pagans came from all over Ireland to worship this false god. Saint Patrick came and destroyed it and people say that he left the track of his knee in the stone. One day a boy was sent to bring cattle off the fort. He started very early but did not return for three days. He came back and worked as usual, but never mentioned what happened to him." [49]

While we know such tales are basically propaganda, grains of truth often run through them. That Derryragh was originally a "principal fort" has been borne out by archeological studies. Indeed, Kevin White's thesis on the subject strongly suggests that Derryragh is a *"previously unidentified minor 'royal' site."* While there is a concurrence of this medieval myth with local folklore, Michael O'Duigeannain in 1940 dismissed this as originating from *"pseudo-learned inventions of the 10th and 11th centuries."* [50] The site was most likely chosen for the epic tale because of its political significance, in order to diminish the Druid backed power of the Samhradhain clan's royal governance.

"A geophysical survey was carried out at the hilltop enclosure site of Derryragh...[that has] disproved the theory that Derryragh is the location of Crom Cruach's idol. The author firmly believes the aniconic stone, the Killycluggin Stone, might have been perceived as Crom Cruach's idol. The geophysical survey did produce evidence of a palisaded enclosure with a funnel entrance, a feature that's found at many of the major 'royal sites'. Analysis of the literary sources and the monuments of the area presents a strong case that Magh Sléct is a minor 'royal' site".[51]

DERRYRATH EXPERIENCE

Maire MacNeill mentions Derryrath in her round-up of Lughnasa traditions, as being associated in local tradition with a Fairy Pass that continues on to Co. Donegal via Bellavally Gap. In tradition it passed by a famous hilltop holy well at nearby Bellaleenan, a Lughnasa festival place overlooking the Blackwater River which flows from Slieve an Ierainn into Ballymagauran Lough. Along this Pass, it was said, *"the fairies were often heard going the way".*[52] A Fairy Pass is perceivable by dowsers as a magnetic, serpentine-shaped current that meanders across the landscape. (Chinese landscape tradition would classify them as Lung Mei / Dragon Lines.) While they are not uncommon, it is very rare for one to be documented. And to be as long, would make it a significant energetic landscape feature. As a dowser, I was keen to look for it and on a visit there was not disappointed!

Just past Ballymagauran we took the tiny lane to the right off the R205. This L5058 Doire Rath road looks more like a driveway, with a grass strip down the middle. (It was probably the first road here.) Rising up over the base of Derryrath hill, we stopped there and talked to the land owner, who kindly told us how to access the famous Darragh Fort, as it's often called. Parking beside his house at the highest point of the lane, we ascended the hill via a timber field gate that gives the closest access. Immediately in front of us, at the base of the slope, were the monument stones he'd told us about, a couple of massive limestone slabs are all that remain of a possible tomb. It was a bucolic scene, with contented dairy cows in lush pasture watching on as we marvelled at the stones and already wide views.

Something felt special around the stones (seen overleaf). Could the Fairy Pass be close by, I sensed? Such earth energy lines often intersect with significant stones. My pendulum dowsing confirmed this. Yes, a relatively huge energy current came surging down the hillside, passed through the megalithic structure, then onwards on its way to far off Donegal. It was an exhilarating discovery and a powerful earth energy to tune into.

We then ascended to the summit, where the oval hilltop enclosure of Derryrath is in a breathtaking location. Here, on the highest hilltop in Magh Sleact at 100m above sea level, can be had views of five counties on a clear day. County Fermanagh is to the north and Slieve Rushen looms large on the right, punctuated by a concrete works that towers above its eastern flank. West to northwest is the line of mountains, Cuilcagh and Slieve Iarainn. Views across Leitrim and particularly Lough Garadice can be seen; to the south east, County Cavan and on clear days Longford; to the east the drumlins of Cavan and in the north east, County Monaghan may be visible.[53] The banks encircling the site with their wild hedgerow plants were a riot of summer blossoms, the flowering elderberries looking splendid. Purple flowering foxgloves graced the bank edges and attracted huge bumblebees that were generously accommodated within their individual flowers.

By dowsing, I followed the Fairy Pass up the hill to its end point, in the centre of the enclosure. Here it finally earthed itself, giving the energy signature of a downward geo-spiral, an earth vortex. The centre is energetically still, just like the eye of a hurricane. Around it I dowsed five, downward spiralling energy rings - unusually large. If the geo-spiral would be stimulated by ritual activities, the number of rings could no dobt increase, I imagined. Sacred sites have been associated with seven ring geo-spirals. This one certainly felt like a neglected sacred site. The folktale mention of fairies dancing around a central Fairy Tree made sense then too. I know that nature spirits love to dance around a vortex and I picked up that they do dance around the one here to this day! Other local folktales connect this site with leprechauns.[54] I'm sure they would be dancing too. The ritual nature of this site is felt in its magical and benign atmosphere. It's easy to get the sense that Iron Age Druids were working strongly and harmoniously with the earth energies here.

KILNAVERT

The best preserved and accessible megalithic tomb in Magh Sléct is the early Bronze Age wedge tomb at Kilnavert (seen overleaf). It's on the left in a farm field on the road to Ballyconnell, some 250 m before St Patrick's Church (where it's easier to park vehicles). An old brown sign before the bend proclaims the site and you can park beside it there, farming activities permitting. The landowner is friendly and happy to share this national monument (as long as you respect the rules of the farm, shutting gates and avoiding proximity to livestock etc). Which goes for all farm land access. The monument is some 200 m from the sign.

This magnetic site with wide views of the hulking mountain range behind is marked on old OS maps as a Giant's Grave. Much stone has been robbed out, but a dolmen type structure of flagstones remains and the outer bank is studded with large flags and a circle of magnificent beech trees that have rooted around them. It's set on a raised earthen platform (75 cm high and 10 m diameter) that must be the remains of the base of its cairn. The tomb has a single gallery with its inner side-walls still standing. The gallery is 3.5 m long and 1.5 m to 1.35 m wide. A single capstone covers much of the gallery.

Amateur digs there in the past found various artefacts. *"It is recorded that teeth, two pots and two combs were found in a cist in the monument,"* White notes. Close by are two standing stones, one just outside the platform to the north, at 1.75 m high, and another 90 m to the south, that's 2.1 m high. According to local tradition one of these stones *"was used as a mass rock in penal times, with two depressions on the surface of the rock being believed to have been used to contain wine,"* he says. [55]

Dowsing the standing stone to the south, between the tomb and road, I detected an earth energy current, a small Fairy Line, joining it to the tomb energetically. On a visit here a 'fairy lamb', that became isolated from the flock and was standing curiously beside this pillar stone, came over to greet us, adding to the magic.

Kilnavert townland has a dozen or so prehistoric monuments, including six possible ring barrows, three standing stones, the wedge tomb described and one stone circle. The six possible ring barrows are located around the Kilnavert church area, but they are mostly marked mistakenly as 'forts' on Ordnance Survey maps. Barrows, circular funeral mounds, are considered to be a hallmark of the Iron Age. With such a concentration of them, it's probably the most extensive barrow cemetery in Co. Cavan.

After the alleged destruction of Crom's 'idols' (which doesn't get a mention in the earliest accounts of the saint).[56] Patrick reputedly established the first Patrician Church in the county,

here in the Rath of Kilnavert, aka Fossa Slécht or Rath Sléch. He was said to have baptised converts here at the holy well Toberpatrick, in the next field in the townland of Corran. The current St. Patrick's Roman Catholic Church was erected in 1864, replacing an earlier thatched church built about 1798, that replaced previous churches all the way back to the original 5th century church, that was called Domnach Maige Slécht.[57] On the 1836 Ordnance Survey map, however, it's called St. Mogue's Church.[58] St. Mogue was born in Magh Slécht in 555AD, on nearby Mogue's Island in Templeport Lough, where he had a monastery. It's more plausible that a local saint established this church and that St Patrick never came here.

You can still see some of the original circular enclosure of the Rath of Kilnavert, in the form of earth banks encircling the graveyard and church, with an area of some 60 m diameter. It must have once been an important rath. Indeed, prior to building the current church, the ringfort was said to have been bivallate (double ringed). *"This fact led O'Connell to believe that Rath Slécht was the residence of the chieftain of Magh Slécht and when he was converted to Christianity he handed over his residence,"* notes White. [59]

While we'll never know if Patrick ever actually came here, we can be sure that his legend was anti-Pagan propaganda. So, did it work? Probably not - the three Patrick's Wells have their annual Pattern Days not on his feast day, but on the last Sunday of July, the day of Crom Dubh, the harvest god, a common enough quirk!

The most famous of the wells, Tober Patrick, is located some 300 m east of Rath Slécht and the present day church. Well pilgrims once moved from the well to the church shuffling on their knees, copying the style that St. Patrick is meant to have used (perhaps emulating Pagan prostrations, in the spirit of- "I can do them better!"). Not surprisingly, patterns at this well died out in the 1860's, perhaps due to sore knees.[60]

Patrick's stories, not written until the late 7th century, centuries after his death, are highly questionable. *"The 'lives' were written as propaganda for the church of Armagh and are not objective history,"* says archeologist Michael Moore.[61] This is why it's impossible to pinpoint an exact site for the confrontation with Crom Dubh, nor confirm if it even happened. The pseudo-legend speaks of Paddy smoting a rock and another twelve in a circle, that were associated with underworld god Crom Dubh, and casting them all into the ground. Actually, there is a stone circle in the nearby townland of Killycluggin and in the 1920s a very important ritual stone was discovered close beside it, one that seems to have been deliberately buried.

The gap of some 15 centuries in these associated events is curious and makes you wonder if the St Patrick legend was re-written subsequent to the discovery of the buried stone? Is it just a co-incidence? Or does it truly go back to the incident when it was actually buried?

KILLYCLUGGIN

The stone circle at Killycluggin is *"probably the most significant monument of its type in the area of Magh Slécht,"* says White. With a diameter of 22 m, it comprises 18 stones, 13 of which are fallen. The two largest stones, on the north east, are flat on the ground but they might have have formed an impressive entrance way when standing upright. [62]

Access is behind the school on the right side of the road. A style on the left allows access over the fence into the field beside the school and from there you can walk up to the top of the low hill and view the stone circle in the overgrown site. Further up the road to the east you can view a replica of the Killycluggin Stone that was found buried near the stone circle. The beautiful swirling, bio-geometric style of its decorations (known as 'La Tene', from the location of important related finds in Switzerland) dates it to the Iron Age. As with the other existing La Tene stone examples, it's highly likely to have been used as a royal inauguration stone. The rare Irish La Tene stones include the Turoe Stone, in Galway and Castlestrange Stone in Roscommon. The original Killycluggin stone, the only one found in situ, is now in the County Museum in Ballyjamesduff (as belw). It's dated to about 100 B.C

The concrete copy (right) sits in the middle of a road junction on the left, a kilometre or so from where it was dug up. An interpretative sign beside it gives a good account of the find. On one visit there I met one of the original stone retrievers, an old gentleman farmer, Mr Bannon, who lives besides it. He reminisced how the location got rather busy there from the 1970s on, with *"busloads of people"*, from America in particular, coming to view the celebrity stone, he told me.

The Killycluggin Stone, when buried had its top sticking up out of the ground and was an obstruction for tillage, so farmers smashed it off, before realising it was no ordinary stone and eventually digging it out, to archeological acclaim. It was first identified in 1921 by Robert Vincent Walker, a Cavan County Health Inspector who was also an antiquarian and place-names expert.[63] There were two fragments found (neither of which joined together) and both were left outside until the 1970's. In 1974 there was a full excavation undertaken by archeologists Barry Raftery with assistance from Eamonn Kelly and a few local lads, and both pieces were removed to the National Museum. A trench was initially dug around the area where the first fragment was found and within it were the remains of two pits, one containing charcoal and burnt bone as well as a flint scraper, the second pit - a mix of stone and grit. *"Raftery concluded that the stone and the stone circle were related* [and] *he believed that the stone may have been deliberately buried to remove it from view, possibly by early Christians who wanted to remove symbols of Paganism,"* says White.[64] So, perhaps the St Patrick stone burying myth relates to that event? But whether it was Paddy that smote the stone a banishing blow, or St Mogue, a bunch of farmers, or other actors, we'll probably never know.

Lissanover

A back road going north from the Killycluggin junction passes first through the adjacent townland of Lissanover. It was a place of early importance and a map from 1750 shows its prominence. Here, on farmland, are located the remains of two rows of standing stone, less than 250 m from each other. Row A is just one stone today, while the 1912 edition of the OS map shows two stones. Row B is a more complete stone row comprising three stones. There is an orientation that points towards a stone circle, as well as the finding place of the Killycluggin Stone, suggesting it *"may have been part of a larger monument or stone circle"*, says White. A ritual landscape, indeed! The stone circle at Lissanover is today in a ruinous state, having been reduced to piles of small stones and one partially buried large stone, he says.[65]

Folklore tells of a castle in Lissanover, barely a trace of which is left today. *"The stronghold of the McGovern chieftain was Lissanover - Lios-an-lubhair (The Proud Fort), overlooking the present Templeport Lake…At the close of the eighteenth century when English sway began to assert itself in Cavan and south Leitrim, McGovern removed to Gleann Gaibhle and the castle of Lissanover fell into disuse… The ruins of it were pulled down some ten years ago."* [66] [i.e. in the 1920's].

After the demise of the Gaelic lords, this castle was the base for a cruel, sociopathic landlord, well remembered in local folklore. A tree outside the castle served as his gallows. Stones in the castle walls were bonded with new milk and blood demanded by him from his tenants' animals, under serious threat for non-delivery. *"If they did not give it, they would be hanged."* [67] …*"Hulmes lived in Lisanover. He succeeded the four brothers that lived in Lisanover. He was a cruel pitiless tyrant. He was a Protestant. When he would get anyone trespassing on his land especially a Catholic he would put them under great torture."* [68]

One sinister tale tells of how he tricked and murdered his brother, the King of Lissanover, and took over his position there.[69] *"Humes was the king that came after McGovern. The (king) last Landlord that lived in the castle, was Lord Ingles. He was a very cruel Lord, he evicted all Catholics out of their lands."* [70]

In this townland a fabulous gold torc was discovered in 1909 and it's on display in the National Museum in Dublin. *"When the Danes were invading Ireland they were very wealthy and they wore golden collars. King Malachy won one of these historic pieces from the invaders and the collar that was found was supposed to be his."* [71] The classic solid gold lunula would certainly have been worn as a symbol of authority and probably originated from the nearby castle. It was found by a farmer in a rock fissure 2.5 m underground, in an old quarry on his land at the edge of Lissanover townland, adjoining Cor Bog.[72]

That this area was previously a borderland zone and scene of territorial conflicts is remembered in local folklore collected by Corran school in the 1930s. *"There is a field near the castle* [at Lissanover] *called the valley of the black pig. It is said that a black pig was seen going down the field and that he will go down the field before the end of the world."* [73]...
"It is said wherever the [black] *pig fed there will be war and that was in Lissanover."* [74]

The remains of a disused railway embankment, that once carried trains between Ballinamore and Ballyconnell, passes through the south western corner of Lissanover. I wonder if its builders may have appropriated a conveniently existent Iron Age embankment for some of their track? This idea is echoed in a line from a Folklore Commission record about another legendary path of the Black Pig in Co. Sligo: *"It is said that the railway line from Collooney to Claremorris is running the way she* [the Black Pig] *went"*. [75]

JAMPA LING

North east of here in the direction of Bawnboy, is the modern legend of Jampa Ling, the Tibetan Buddhist meditation centre. It's set within the beautiful grounds of Owendoon House, with mature trees and a lake frontage to Lough Bunerky, is open to the public and a lovely, chilled-out place to visit. You can walk the beautiful gardens, visit the shop that features crafts from Mongolia (such as cosy wool felt slippers), or attend events there. There are various retreats, rituals, celebrations and programmes. Self-catering hostel accommodation is also available.

The centre is presided over by The Venerable Panchen Ötrul Rinpoche, a senior and highly respected Tibetan Buddhist scholar of the Gelugpa School, who teaches regularly in Ireland, Europe, North America and Asia. Ven. Rinpoche also visits Mongolia each year, where he is heavily involved in charitable work and the re-emergence of Buddhism. In 1990, Ven. Rinpoche, who attended school with the Dalai Llama, was asked by Irish students of Buddhism to become the spiritual director of Jampa Ling. [76]

BALLYCONNELL AND BALLYHEADY

Continuing along the R205 road from Ballinamore and you get to Ballyconnell, a pretty Co.

Cavan town. The town is situated in Tullyhaw on the Woodford (Grainne) River, that was canalised as part of the Shannon-Erne waterway, the river being the eastern border of Mag Slécht and of Tullyhunco. A ford on the river there was the traditional site of the killing of its namesake, the great Ulster warrior hero Conall Cernach.[77]

Ballyconnell's name, from Béal Átha Conaill, means the entrance to the ford of Conall. Conall's grave is said to be in a hilltop cairn around 5 km south of Ballyconnell at Ballyheady, also on the border of Magh Sléct. The stone mound, now surrounded by a conifer plantation, is a monument of some 3,000 years age, which is much earlier than Conall's time.[78]

It's the topmost one of three cairns in the townland of Killarah. These are aligned in a roughly straight line, west-north-west to east-south-east, running from the top of Bellaheady Mountain down to the Woodford River, 550 m away. Prior to the forestry, the site had extensive views of the surrounding area and itself could be seen from afar. The large cairn, known locally as The Cairn Stones, was visible from Ballyconnell as well.[79]

Now much denuded of stone, inside the mound a cist burial was found by council workers as they were removing material for re-use in road construction in the 1930's. It was then examined by archeologist Sean O'Riordain, who recorded the remains of three people and a number of cremation burials, but no grave goods. O'Riordain concluded that the cist was a Middle Bronze Age addition to the original cairn. First written about in 1739, it was reported that two of the large mounds were found to contain *"small apartments and urns in them. In the first there was found, about 40 years ago, a golden chalice of considerable value by a farmer, who thinking it to be brass made a present of it to Capt. Ellis his landlord."* [80]

A Ballyconnell resident informed students of Munlough Nth school in the 1930's that - *"Conall Cearnach was one of the Red Branch Knights who lived in Ulster. He was a cousin of Cuculain… Ulster at that time was at war with Connacht. There was great enmity between the two provinces…Ballyconnell was at first called Ath na Mianna. Conall's son was called Miann. He engineered the building of the Black Pig's Dyke from Dundalk to Donegal, made to keep the Connacht men from coming into Ulster. At that time Connacht was the strongest of the four provinces".*[81]

Across twenty different sagas of Ulster, we see Conall cast as an archetypal warrior hero, a major demigod of a character, who tirelessly defended the borders of Ulster, protected individuals and the honour of his friends, and the very honour of Ulster itself.[82] The role he plays is of sacred guardian, the Divine Masculine aspect of the sovereignty of Ulster.

Up until the early 20th century Ballyheady Hill was visited annually during Lughnasa celebrations of Bilberry Sunday. People played games and danced to the fiddle and flute, and they picked the ripe bilberries on the hill. There is no known connection between the assembly and the cairn.[83] But it could hardly be a coincidence?

TOMREGAN AND MULLYNAGOLMAN

Ballyconnell has a most mysterious carved stone, known as the Tomregan Stone, that's now kept securely inside a church. Probably once taken from the top of a medieval church window, it was found in 1961 lying face down in a drain, a kilometre away from where the former monastery of Toomregon stood, in the townland of Mullynagolman.[84] It then spent years mouldering outdoors in the churchyard.

While some have called it a 'sheela-na-gig', the carving appears to more likely depict local hero St Bruicu / Bricin / Dreccan, though it's a very weathered and hard-to-define image to discern today. The name Tomregan is a corruption of Tuam Dreccan, the tomb of the saint who headed a famed monastic college, Bricin's School or the University of Tuaim Drecuin. Tomregan is now the name of the parish, as well as a nearby townland with the further corrupted (or typo error) name of Tonyrevan. Founded in around the 7th Century, the college became famous across Europe for its schools of classics, law, medicine and history. Bricin was especially renowned for his skills of brain surgery, after he saved the life of Cenn Faelad, a prince who was injured in battle.[85]

Archeologists have found remains of a round tower and church at the site in Mullynagolman, indicating its great importance. (Ireland's substantial stone Round Towers of up to 34 m in height were a great status symbol and treasures were kept in the upper stories, where they were traditionally safe from pillaging. Round Towers were often associated with pilgrimage, acting as a signpost for travellers, students or the sick to find their way there.[86]) Bricin's university is thought to have closed sometime in the 8th or 9th Century. In Dublin, St. Bricin's Military hospital was named in honour of this saint.[87]

The semi-monstrous looking Tomregan carving is much eroded, but some have suggested that it depicts St. Bricin holding a skull in one hand and a surgery tool in the other. This most curious piece is now housed in a church just inside an entranceway and half hidden behind a table, as I discovered on my visit. To view it, after entering Ballyconnell, take a left at the crossroads (towards Doon). The pretty Church of Ireland church is some 300 m later, on the right. The Tom Regan Parish Hall is opposite it on the Doon Road and a few doors down on the left is the home of Mrs Brennan, who lends the key to the church to visitors.

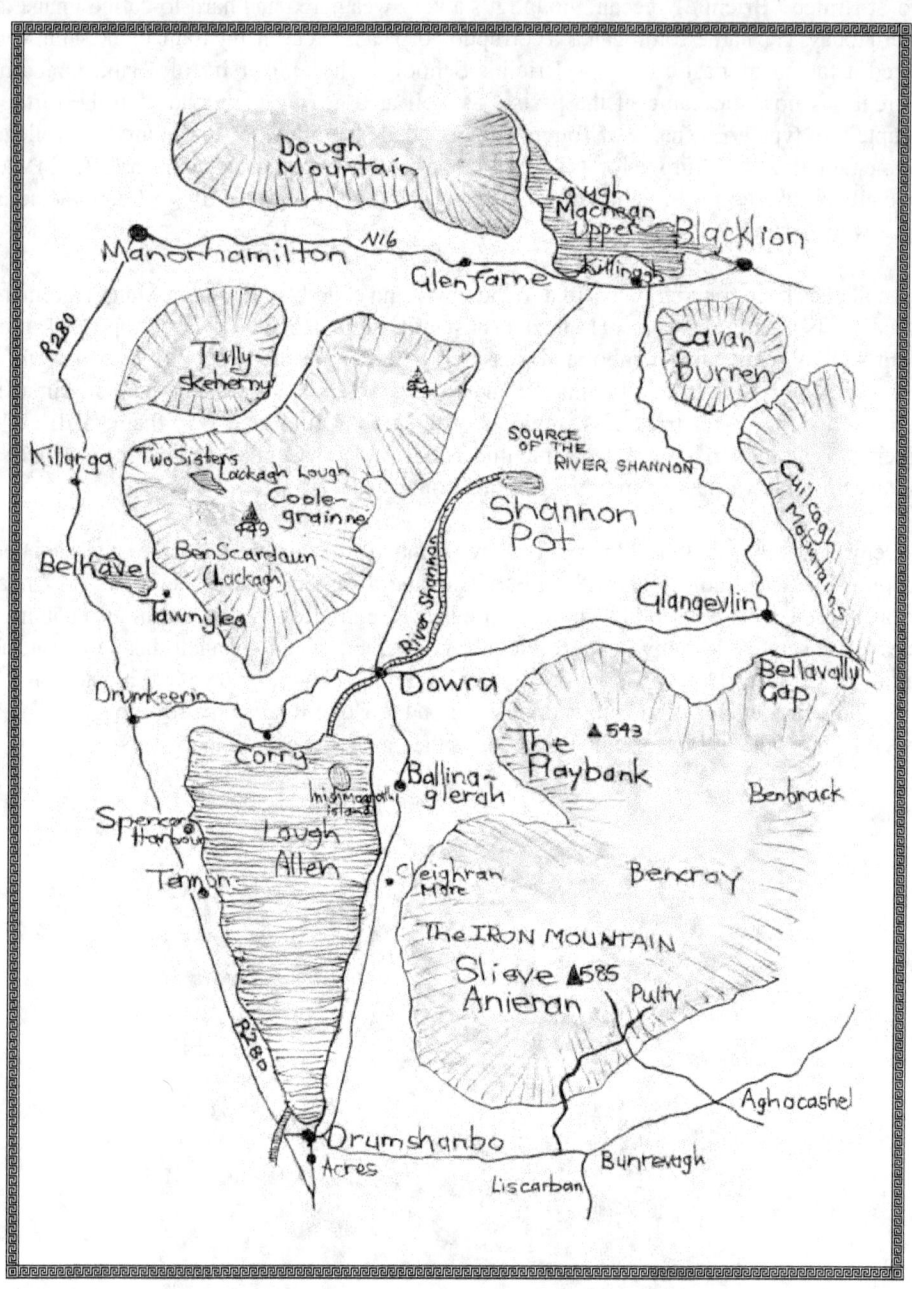

Chapter 8
Iron Mountain

Coming of the Iron Age

The Irish Iron Age was a relatively late development that began around 500 BCE and ended about 500 CE. The new art of iron making allowed the creation of cheaper and more effective tools and weapons for the common people. No more were weapons the status symbols of a warrior elite, as it was in the Bronze Age, when only wealthy and well-connected people could import the metals required. Iron was much more freely available and made better tools, these ushered in advances in agriculture, technology and a scaling up of warfare. It also brought deforestation to a new level.

It's not that the forging of iron implements was easy to do. It was just more egalitarian and it must have greatly changed the balance of power. *"Though occurring naturally over far more extensive areas and in far greater quantity than copper and tin, its extraction required a more complex technology and a higher temperature for the chemical changes to take place. Once the ore had been reduced, the spongy iron bloom had to be reheated and beaten many times to remove slag. Finally, when the iron was pure enough, a number of blooms would be beaten together to form an ingot of sufficient size to allow tools and weapons to be forged"*.[1] Not surprisingly, iron workers were highly skilled and powerful technicians who were considered to have great mystical powers, such as Irish blacksmith god Gobniu. Great reverence was paid to metalworkers, who creatively transformed the elements - metal, fire, air and water. They were the alchemists of their day, who facilitated food and security, life and death.

The saga of the arrival of the mythic Tuatha da Danaan to Ireland located them in Co. Leitrim, high up upon the misty mountain of Sliabh an Iarainn, the Iron Mountain. This tribe were followers of the goddess Dana, the mother of the gods - a typical Celtic naming protocol. However Dana is not a name that we see much elsewhere in Ireland, apart from derivative names Anu and Ana. Whatever the provenance, the invaders, wielding their superior iron weapons, were able to overpower the incumbent tribes on the battle ground. (O'Connor suggested that they represent the Fir Belgs.) Debate has raged over where the described battles took place (and if at all). However a version of the tale in Leitrim's folklore gives a plausible setting for the legendary events, keeping it within the Sliabh An Iarain area.

"When the Tuatha-De-Dannan came to Ireland it is said they landed at Sligo, crossed Lough Allen and went in hiding on Sliab-an-Iarainn. They found iron on Sliab-an-Iarainn, hence the name [Iron Mountain]....*A battle was fought on Sliab-an-Iarainn between the Tuatha-De-Danann and the Firbolgs, and it is said that the Shannon ran red with blood after this battle. The Tuatha-de-Danann were victorious in their battle in Mag Rein."* [2]

The Tuatha-De-Dannan were said to have arrived bearing particular icons, the touchstones of their culture. These included an invincible sword and a cauldron of plenty that could never be emptied of food. The top god Dagda (Good God) owned this legendary cauldron, which you might call a metaphor for the bounty of the Earth. They also brought the Stone of Destiny (or several it seems) that was used for the inauguration of kings and there are multiple possibilities for these in Ireland. The best candidates are the handful of La Tene (Swiss Iron Age style) stones, beautifully carved boulders some 2000 years of age. The three best surviving examples being the Turoe Stone from Rath Ferach in Galway and, on the edge of Roscommon, near the Suck River that once divided Ulster and Connaught, the Castlestrange stone. The third is the Killycluggin Stone of Magh Sléct, also found in a border area, near tracks of the Black Pig.

In the Iron Mountain legend, the locals were oblivious to the presence of an invading tribe that had arrived on its slopes and stayed stealthily hidden in forests of mighty Oak, Ash and Elm trees. They kept invisible in leafy clouds of mist and twirling clouds of smoke. Here, in mountain boglands and along stream banks they found lumps of iron ore and, from the abundant trees, made charcoal to heat it to the right temperature to make their superior iron blades and axes. Iron gave the Tuatha da Danaan the edge over their Bronze Age cousins and their technological superiority was later confirmed on the battle fields. But these were not human beings, more warrior gods than flesh and blood. To satisfy the church, it's typical to find the old deities relegated to a lower status in the literature. The Tuatha da Danaan are an emasculated tribe of gods, a pantheon of human-like deities, representing the flavour of their times. They were the face of a new order, an industrial revolution that changed everything.

ACRES

Heading north from Carrick on Shannon towards Drumshanbo, you pass through Acres. Acres Lough is on your left, with its marina and canal. It's worth stopping here, as a visitor information centre features some local history and folklore. The jewel in the crown of the lake is the floating boardwalk that has you walking or cycling over the rippling waters, in summer passing blooming water lilies, nesting swans and other beauties. The 600 m boardwalk, Ireland's first, is the start of a 6.5 km linear walking and cycling trail from Acres

Lake along the canal banks to Battlebridge Lock, near Leitrim Village.[3] Lough Allen Canal leaves the southern end of Acres Lough and bypasses the shallow part of the Shannon, entering the river after Battlebridge Lock at Drumhierney, where there's enough depth for navigation. By the time the canal was finished in 1820, it had already been superseded by a railway line and so was little used. When Lough Allen was controlled for electricity production, water levels fluctuated too much for the canal to be used by boats. Reopened for boat traffic in 1996, lake levels are now kept constantly at a level suited for navigation.[4]

DRUMSHANBO

Drumshanbo is a lovely village with a charming old world streetscape. The name Druim Sean Bhoth means the Ridge of the Old Hut. Today a modern brewery is the town's greatest economic success, while in its hey day, Drumshanbo was a town drunk on resource extraction. Local iron mines and forests fuelled an industrial era of frenetic intensity. On the edge of the village, the townland name Furnace Hill reflects this legacy. The forests were fully wiped out by 1765, but then a coal seam was discovered nearby in the hills above Arigna, in Co. Roscommon, and this allowed the industry to continue for a bit longer.[5]

The hollowed out landscapes paid a high price for economic gain. And whose gain was it anyway? There was little local benefit to people who were fundamental to its operation. Technical know-how was kept in-house and profits channelled elsewhere, while permanently impoverished workers could only think of the next meal. A smelting furnace in the townland of Druminalass built by Sir Charles Coote about 400 years ago was described thus.

"The workers, it is said, came from Holland and England. The Irish were given no work at the furnace, their duty was to carry the iron-stone from Sliabh an Iarainn and work in the corn-mill which was attached to the furnace. Their pay consisted of meal from the mill." [6]

Coote had established ironworks at Arigna, Creevylea, Dromod and Ballinamore. It's estimated that he employed 3000 men altogether, but not a single one was Irish. J J Guckian explained why this was the case - *"His foundries produced cannon for the Army and Irish workers could not be trusted in the process of their manufacture."* [7] It's not surprising then that all of Cootes' ironworks were destroyed in the Rebellion of 1641. But they were re-started after 1690. [8]

When peak coal, peak forest and peak iron had passed, it was the end of a hectic and environmentally devastating era. But I suppose it would have been a relief for the exploited workers, perhaps allowing them to return to their original, independent lifestyles, enjoying the primordial peasant economy, that seeks only to produce happy, healthy families, rather than being the wage slaves of others, at the mercy of the market economy.

Today Drumshanbo has a great reputation for its vibrant traditional music scene, with festivals and cultural events attracting people from across Europe and beyond coming to join trad sessions, master classes and music courses. As well, it's the gateway to the vast expanse of water that is Lough Allen.

LOUGH ALLEN

The lake, some 11 km long and 4 km wide, is the county's biggest by far and is the first on the River Shannon. Set in a dramatic backdrop of mountains and hills wrapping around it on three sides, it can be grey, windswept and moody at times, but the cultural landscape is brightly saturated in stories and myth. The lough has been a focus for human habitation since Mesolithic times, going back to some 9,000 years ago, with artefacts from then found here. [9] Finds from the later Bronze Age have included a bronze dagger from a bog, several dug out canoes and a beautifully decorated bronze horse bit found on Duck Island, off Cormongan.

In the Bronze Age the lake levels were much lower. After works reduced the lake's elevated water level in the 1930s, a dug out canoe and crannogs were discovered in the Derrintober area, near the southern tip of the lake. This included a line of eight crannogs some 80 m in from the shore. This possible lake village consisted of stone platforms about 4-6 m in diameter, with an extra large one that may have acted as a main fortress. To access them, an underwater stone path 5 m wide had been constructed. The Leitrim Observer reported what an important find this was. However all were subsequently destroyed. [10]

When the Iron Age came, the presence of iron drew people to this lake region like never before. *"The mineral resources of the Lough Allen area in counties Leitrim and adjacent Roscommon are amongst the richest in the island of Ireland,"* Susan Hegarty explained.[11] Iron ore was an important attraction, being mined around Lough Allen from the 15th to the 18th century, if not earlier, while coal mining became more prominent by the 19th century. Coal was also mined to the east of Lough Allen towards Sliebh An Iarain, and to the west of Arigna. But these coal seams were later exhausted as well.[12]

It's hard to imagine a landscape of thickly forested hills around the lough when you see them today. The forests finally succumbed to the numerous ironworks in the region by around 1765 and they remain mostly bare to this day. In 1832 an observer, Isaac Weld, reported *"there can be no doubt that the hills were freely not only covered with trees but very large ones, judging from the size of the stumps and roots which can occasionally be traced."* [13]

Lough Allen's most notable island, Inishmacgrath is situated in the north-east corner of the lake, close to where the Shannon enters the lake, having dropped in elevation some 100 m. Some 3 ha or so in size, ancient church ruins here are associated with St Beog of the 12th century. The focus for the old parish of Inishmagrath, the graveyard is now disused, but in the past it was so popular that people went to the trouble of ferrying their dead across to it. It was especially inconvenient for them when the weather prevented a boat crossing and sometimes the mourners waited beside the coffin for days for it to improve, at a point of land jutting out into the lake known as Deadman's Point.[14]

"Inch (nó inis) Island is situated in Lough Allen about one mile from the mainland. The tradition in the neighbourhood is that the Franciscan Fathers - who had a Monastery at Fenagh, Creevalea, and other places, had a Church built on the island, to which they came frequently to make Retreats. The remains of a Church is plainly visible, and the older inhabitants of the locality remember that there was a graveyard there too…Tradition has it there was a large flat Flag-stone which floated in to the mainland, and that it was on this stone the coffins for burial were placed when being taken to the island. The Stone was looked upon as enchanted".[15]

The lake's surrounding hills are mostly rough pasturelands. Flora and fauna in the lake are not greatly abundant nor diverse, for the waters are quite nutrient deficient, without the cyclic enrichment to the soil that trees bring. This is coupled with the problem of iron that washes down from the bare ground, both factors that are not conducive to fertility. Reed beds are few, except for at the north end at Ross-more, where there's an important wetland refuge for birds. And at Kilgarriff are other important wetland habitats, with both freshwater crayfish and otters thriving there. The Eurasian Otter was called the Dobar-chu in Irish, meaning water hound. [16] The Dobar-chu was also a name once used for water beasts regarded with terror as supernatural and dangerous.

There were many mysterious experiences recorded around Lough Allen, that was said to be the domain of fickle lake goddess Aillfhion, who could be vicious and take lives.[17] While this could be just another case of medieval character assassination, the lake can be a dangerous place. Sudden storms can arise here and winds can be fierce, drownings have been numerous. It's not surprising to read accounts of a treacherous female lake spirit with a serpentine form. [18] But local folklore also casts her in a benevolent light and describes her other form. In the following stories she is life-saving.

"About two years ago [in the 1930s] *a Mermaid was seen on Lough Allen near Ballinaglena by two men. The priest in Ballinaglena preached about it and warned the people not to touch the lake, as it was expected that someone would be drowned".*[19] Only recently, local folksong enthusiast Vicky Crawford spoke of coming across *"stories of the 'mermaid' or 'beautiful lady' who was spotted by various people on the shores of Lough Allen…Some say she appeared as a beautiful lady to warn people off sailing on the lake at a particular time, others that she guided them in some way."* She related that in both Lough Allen and in Lough Melvin further north, people in recent times have encountered 'beautiful ladies' and seen 'dragons'. The dragons are described by clairvoyants as being coloured blue, with lovely turquoise wings.[20]

Another typical Irish water spirit known as a Water Horse used to be seen around the lake on occasions, as in a tale collected from a school student's father in the 1930s. *"Once a water-horse came up out of Lough Allen and stayed on a mans farm for three days. The man did not know to whom the horse belonged and on the third day he yoked him to a cart and used him for carting. While he was carting, the horse ran away into the lake, bringing the cart with him and was never seen again".* [21]

SLIABH AN IARAINN

Sliabh an Iarainn rears its mighty hulk above the eastern shore of Lough Allen, a continuation of the Cuilcagh Mountain range. It towers over the other big hills at 585 m in height and is fortunate to be relatively unspoiled. Once covered with luxurious forests, back in 1680 the shrinking forests were described by Breifni chief Tadg O'Rourke, who reported that - *"There are very good woods of Ash, Oak, Alder, Birch, whereof a great part is consumed by several ironworks around the region."*[22]

Previously known as Sliabh Conmhaícne, the mountain of the Conmaicne Rein[23], this richly mythic mountain that overlooks South Leitrim is a monument to extractive industries and unsustainable development. The iron here is in the form of nodules, found within the Namurian shale beds that form much of the bedrock around Lough Allen. Nodules were washed down along streams to the lakeshore, where local people gathered them up and carted them to furnaces.[24] The bare slopes of these mountains are stark. They should have been reafforested centuries ago, but the colonial powers were only looking for short term gains. Now chequered with heather, bogland and monoculture blocks of Sitka Spruce plantations, it remains largely a wildlife desert, compared to the original woodlands.

Despite looking inhospitable, this mountain land once welcomed the fleeing Ultach, refugee families escaping persecution, who flooded down from northern counties from 1795. They found no spare arable land in Leitrim, so they had to make their own soil on the mountainsides - combining burnt heather and limestone (lime), sand dragged up from river banks and composted green waste and manure. Incredibly, they managed to survive and thrive. But many of their homes have long been abandoned and, being totally biodegradable, are dissolving back into the landscape.

Leitrim's mightiest mountain is drenched in myth and likewise is Lough Allen beside it. Archaic origin legends cast gigantic spiritual forces as landscape creators here, as recorded in the 1930s. *"The are a number of old legends as to the origin of Sliabh an Iarainn and Lough Allen. According to one story, two giants met where Lough Allen now stands and began to quarrel. Each of these giants carried a great enormous iron sword and after a while the swords broke into pieces and sank into the ground. As they had no swords to fight with, they threw 'clabar' [mud] at each other, thus forming Sliabh an Iarainn and the Arigna mountains, at each of which iron is found. The holes from which the mud was scooped filled with water thus forming Lough Allen".*[25]

The mythic mountain has also served as a weather gauge for local people. *"One of the best known signs of rain in this district is to see the mist or fog coming down the sides of Sliabh-an-Iarainn - the only high mountain in South Leitrim. If, on the other hand, the mist goes up the mountain people have no hesitation in proceeding with their haymaking or other fair-weather occupation."* [26]

PULTY

Just below the highest point on Slieve Aneiran's southern slope at Mullaghgarve (the Rough Summit) runs a legendary mountain stream that drops suddenly into a deep rock fissure, reappearing above ground some 1.6 km further down the slope. When the stream is in spate, the sound reverberates greatly as it disappears down the hole. The hole, called Pulty (Poll Taighe Cochlain was an earlier name) is a scary place in that livestock and people were said to sometimes disappear into it, never to be seen again. It gained a reputation as being an entrance into the Underworld, a gateway to Hell, and was associated with a dangerous serpent spirit, described as a "horrible worm" in one account. But the Pulty also had a great power of attraction to it.

Here was the venue for an annual celebration of Lughnasa, the start of harvest, every Pulty Sunday, also known as Donagh, Patron and Fraughan (local name for bilberries) Sunday. Up until WW1 people would attend from around 8 km distance around. It was popular to throw a stone down into the hole and say *"Away you go!"*, then listen to the long resounding echoes of it. In an adjoining townland, a holy well dedicated to St Patrick was a pilgrimage ritual point on the Patron day. People also enjoyed picking fraughans, buying sticky buns, lemonade and other fruits from stalls, and participating in sports such as rock throwing and weight lifting. Pipers played dance tunes and the whole community had tons of fun. The event ended around 8 pm, but some dances were then held in farm houses afterwards.[27]

The possible location of St Patrick's Well on the archeological record is at the base of the mountain south of Mullagarve /Pulty Hole, in Bunrevagh townland, where it borders Liscarban townland. Located in rough pasture, a stream flows by some 5 m from the well. The overgrown natural spring was long used as a water source, but no local knowledge of veneration was noted by archeologists, so maybe it was elsewhere.[28] Mairie MacNeill wrote that *"it is said that St Patrick blessed it* [the well] *on his journey from Magh Slecht to the Shannon; and it is reputed to cure warts and toothache. Rounds were made at the well as part of the day's outing."*[29]

In the following accounts we learn of a Druid altar stone that was nearby, but is now unknown, and the determination of the saint to combat Paganism. *"St Patrick passed through Co Leitrim on his way from Co. Roscommon to Mag Sleact in Co Cavan to destroy the chief idol Crom Cruac. He also passed through Liscarbon on his way to Sliab-an-Iarainn to put a stop to Druids worship there…Tobar Padraig is the name still given to a well in Liscarbon."* [30]

"On Sliab an Iarainn a short distance east of Braveiga [Bunrevagh] *stone, which was supposed to be the altar of the Druids worship, there is a big hole known as Polltaí Hole. Pagan worship was supposed to be carried on at this hole until St Patrick finally put an end to it. Until about twenty five years ago* [circa 1914] *the boys of the district gathered at Polltaí Hole on Garland Sunday which is the last Sunday of July. They spent the Sunday throwing stones into the hole and lighting fires in the heather."* [31]

St Patrick's possible well site is beside the road that leads up the mountain towards the Pulty Hole and with tales of a ritual stone also in the area, it's starting to sound like an ancient pilgrimage path in a sacred ritual landscape. The Lughnasa well pattern being a continuation of this landscape reverence. Early efforts to stamp out Pagan practises are ubiquitous in the monastic tales and in local folklore, while shining a sliver of light onto the location of ritual hot spots. Today only scant traces of the stone and well remain, but their memory persists.

SWEATHOUSES

"The inhabitants of every town-land in the parish had their own sweat-house. Every Saturday the sweat-house was heated. One Saturday morning a large turf-fire was lighted in the sweat-house. The sweat-house was heated to a very high temperature. In the evening a person used to go to the sweat-house, close the door and remain there till he was literally 'bathed in sweat'. The people of olden-times believed that by perspiring in such a manner rheumatism was prevented." [32]

Sweathouses are small, drystone or mud structures that typically have a corbelled roof and flagstone floors. Usually built into hillsides, or made on flat land as mounds covered with sods of earth, they were filled up with turf that burned for up to two days, with the tiny doorways blocked up. Up until the early 1900s they were used as a type of 'cure-all sauna' for people. Their proximity to water allowed for immediate refreshment afterwards, with people plunging into cold water for better recovery. Or they wrapped up in a blanket and went off to home and bed.

Leitrim has the remains of 116 recorded sweathouses, making it literally a hot bed for what were the saunas of their day. This is the greatest concentration in all of Ireland. They are mostly located in north Leitrim and the Lough Allen area, although there are recently confirmed to be three outlier occurrences east of Mohill. Very few are in good condition and only around half them still have walls intact. A well kept example at Annagh in Glenfarne Demesne has been likened to a small passage tomb in shape.

You would imagine they would have been popular with miners, whose lungs and skin were riddled with dust after a grimy day's work underground in poor working conditions, but a 2021 heritage project found no evidence for this. Rheumatism was the most common ailment they sought relief for in folktales.[33] Considering the cold and dampness of the typical old Irish cottage, it's no surprise!

"The list of cures is long but here, in Leitrim, treating aches and pains, fever and tuberculosis appear to be the main reason for their use. There is no memory of them having been associated with any specific industry such as mining or flax but instead simply the normal labour-intensive life of 19th century rural Ireland," wrote Aidan Harte, the archeologist co-ordinator with the Leitrim Sweathouse Project. (Local people are engaging in this project and sharing their knowledge with it.) [34]

Photos previous page - Archeologist Sam Moore at St Hugh's Sweathouse and the well nearby.

BALLINAGLERA

St Hugh's Sweat House, about 11 km north Drumshanbo in Cleighran More townland, is a wonderful, well-preserved example of a sweathouse that's easy to visit. A holy well is close by too. it's dedicated to St Beo-Aodh (Hugh), the patron saint of Ballinaglera (Baile na gCleireach, Town of the Clerics), who founded the church on Inishmacgrath Island in Lough Allen (which can be seen from the well site). Hugh's death was recorded in the Annals as 523; the saint's feast day of March 8th was the day of pilgrimage to the well. [35]

Before you get to Ballinaglera from Drumshanbo, turn right after crossing the Stony River. Access the sweathouse area via a little stone bridge and enter the shady grove. The well housing is a simple beehive structure of stones. A high level of iron and other minerals in the water is evident where the water and stones are stained orange-red. Adjacent to it is the sweat house, in a bank by the stream where people once cooled off after a good, long sweat.[36]

THE PLAYBANK

On the north western summit of the Slieve An Eiran massif people once gathered en masse to celebrate the start of harvest. On the last Sunday in July, known as Garland, Donagh or Bilberry Sunday, up to 2,000 people attended the event in the townland of Urbal Barr, above the village of Ballinagleragh, to *"give the last salute to summer."* Here they picked bilberries as they ascended upwards to the level plateau on the summit known as the The Playbank, or Playground (bilberries not being found on the summit itself). They picnicked and frolicked there from the afternoon until evening. Dance performances and competitions were held, fiddlers and flautists provided the music. There were sports events such as jumping and weight throwing. Being the main festival point for people from surrounding parishes, it was fun central here! The day wound up by 8 pm and as they left, people raised a loud cheer. Some farm houses hosted dances for the youths afterwards. The last big gathering was held in 1917, but people still climb the hill and pick bilberries, while dancing and sports are *"a thing of the past,"* noted MacNeill in 1962. [37]

DOWRA

A little north of Lough Allen, Dowra is the first town on the River Shannon. It's located beside an ancient river crossing, that was still visible in the 1930s, as attested by the folklore.

"Quite near the School there may be seen a remarkable set of large stones, which were used as stepping-stones across the Shannon. This was the 'Ford' which enabled people to get across the river, when no bridges or roads existed... The old tradition about the name Damh-Shthrath is, that along the Sráitheanna immense droves of oxen or bullocks grazed, hence the name Damh-Shthrát - Plain of the Ox."

Dowra was once a busy corridor of enterprise and industry. An iron works may have been the origin focus of the town, as it harnessed the steady flow of river water available there. *"At an early date there were Iron-works carried on near the village - and a place now known as the 'Wastry' may be seen; this was an artificial waterway for the waste water of the river to flow, after it had been used for the purpose of smelting the iron. A heap of Pig-iron is still* in existence near this place". [38]

The Black Pig passed by this way, placing Dowra within the Valley of the Black Pig and thus within Ulster. The line of the Black Pig's Dyke is first shown on the second edition OS map (1876-80). It's located to the south-west of the village, commencing at the bridge over the Shannon then proceeding in a southwest direction along the river, appearing intermittently on both banks. *"After 2.92 km it branches in two, with one branch continuing in a southwesterly direction along the River Shannon for a further 669 m and the other travelling northwards along the Owennayle River for a distance of 821 m. The Archaeological Survey of Ireland noted that no trace of the monument was visible on the ground, nor was there any local knowledge of its existence....* [while] *both river banks have heavy tree cover, which makes identification difficult."* [39]

It isn't a surprise then, to see that the border of Leitrim and Cavan here is still following the course of the Shannon and Owennayle rivers. Three townlands adjacent to where the R200 crosses the Owennayle River are Glebes, so they must be fertile lands, that were confiscated and assigned to the church.

GLANGEVLIN

Glangevlin, in Irish Gleann Ghaibhle, the Glen of the Fork, is a village in the northwest of Co. Cavan at the junction of the R200 and R207 regional roads. It is surrounded by the Cuilcagh Mountains and borders Leitrim and Fermanagh. The lush valley pastures around here are home to tales of the Glas Cow, who could never be milked dry as she ranged up and down along the river banks.[40]

"Sometime ago there lived a blacksmith in the townland of Derrynatuon. The blacksmiths name was Geiblin Gab. This is the way our parish derived the name Glangevlin which means the Blacksmith's Glen. He owned a cow and her name was Gas Gaiblín. ... It has also been said that her udder was so large that it took a piece out of the mountain when coming home. The Gap [Bellavally Gap] *is still to be seen on the mountain".*[41]

Glangevlin was the last place in inland Ireland where Irish was widely spoken, up until the 1930s. Glangevlin is also known to be the last place in Ireland to have a glacier remaining from the Ice Age, in the Cuilcagh mountains, the last ice affected part of the island of Ireland. [42] Magic and mystery have also long lurked in these hidden hilly parts. An acclaimed healing tradition in the following report from the 1930s is similar to one belonging to members of the McGovern clan of Tullyhaw. A regional healing speciality, perhaps?

"The [hydrophobia, a symptom of rabies] *cure was known to one man in Glangevlin, and he lived down in Legnagrow.... It is said that the cure was handed down from generation to generation to this family and this man was the last who held it* [and] *people came from far and near for him to make up the medicine and give it....The only things we know were used in it were nuts and herbs and the rest was kept as a secret. Before getting the medicine, the person suffering would have to be fasting three days and of course kept in bed. If he would not be recovered before nine days he was past curing."* [43]

Heading further east on the R200, a large stone outcrop known as Maguire's Chair sits on the south side of the road, some 8.7 kms from Glangevlin village, in the townland of Altachullion, at Bellavally Gap. This was the inauguration site of the ruling Maguire clan back in medieval times. From here the local chiefs had a magnificent view of their domain. Locally, known as a Wishing Chair, it's said that if you go and sit on it on the last Sunday in July and make a wish, it will come true (a piece of later mythos).[44]

"Enormous gatherings with no religious observations attached were held, well into the twentieth century at...Maguire's chair", this being an echo of Pagan Lughnasa traditions. [45] Also known as the Black Rocks, the gathering was attended by folks from far and wide. There used to be games, dancing and athletic competitions. It was a great day for the youth and once famous for 'runaway matches', a custom peculiar to Ulster. As well, *"Everybody knows that the Black Rocks is a great place for the fairies"*, Maire MacNeil was told. Derryrath in Magh Slecht is also visible from here. [46]

TOBAR MUIRE

The lost village of Tobar (meaning 'well') once existed between the towns of Blacklion and Dowra. It was famous for a holy well called Tobar Muire. The well still exists, but the once substantial village is no more.[47] Tober and the well are on the OS map 26, a few kilometres north of Dowra. But nothing can be seen from Google Earth and the location remains rather elusive.

SHANNON POT

In the mountain fastness of this wild borderland country rivers are spawned, the most notable of which is the River Shannon. The source of the Shannon is Log na Sionna, or Shannon Pot, purportedly named after mythic femme Sionnan. It's a small pool some 16 m across and 9 m deep, set in a grove of graceful willow trees. The gurgling brown waters emerge under pressure from a limestone hole in the ground, gushing with whirling bubbles. However the water doesn't originate from just here, it has already travelled beneath the Cuilcagh Mountains of Co. Fermanagh. Wherever it starts, this is the traditional source of the river.

Myths of the Shannon Pot follow the norm of oft repeated themes of medieval literary tradition. Beautiful elite woman/princess/goddess seeks forbidden knowledge in the sacred waters and her punishment for this is to be drowned in the nascent river, that is then named after her. The story may well originate from patriarchal paradigms designed to denigrate and stifle women's aspirations. Happily, it isn't the original origin tale. Sinann is not a goddess that turns up elsewhere and it makes the tale sound contrived. When we consider that Greek geographer Ptolemy, at the turn of the 2nd century, called this river, on his famous map of Ireland, 'Sennos', this equates it with the modern name of the River Seine in France, of the tribe of the Senones. In Ptolemy's time incoming Celtic tribes brought their topographical names with them to Ireland, to remind them of their homelands.[48]

Older origin myths for the Shannon have been recorded with more genuinely archaic themes. There are several themes woven into the following tale recorded in the 1930s by a Carrick on Shannon school. Just to introduce the characters in it - the Great Worm represents the serpent forces of the landscape; the sea maiden with her magic comb - an all powerful sovereignty goddess; and the man with the plan - the coming of Christianity. It paints a primordial mythos, with perhaps a touch of Norse, in that the name 'worm' is Old Norse for serpent/dragon.

"A druid foretold that a man was to come to Ireland who would banish all dragons or serpents. At this time the great Ollpheist of the Shannon was in a hole in a lake near Arigna. When it heard about this man who was to come, it made up its mind that it would leave Ireland and make his way for the sea. It cut a channel out of the hole to try and make its escape to the sea. On its way it committed the most horrible depredations... The great Worm went on until it came to a place which is now known as Lough Derg. There all the venomous serpents were

gathered and they gave it battle. ...They fought for a month and no side had victory but at the end of the month the Great Worm won. Then the Great Worm leaped into the air and it came down on the serpents, making mash of them. The Great Worm was all cuts and wounds after the battle. Then it ate all the serpents that were killed. The lake was 'dearg' [red] *with blood. Some people say that it is why it was called Lough Derg.*

"As soon as its wounds were healed and it had taken a rest, it started work again. ...Then it ...made the river wider from that to the sea, because it was not hindered by anyone. As soon as it went into the sea a great whale attacked it and it was nearly beaten when a sea-maiden came along and helped it and they killed the whale. The Great Worm and the sea-maiden went along side by side until they came to a village in the coast. There were three score of fishermen fishing. The Great Worm was very hungry and he swallowed them greedily, both men and boats.

"Then the sea maiden spoke and said it was a shame. This angered him and he attacked her, but she was too clever for him. She drew out a golden comb with venom in it and threw it into the Worm's eye. Then the sea-maiden drew out scissors and she put a hole in his stomach and he died. The water was ebbing out and the Worm body was left on the strand at Bantry Bay until the people of the village opened its body and they found the men sleeping in their boats." [49]

It's all very reminiscent of the classic myths of a serpent spirit being who carves the river out of the landscape with its sinuous body. Similar to Australian Aboriginal origin mythos of the Rainbow Serpent making the water ways.[50] The original story probably came out of Africa. It's an extraordinary survival of archaic global mythos.

There's now a 14 km walking trail, part of the Cavan Way, that closely follows the course of the River Shannon, starting from the Shannon Pot and leaving its side at Dowra, to the south. In 2025 an interpretative visitors centre is being built at the Shannon Pot. (I hope the resident mermaid family in the Shannon Pot are not disturbed!)

CAVAN BURREN

Renowned for its numerous megalithic sites, Cavan Burren Park has been heavily promoted and is served by an interpretative centre, so it will only get a brief mention here. It's located on a limestone plateau at an elevation of 295 m, under the shadow of the mighty Cuilcagh Mountain. Widely recognised as one of the finest prehistoric relict landscapes in Ireland, it's part of the Cuilcagh Lakelands Geopark and is designated by UNESCO (the United National Educational Scientific and Cultural Organisation) for its exceptional geological heritage too. Geoparks highlight the culture, archaeology, wildlife and history of an area.

About 13,000 years ago, during the last Ice Age, huge boulders of sandstone from elsewhere were deposited by glaciers onto the limestone bedrock of Cavan Burren. There are lots of these glacial erratics throughout the park. They sit on pedestals of limestone making them very visually distinctive. Some have carvings of cup and ring marks and other symbolic patterns on them. The landscape was altered with the arrival of people from around 4,500BCE, when the first Neolithic farmers came. Remains of their settlements are evident from magnificent archaeological monuments, such as the Giant's Grave wedge tomb, plus the remains of archaic field walls, etc. There's much online - https://www.cavanburrenpark.ie/
A fascinating visual survey of prehistoric settlement features, boulder monuments, rock art and sculptings in the Burren can be found at www.cavanburren.ie.

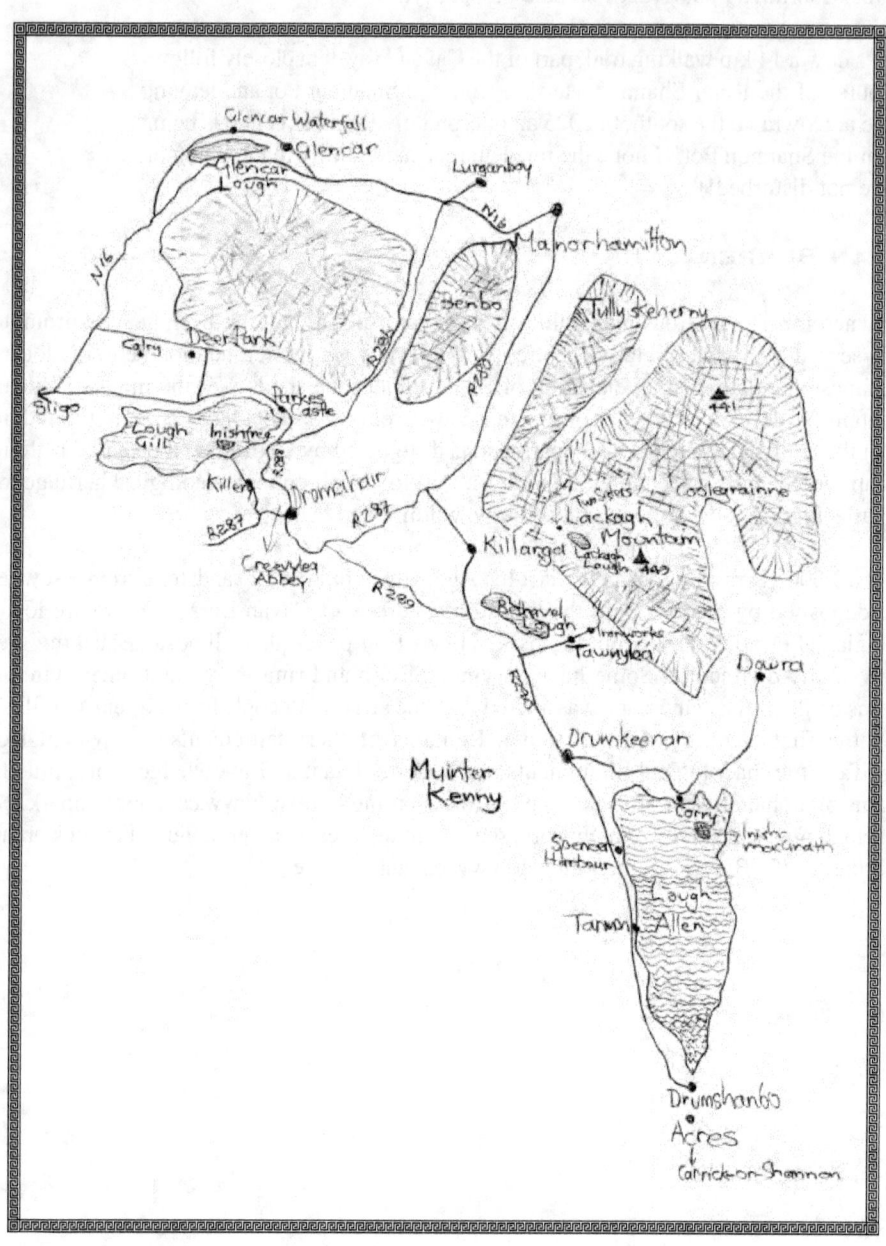

Chapter 9
Wild West Breifni

Heading to north Leitrim from Carrick on Shannon, we skirt the western shore of Lough Allen and traverse lands running west to the Roscommon border, once the territory of Muinterkenny, whose chief town was Drumkeeran. The ruling clan here was the MacConSnamha, later known as the Fordes. In this district there were several early ecclesiastical sites and it was a bustling centre for metal working and other manufacturing.

Tarmon

Early Christian sites were established on the western lake shore of Lough Allen and the most accessible site today is at Curraghs South, on a small point of land running into the lough. This Abbey of Tarmon, Teampul na gCorrachai, is named for the monks who navigated the waterways in their little oval boats made of hides, called curraghs. It is remembered as being run by 'Black Friars', named for their sombre outfits.

To get to Termon (An Tearmann, the Sanctuary Land), at a right hand bend on the R280 road, take the right turn where the old white sign post points to the Abbey of Termon. Go down the end of tiny lane to the old church site and graveyard. The ruins of St Patrick's Church are in a picturesque setting, surrounded by trees, the lake wrapping around the site. (It may have once been an island, when lake levels were higher.) The small Protestant graveyard has graves mostly from the 19th century.

"The church at Curraghs was built in the 6th century by a family the name of O'Rourke... [who] *proposed that eight townlands should pay to the up-keep of this church; these were called the Termons and that is how this district got its name. This church remained there until the 12th century. A community of Benedictine Monks came then and built a monastery there and a school also...[that] flourished until the coming of Cromwell."*[1]

Another church ruin lies south of Curraghs, in Cartronbeg, close to the county border with Roscommon. It's on the next peninsula, that juts out to the north. Once known as Nunnery Point and before then Gubb, this may have also been an island once. Here are ruins of the Convent of Conagh, the Teampull na gCailleacha Dubha, or Church of the Black Nuns.

"There was also a community of Benedictine Nuns in a convent at Gubb. At that time the chieftain of this district Garret Forde lived in Corry. [In 1642] Sir Fredrick Hamilton... killed him. Garret Forde's two daughters escaped and came to the nuns at Gubb. [Hamilton] followed them and killed them and killed the nuns also. The ruins of the convent and monastery are still to be seen on the shores of Lake Allen".[2]

SPENCER HARBOUR

North of Termon, 4 km south of Drumkeerin and just off the R280 road, signposted with a brown sign on the right, Spencer Harbour gives good public access to Lough Allen, with boat jetties, picnic tables and vistas of the vast lake and mountain backdrop. Human history goes back far here, with archeological discoveries of finds including Mesolithic era stone knives and arrowheads; plus unpolished axes dated to around 3,500BCE.[3] The earliest hunter-gatherer people must have had good pickings in these lush surrounds.

Here was also a hot spot for trade and industry. On a peninsula just north of the harbour a brick chimney can be seen (below, top left), at the site of a 19th century iron works. Festooned with ivy, it stands 20 m high and has four furnace inlets at its base.[4] The wooden piers of an old jetty on the nearby lake's edge are visible too. There were other industrial complexes here, now largely erased from view, but they remain in folk memory.

"There was a clay works at Spencer Harbour about 65 years ago [ie 1860-70's]. There were roofing tiles, sewerage and drainage pipes, and crockery ware of every description made at

it. There were....bricks made at it also... [some] made from clay that was brought from Athlone in boats. The sewerage pipes and drainage pipes were made from clay that was got in the hills. There were about twenty men carting coal every day. The coal was brought down as far as the levels on an aerial rope." [5]

"[The clay works] *gave employment to about a hundred people...The clay that was got in the hills was brought to the factory by a bogey which was drawn by a pony on a tramway. There was a store at Spencer Harbour and steamers used to come from Limerick with meal and flour. The steamers used to leave with a cargo of bricks or coal."* [6]

It's hard to imagine the hustle and bustle of those times, when now the shores are largely silent, apart from the occasional squarking coot or whooping swan. What seemed like a thriving economy that would last forever was limited by the colonial approach to the exploitation of resources, where no forward planning, such as forest management, was attempted. Short term gain was the plan. When all of value had been extracted and profits made, it was time to give the colony its independence, a pattern repeated the world over.

CORRY

Corry (the Weir/Rocky Ridge) on the northern lakeshore, was once elite central, with an identified moated site that's one of just three in Leitrim on the archeological record.[7] Forde's Castle, on a bulbous peninsula jutting into Lough Allen, was the power centre of the MacConsava clan, who were minor Gaelic lords in the mid to late medieval period. There is a reference in the Annals to a wooden house that was possibly located here, that was destroyed by the O'Donnells in 1530, in a rampage that included other castles and towns.[8] *"The best wooden house in all of Ireland,"* it was called. The castle was set within a rectangular earthen walled enclosure (the moated site), 38 m by 34 m, with a bank up to 2 m in height and a wet ditch to the south, in woodland on a summit near the shoreline.[9] Later, a masonry castle (tower house) was erected over part of it, at Corry's Fosse. In tradition this tower house was destroyed by Hamilton around 1640.[10]

Corry Strand is the only designated swimming place in north Leitrim and it's where school children have swimming lessons.

DRUMKEERIN

North west of Lough Allen, Drumkeerin (Droimm Caorthainn, Ridge of the Rowan Trees) is a small town that was once the seat of the rulers of Muinterkenny. On the archeological record there are five bullauns located within 5 km of the village - an unusually high concentration with none located in a church setting. None are accessible to the public.[11]

Bullauns are mysterious monuments, the Irish word can mean a circular boulder, a boulder with hollows, or sometimes a circular clearing in a landscape.[12] Typically, they are boulders with one or more circular hollows that suggest the function of ritual grinding stones. Usually found at early church and holy well sites, they are also found in important cashels and raths, and no doubt have a pre-Christian origin. They were possibly used for ritual grain grinding at the start of harvest, at Lughnasa celebrations. No better way to make sacred cakes in a ritual communal setting!

BELHAVEL LOUGH AND BEN SCARDAUN

Heading north west from Drumkeerin on the R280 you pass Belhavel Lough on your right. The lough is about 2 km long by 300 - 700 m wide. Behind it looms the large triangular highland mass of Lackagh Mountain, also called Ben Scardaun, that overlooks the lake and Killarga village. A couple of roads turn off the R280 to the right towards it. A Lammas Fair used to be held at Belhavel, on the day after an annual gathering on top of Ben Scardaun. It would have been enjoyed as the most eagerly awaited, fun filled event of the year.

On the last Sunday of July, locally called Garland or Ben Sunday, hordes of people used to visit the mountaintop. Before ascending it they'd eat a big pot of colcannon, made with new potatoes and cabbage. Then they gathered together near a small lake, Lough na Wellian, or Lackagh Lough, beside two big round stones some 6 m high, known as the Two Sisters. Musicians would play various instruments there and people sang. Then around 3 pm they'd make the ascent to the summit together to the playing of music. Reaching the top, they re-assembled around a mound of stones. Berries and flowers were picked, some bunches taken home to be left at doorways to bring luck, and others made into garlands to be left on the summit as an offering. People enjoyed their revelries until sunset. MacNeill tells us that *"children kept close to their parents, for there was a tradition that leprecauns used to be seen on the mountain on that day."* [13]

Belhavel once had a 'castle' overlooking the lough at its western side, from the end of a north - south rocky ridge. In tradition the fortified house was built by the Montgomery family, possibly in the late 17th century. Only a single cut stone piece remains of it. The folklore records tells us a little. *"Belhavel Lake (or as it was called in former years Lough Lein) ... got the name Belhavel from the landlord Montgomery's wife. Her name was Belle Havel. She was a French lady."* [14] ... *"[She] lived there in a castle overlooking the lake. All traces of the castle have now disappeared, but some of the stones have been built in a house which stands where the Castle stood."* [15]

Just below the castle site is a crannog about 200 m from out the shore. It's an overgrown circular island 20 m across, with no obvious evidence of man made construction. But close by on the shore, a 60 cm wide sandstone quern was found and is now kept in a house nearby. [16]

South west of Belhavel about 6-7 km away, a hill called Corran used to be the focus of a Lughnasa festival that was held in the townland of Killavoggy (Coill a Bhogaigh, the Wood of the Bog). From its summit there are fine views across Leitrim, Sligo, Roscommon, Mayo and Cavan. People gathered on the hill on the last Sunday in July to frolic and pick bilberries. [17]

TAWNYLEA

Just below Belhavel is the Tawnylea area (Tamhnach Liath, the Grey Green Field), about 6 km north-east of Drumkeerin. Here Sir Charles Coote, a major landowner as a result of the Plantation, established a smelter to exploit local iron deposits in the early 17th century. Its remains are north east of the village in Knockacullion townland, at the base of Lackagh Mountain. Coote brought in English and Dutch miners, and no Irish were employed there. The Creevelea smelter was the most significant iron works in all of Leitrim.

In this Creevylea area the Dergvone Shale Formation shales include nodules of siderite (an iron carbonate mineral) up to 60 cm in diameter. These big nuggets of iron were easily found after being washed into stream beds by rain. They had long been scavenged there, with iron working in the district dating back to the 16th century at least.[18]

First the iron works consumed all the local forests for wood charcoal. Later, coal from nearby Arigna was used, until it too ran out. Sandstone, used as a refractory lining in furnaces and limestone for use as a flux, were both also locally available, helping to minimise production costs. Thanks to these local resources, the ironworks was making good profits until 1866. But despite making good quality iron, it could not compete with cheaper iron produced on a mass scale in England. (It was also situated too far from its markets.) When the price of iron fell, the works was out-competed and by 1872 it was abandoned - ending iron mining in Leitrim for good.[19] A 1905 photo of the works called it *"the last place in Ireland where iron has been manufactured."* [20]

The ruins of Creevylea Ironworks can be seen near the end of the Tawnylea road at the base of the mountain. The archeological record shows an impressive looking and still largely intact blast furnace that was built in 1852. This is the most substantial remnant of a once big industrial complex. There are also some parts of walls of the engine house still standing beside the furnace, while sluice and weir type structures survive in the river channel. (Stone from demolished buildings was taken away for road-making.) The site, beside the road and not far from an old sweat house and school, is on private land. [21] You can park there near an empty house just before the ironworks ruins and walk down to it.

I was taken to the site by a local woman who had grown up in the area. She hadn't been there in years. We followed the tiny road along from Tawnylea village towards the mountain. Approaching the site, in a neglected, overgrown gully, it was hard for her to recognise it. She was shocked to see it so overgrown, almost obscured by the cover of vegetation. It was also shocking for her to see the condition of the chewed-up road, from truck movements for the erection of wind turbines that were going in, above us on the mountain. A very large access road going up the slope had been made right in front of the ironworks, disturbing the scene even more.

KILLARGA

A focus of continuing devotion, the holy well near Killarga is a well worth visiting. It's just before you get to the village on the R280, on the right at the well sign, where there's parking space. From here you can take the short pilgrimage walk to the sacred spring site, first going past an old lime kiln in the cliff face. This is a niche cut into the limestone where lime rocks were once heated before being crushed into lime. This was used for sweetening the soil, whitewashing buildings and as a disinfectant. Walking the well trail in springtime is a treat, with bluebells carpeting the scrubby hillside. At the far end of the field and path you reach the little sacred grove, a peaceful place of green nature and gushing, pure waters, plus kitschy statues and ornamentation, somewhat like a Lourdes grotto. In tradition it was associated with a church of the 6th century, Cill Fearga.

"This well is called the well of Saint Fearga. On the 15th of August people go to Killargue holy well and make rounds there. When they are making rounds they leave relics near the well. Cures

are made at Killargue holy well by washing the part that is ill in a stream flowing from the well." [22]

St Mary's Well, as it's now known, is set in the south facing base of a low limestone cliff face. Spring water gushes up from a natural cleft in the limestone rock, a stone wall has been added and it's nestled within a small rectangular enclosure. A host of small statues, trinkets and varied offerings deck out the scene, while a rag tree grows in another enclosure, beside the well. People leave little pieces of cloth tied on it, symbolic of leaving their illness behind (they are supposed to rot away, so synthetic materials don't work). An old stone lintel and cross here were probably relics of the early local church. The site is still venerated by local people at a Pattern Day held mid August, a time coinciding with old Lughnasa type celebrations. [23] Stations were also performed on the other days dedicated to Mary - February 2nd, March 25th and September 8th.

The name change to Mary was possibly the result of a visionary experience recorded in folklore. *"A young girl named Mc Morrow lived near where the well is now. One summers evening as she was out at her own home she saw a beautiful lady walking on the rocks. This was supposed to be the blessed Virgin. She fell sick next day and she never got better. She died soon after she saw the Lady. Before she died she was always talking about the beautiful lady she saw on the rocks. At the foot of the rock, where she saw the lady, there sprung up a well. The Bishop came and blessed it and there is great devotion towards it on the 15th August."* [24]

In Killarga village itself, on a low east - west ridge, are the ruins of the old Roman Catholic church. Built in 1791, it has two walls still standing in good condition, within a rectangular burial ground. It replaced an earlier church. Perhaps here was once the Cill Fearga, the Church of Fearga, but the record is so-far mute. A 12th century manuscript details that the name of the saint was Findchad. *"Later Fionnchadh, nicknamed faoilidh, 'the joyous'...[and the]* variant form...*Fheargna no Fhorga,"* writes Nollaig O'Muraile. [25]

North east of the village in the townland of Blackgardens is the remains of a sweat house. The now roofless circular stone chamber, with an interior of 1.9 m diameter, is set into the bottom of a west facing slope and is built on a plinth. [26]

DROMAHAIR

Heading further north-west, the charming village of Dromahair is set amidst verdant landscapes of rolling hills. Beside it the River Bonet, that flows into nearby Lough Gill, is close to the border with Co. Sligo. A grand vista here of rounded mountain shapes of Keelogyboy, Leean and Benbo suggest a Sleeping Giant formation in tradition. This can be seen as you approach the village (as well as views of Slieve Daeáne and Killery mountains to the west). Passengers on the Lough Gill tour boat from Parke's Castle also get a fine view of the Sleeping Warrior from the middle of the lake. You can view it from the nearby Creevylea Abbey, as well.

Dromahair was redesigned in the late 18th century by a benign British landlord, George Lane Fox, who modelled it on a village in Somerset. Unlike the typical Irish village, houses were set back from the road with little gardens out the front, while street trees and fine buildings contribute to its ongoing attractiveness. The central streetscape still follows this pattern.

Village life once buzzed with livestock fairs and markets, there was a court house, a grain mill, bakery and a renowned pub. A quay on the River Bonet below the village took local produce by boat to Sligo and beyond, while boats came laden with grain for Dromahaire's mill.[27] On the main street in the heart of the village, the Stanford Village Inn is Leitrim's oldest pub, at around 250 years age, and still going strong. It was the go-to place for refreshments for visitors on Lough Gill cruise boats. Current publican Laura McGowan is a local history enthusiast and sometimes tour leader. W. B. Yeats used to visit Dromahair regularly en route to the island of Inishfree on Lough Gill, or to visit his friend the parish priest, who was the subject of his poem The Old Priest Peter Gilligan, while Dromahair is also mentioned in his poem The Man who Dreamed of Faeryland.

Located on a ridge above the Bonet River, Dromahair gets its name from this ridge, where the church of Drumlease was located. An early foundation of possibly 5th century age, currently a Church of Ireland parish church is there, built in 1816 on land donated by the landlord family. It replaced the previous Church of St Patrick that was in another location, in the townland of Drumlease around 1km away. The earlier medieval church had served the parish for centuries, but local historian Des Gillmor thinks it had to be replaced. An old parishioner told Des of how the roof had collapsed just after a Sunday service.[28]

The Old Drumlease site is hidden from general view, up a hill at the end of a laneway, off the small lane L4165 that runs southeast of Dromahair. With views of land sloping down to the River Bonet, the now overgrown graveyard is traditionally regarded as having once been the site of a monastery established by St Patrick, when it was called Drumdara, the Ridge of the Oak Trees. Back in 1922 a substantial church ruin was visible and written about, but there's no evidence of it now, just the mortared stone walls of a sub-rectangular graveyard that measures 53 m by 18 - 24 m. A survey of grave slabs in 1914 found some (for the Carter family) going back to 1735, while Stuart was the commonest family name of those interred.

"It seems that it was a significant ecclesiastical place as early as the late 7th century... Worship may have been continuous on the Old Drumlease site for 14 centuries," Gillmor wrote. In two old manuscripts Drumlease is mentioned for the presence of a hospital too. The name Drum-Lias is generally translated as the Hill of the Huts and it's presumed that this referred to the monks' huts.[29]

The name Dromahair, Droim Dhá Ethiar, is thought to mean the Ridge of Two (air) Demons, but it could also be a corruption of another name. Archeologist Sam Moore translates it as the Ridge of the Western Ford, which sounds more plausible. River fording places are always significant and in the late medieval period Dromahair continued in importance, becoming the capital of West Breiffne. Here the O'Rourkes had their most important stronghold. The site of their castle, built circa 950 (with Villiers Castle there now), plus probable banqueting hall, are still present in the south end of Dromahair village, just off the main street, but they now share the site with holiday cottages and have been off limits to the public.

Dromahair was purportedly the location from which Devorgilla (wife of Tiernan O'Rourke) was abducted by Dermot McMurrough (the King of Leinster) in 1153. This event is cited as the initial cause of the Anglo-Norman invasion. But the reality may be differently interpreted. Tiernan O'Rourke's strategic/arranged marriage to Princess Dervorgilla of Meath might have started off badly. When O'Rourke went away on pilgrimage, she packed her bags, cows and servants and went off to the court of his enemy King Diarmuid MacMurrough, in the province of Leinster. But a peace treaty was made and she returned and undertook her queenly duties with him. However it seems that Dervogilla has been pseudo-mythologised as having eloped with King MacMurrough and that this was the cause of the Norman Invasion, with Tiernan supposedly inviting the foreigners over to help him get her back. But it has been pointed out that she seems to have had nothing to do with the invasion and that she had actually been the Queen of Breifne for 20 years before the Normans arrived.

Does Dervoglla deserve to be so maligned in history? Was an invasion agenda served by a distortion of the facts? It seems so. She probably went to him willingly for safeguarding. Many historians agree - *"There was no elopement and no romance. Dervorgilla, in our judgement, was taken away for safety and as a hostage with the consent of her family,"* O'Cleraigh stated. A.M. Sullivan in his Story of Ireland claimed that *"Dervorgilla was badly treated by history"*, and adds that *"both the eminent historians O'Donovan and O'Curry were of the same view."*[30]

A castle was later constructed on the site for Sir William Villiers in circa 1629, after he was granted over ten thousand acres in the Plantation of Leitrim.[31] A fortified manor house, Villier's Castle was probably made with stones from the demolished O'Rourke's Hall down the hill. The ruins are in the grounds of The Lodge and fourteen holiday cottages built in the 1980's surround them. (These have since been abandoned to nature.)

Villiers Castle (seen overleaf) looms over the main street, behind a stone wall and opposite the town bus stop, its mantle of ivy threatening to destroy it further. The u-shaped three storey building of limestone and sandstone is an unusual design. Apart from the front, south-west facing wall, it survives somewhat intact, including the fireplaces and seven chimney stacks. It's set within a rectangular bawn (fortified courtyard) 48 m by 35 m, of which only the north east and north west walls remain, with ten gun loops in them and a fortified gatehouse 10 m by 5 m with five gun loops. The defensive nature of Villiers Castle is in sharp contrast with the non-defensive architecture of the earlier castle/hall of the O'Rourkes. Breiffne king Brian O'Rourke was imprisoned in London in the 1620's when George Villiers, a favourite of Catholic King James 1st, was granted his land in Leitrim. But, soon after, Villiers was assassinated in Portsmouth and the estate passed to his brother William, the builder of the castle.[32]

Below Villiers Castle, 60 m to the south of it, is the ruin of O'Rourke's Hall that overlooks a gorge of the River Bonet. This open plan hall-castle remained a haunt of the O'Rourkes until the 17th century. The rectangular structure of mortared limestone walls measures 21.5 m by 7.4 m. Only the ground floor remains, with all the decorative stonework robbed out, making its age hard to determine. An old engraving showed it in a more intact form (seen on the right). A standing stone is located about 100 m to the north of the ruin, close to a gatehouse, but this could be modern.[33]

O'ROURKE'S HALL, CO LEITRIM

O'Rourke's Hall has recently been confirmed to be *"a 15th or 16th century Gaelic Irish hall, which functioned as part of an O'Rourke castle complex,"* wrote J J MacDermott.[34] It didn't

have defensive features. Hidden away in the wild and rugged landscape, it relied on isolation and the largely inaccessible nature of the surrounding territory. The hall was a legendary place. In the 1500's it was the scene of lively Christmas banquets, that were immortalised in a popular song set to music by Turlough O'Carolan, the famous harpist. The song, a comical description of a feast held there, amused Jonathan Swift greatly when he visited Leitrim in 1720, and he requested a translation from the Irish original, 'Planxty O'Rourke'. [35]

Further up the River Bonet and within an old loop of it, in an area of 80 m by 40 m, are the remains of Harrison's Castle. Walter Harrison received a Plantation land grant of 1,500 acres, called the Manor of Dunbrandon. A sheriff of Sligo town 1612-1622, he built it around 1621-22. [36] The river loop, now silted up, would have once served as a natural bawn or court, ideal for protecting his substantial fortified house of three stories or more. It's possible that previously a 16th century Gaelic Irish tower house was here and it was incorporated into the new house.[37] In local tradition this castle, in the townland of Sradoon, is the location of Dervogilla's alleged elopement with King MacMurrough.

Today there's just some curving wall surviving from a corner tower, a bit of castle wall and a window at first floor level. Through this window Dervogilla escaped with her lover, goes the tale.[38] However, her story is set in the 12th century, so it may have been the first floor window of a previous castle. Or she simply used the door, as no elopement was actually happening.

CREEVYLEA ABBEY

Just across the river from the village of Dromahair are the impressive ruins of Creevylea Abbey (it's actually a friary rather than an abbey). You can walk there via a lovely walking track, the Creevylea Abbey Loop, that begins beside the Abbey Hotel. The site is on a rocky height overlooking the river on its southern side. It was originally called Carraig Phadraig, St Patrick's Rock, and it was written that Patrick founded the first church here. Or perhaps this is a confusion with the Old Drumlease monastery site? Or he never came here.

One of the last Franciscan friaries to have been built in Ireland before Henry the VIII's dissolution of the monasteries, it was founded in 1508 by Breifne chiefs Owen O'Rourke and

his wife Margaret O'Brian. Their magnificent tomb near the altar, mentioned at the end of the 1700s, is nowhere to be seen now.[39] The Friary went on to have a battered history, being burned down accidentally in 1536, then overtaken by Richard Bingham, the Governor of Connaught, around 1590 and used to camp in and as horse stables, the soldiers burning the fine furniture and precious art for firewood. Friars returned in 1601, repaired the church and used it until 1649, when Cromwell's army forced them out and the buildings fell into ruin.

Much of it is well preserved. The substantial ruins include the church, cloister and domestic buildings.[40] The tower, that stands above the church and would have originally served as a bell-tower, was used for a while as a living quarters by Walter Harrison.[41]

Road access to the abbey is on the R287, just out of Dromahair heading south. It's signed on the right, turn there and right again at the abbey sign. Alternatively take the lovely tree lined walk from the centre of the village, starting beside the Abbey Hotel, and crossing the river over a foot bridge. The abbey ruin is just up the hill, opposite a modern graveyard. It's quite expansive.

Inside the abbey are some notable features on cloister pillars. There are two carvings of St Francis of Assisi. The monks followed the teachings of this nature friendly saint. One carving shows him preaching from a pulpit to the birds perched in a tree beside him (or maybe they are preaching to him?) Another shows him with the stigmata on his hands, as in the photo above. Another intriguing carving is of a head wearing a helmut with two tall pointed horns, as depicted on the interpretative sign (on the right, carving not shown).

The last Franciscan monk here was Friar Peter MacGovern, whose grave became a mecca for effecting cures, with people removing clay from it.[42] They took three spoonfuls of the clay home with them and left the spoons behind at the grave.[43]

From the abbey location you get a good view of the Sleeping Giant formation (seen on the previous page). Looking down towards the village you can see the large Grain Store / Mill (now converted into apartments) and old Club House buildings. This was built in 1909 beside the railway station, to which it was linked by a private railway to the SLNCR railway line that connected Sligo and Enniskillen. The line opened in 1881 and closed in 1957. But now it has a future incarnation being planned, as a long distance walkway.

KILLERY

Not far from the abbey is a small, but intriguing magical site located within the Killery churchyard, on the small road that leads to Lough Gill and the Isle of Inishfree (made famous by Yeat's poetry). Cill Oiridh, the Church of Oiridh, was an important establishment in it's day.

Heading south from Dromahair, take the right turn onto the R287 towards Sligo, go a few kilometres and turn right at the next crossroads towards Lough Gill. The Killery churchyard is on the left, about 1.5 kms from the turn off. It's on top of a small hill in a commanding location, beneath Killery Mountain.

The ruins of the ex-Killery Parish church, St Theresa's, measures some 19 m by 7.4 m on the exterior. The interior is grassy and wild, a grave slab there is from 1830. The eastern gable and two sidewalls are still standing. The north wall is of uncoursed 90 cm thick cyclopean masonry with massive quoins; the south wall is different and only 55 cm thick, its top missing and seems part of a re-build in the 18th century.[44] The church had its west end walled off to probably provide living quarters for the clergy, a not uncommon arrangement in old country churches.

St Theresa's was a place of importance to warrant several mentions of its erenaghs between 1333 and 1416 in the Annals. And a shocking, sacrilegious outrage in 1346 is also recorded for here. It tells of clan chiefs Ualgarg O'Rourke and Rory O'Connor being chased by enemies, the O'Connors and McDonoughs and, to save their lives, they sought safety inside Killery Church. But the sacred right of sanctuary was ignored, their pursuers torched the church and, as they tried to escape, they were slain.[45]

The site would have been like a village then, with huts for living, a forge, bakery and scriptorium, etc. This allowed them to be a fairly self-sustainable community. In the popular burial ground, amidst the usual grave slabs, there is something quite different featured, that sits quietly and unannounced. A circle of seven small round, water washed stones are set on top of a now broken, thin stone slab 75 cm by 80 cm; they surround an angular, taller central stone about 30 cm tall, that's partly wrapped around with cotton strings, known as 'straining threads'. The unusual mini-lithic stone arrangement is also called the Straining Threads, as well as Holy Stones and Curing Stones on the archeological record. It was purportedly created by St Patrick to cure his horse's sprained ankle, after he had blessed the threads and wrapped them around it.[46] (It isn't a unique site, however,

because another unusual Straining Stone is located some 3.5 km to the north east in a graveyard in Cartronhugh townland). [47]

By a tradition of ritual curing, sprains and strains are treated exclusively here, and you can even take the cure home. Both humans and animals can benefit, including horses, in particular. A local family are the custodians of the site with the responsibility for the cure. They help to maintain the stones and keep the central stone re-stringed as required.[48] To receive the cure, the tradition is to say three Hail Marys and one Our Father, removing a thread from the central stone and, attaching it around the strained part of the body. By the time the thread has worn off, one expects a cure.

KILLERY HEALING STONES EXPERIENCE

On a warm spring day when I visited last, the big blue skyscape and cottonwool ball clouds showed off the lovely elevated location, beneath the massif Killery Mountain and above the glistening Lough Gill. There, in the north east quadrant of the graveyard, were the low-key Curing Stones I'd come to show friends. This time a new object was amongst the rounded stones. A take-away meal container with replacement threads had been incongruously added to the stone altar. Though crass, it did give a Plastic Age solution for string hygiene. And it keeps an amazing tradition, an ancient continuum, alive forever too.

No doubt a remnant of Pagan paradigms, the mini-lithic arrangement is a point of high energy and my pendulum always spins wildly over it when dowsing it on my visits. I didn't know why this was the case and didn't pursue my dowsing quest there. Later, I found out that *"according to a caretaker in 1913, there was a 'spring of good water under the slab'."* [49]

Aha! That would explain the fountain of energy gushing upwards. That spurred me on to remember the Healing Stones site and from the comfort of my home and being undistracted, I was able to distantly dowse the location. My pendulum reacted decisively to the energy of water under high pressure, rising upwards from beneath them. It has the form of an energy vortex spiralling upwards and makes for a big energy field around the stones. Perhaps there was a spring here in the past, that was blocked up? My dowsing said no, the water was deep. The energy form it was expressing is what some English dowsers would call a 'blind spring'.

PARKES CASTLE

Following the shores of the beautiful Lough Gill, a scenic drive takes you from Dromahair to Parkes Castle, on the north shore. As its Irish name describes it, the lake waters can be bright and sparkling, and they are traditionally associated with a lake goddess and mermaid spirit beings. [50]

Once an older O'Rourke stronghold, it later became the home of English planter Sir Robert Parkes. The castle was built onto the original bawn (fortified courtyard) around O'Rourke's tower-house, whose foundations can still be seen in the courtyard. The last native owner, Sir Brian O'Rourke, was described by the English governor as *"the proudest man this day living on the Earth."* O'Rourke had resisted crown rule and fled Ireland, but was eventually captured and thrown into the Tower of London, tried and finally hung in 1591.

After 1677, when two of Parkes's children drowned in the lake, the castle fell into disrepair. But in the late 20th century it was restored, using traditional Irish oak timber and craftsmanship and opened to the public. A permanent exhibition of artefacts from the 17th century, including replica period costumes and furniture, is on display inside. Guided tours of the castle and an audio-visual historical presentation are available, while boat tours of Lough Gill leave from Parkes Castle, but only in the warmer months. [51]

DEER PARK

Continuing around the north side of Lough Gill on the R286 amidst stunning scenery, you enter Co. Sligo. Turn right onto the Ballinamona Lane and then left at the intersection with the R278. Turn left again and 350 m later on your left is the megalithic ritual landscape of Magheraghanrush, better known as Deer Park. As the name suggests, it was once an enclosure for deer hunting for the English gentry. Fortunately they also preserved in it an ancient court tomb, dating back to the 3rd millennium BCE. Known locally as the Giant's Grave and considered one of the finest (if not, the actual finest) of its type in the country, this Neolithic treasure inspired Ireland's greatest poet W. B. Yeats.

The huge central court tomb is accessed by an uphill walk and is located at the highest point. That's typical for hill monuments, that have sight lines to other notable hilltop features, but it is unusual for a court cairn to have such a location. Stone cairn material that once covered the megalithic structure has all been robbed away. What remains is a structure that can be compared visually to a human body shape, with a large belly-like central court and several protruding burial chambers that suggest a head and legs, as on the right.

Nearby, there's also a stone circle close to the walking trail, with a cashel, wedge tomb and souterrain in adjoining lands, that are also accessible from the trail.[52] When I first visited this site it was within a dense conifer forest, so dark, gloomy and damp. Without seeing it in the context of the wider landscape, I couldn't get a proper sense of the place. But this has all changed. Nowadays, excellent hilltop views to the east can be had from here, including to other megalithic hilltop bumps on the skyline. The magnificent panorama was only recently restored when surrounding commercial forest was removed.[53]

GLENCAR

Continue heading west from Deerpark along the R278 Sligo road and turn right at Faughts Lane towards the N16, turning right when you reach the intersection with it. You are now heading into the beautiful Glencar Valley. The name means the Glen of the Standing Stone, but it's mostly known for the Glencar Waterfall, another inspiration to Yeats and featured in his poem The Stolen Child. Situated 11 km west of Manorhamilton, the waterfall is beside the equally beautiful Glencar Lough. Looking like a fairy mantle spraying down the steep, verdant valley wall, it has a truly magical, gentle atmosphere. A short, wooded walkway leads to varied platforms for viewing the waterfall, that has a height of 15 m.

There is a car park, picnic area, public toilets, children's playground and a tourist information point. The site is wheelchair friendly. A cafe with views overlooks Glencar Lake and the 7 km

Glencar Hill Walk starts from the carpark.[54] More waterfalls can be visible from the road to Glencar, depending on rainfall. The Devil's Chimney, the second most famous one, is not far from the Glencar waterfall. At 150 m it is Ireland's tallest waterfall.[55] Enigmatically, its falling water is blown upwards into plumes of steam-like spray by even the slightest of breezes. Its original name srut i n-agaid an aeir means the Stream Against the Air.

Straddling counties Sligo and Leitrim, Glencar Lough lies in the Glencar Valley framed by high heather clad mountains with dramatic cliffs. The beautiful freshwater lake is 3 km long and 750 m wide.[56] On the eastern end of the lake there is a crannog, Glencar Island or Castle Carr, that was a stronghold of the O'Rourkes, until inter-tribal war, when two branches of the O'Rourke family disputing its ownership, ended up destroying it in the late 15th century. Nothing remains today.

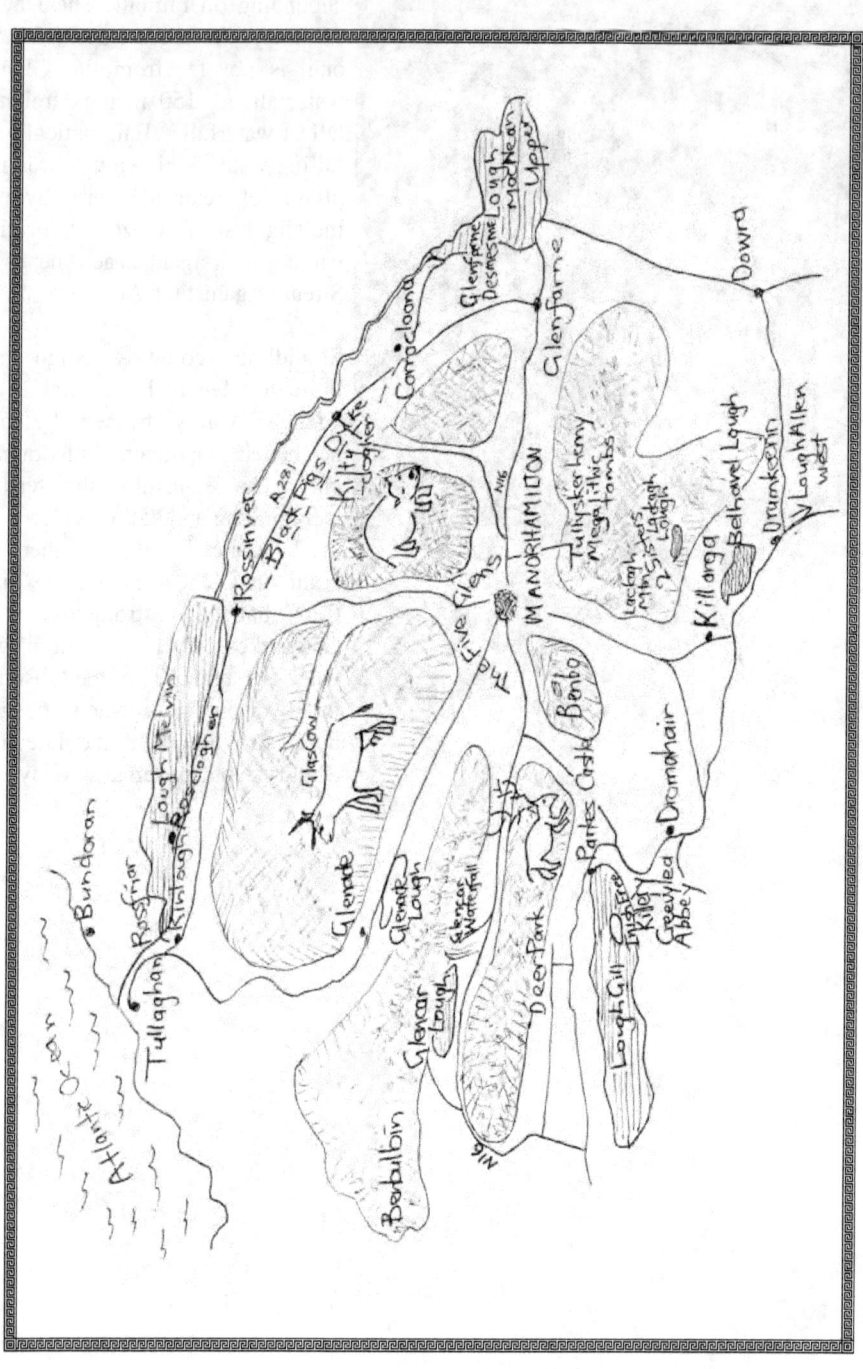

Chapter 10
Bastions of the North

North Leitrim is rugged frontier country bordering Northern Ireland. A wild mountain fastness, the plateau is rent into a huge star shape by long lush valleys carved out by glaciers. Here, primordial mythos and the old Celtic culture was protected and survived long.

To fortify Leitrim's border in the north to north-east and keep invaders from Connaught at bay during the Iron Age, a natural necklace of sparkling lakes and rivers was interconnected by linear embankments - the Black Pig's Dyke, or Great Wall of Ulster. This defensive structure mirrored the settlement pattern used by the continental Celtic tribes, who lived within oppida, as Caesar called them, or walled territory defined by linear boundary banks connecting up to impassable landscape features. The purpose of these defensive structures was more about restricting the movement of cattle and preventing their theft, than of keeping people out.

Perhaps they also provided trackways for garrisons patrolling tribal borders. This was suggested by the following folklore from Edenville school, near Kinlough, recorded by pupils in the 1930s. *"Although a great many people say that the 'Valley of the Black Pig' ran from Bundoran to Dundalk, a man who is now about 40 years dead (John Mac Morrow, Agharroo Kinlough) said that he often heard of the 'Race of the Black Pig'. The pig, which was the shape the Devil assumed when he was hunted, started from Glenade and took its course through the middle of the County, by Lough Allen, on to Athlone and then south to a mountain which he thought was the Devil's Bit...John Mac Morrow told that he heard an account of O Donnell's March to Kinsale about 1600. They passed through Kinlough, according to his story. Kinlough was then part of O Ruarc's territory and was a friendly land. O Donnell would have had many enemies had he taken the coast road through the O'Connor territory. He says the Army followed the race of the Black Pig for at least a great part of the way."* [1]

Musing on their function as throughways, I imagined the garrison following the Black Pig's Dyke coming to boggy sections and relying on guidance perhaps, making their way through bogs on an elaborate network of toghers, woven bog pathways. If you didnt know which track to take, you could end up drowning in a deep bog hole! This scenario could be an interpretation of one aspect of the labyrinthine network of trackways uncovered by archeologists in Edercloon (page 100) in what was the most extensive archeological investigation ever made in Ireland of bog land. [2]

Glencar Valley

Coming from Glencar, follow the N16 road along one of the five glens that run towards Manorhamilton, the capital of north Leitrim, that's situated at its heart. It's another classic glacial valley that was cut deep into the north Leitrim plateau in the Ice Age. A verdant riverland valley, in folklore it was pastureland of the legendary Glas Cow, sacred bovine spirit and descendent of the Holy Cow of Indian tradition.[3]

Before the Lurganboy turn-off you can see, on your left, Castlecar, the Castle of the Rock. A bombastic looking tower house ruin atop a rocky outcrop, the rectangular three storey structure in Castletown townland has only the west gable and adjacent parts of the north and south walls surviving, with a fireplace and some tiny windows.

It was here in the O'Rourke Castle of Car that the earliest use of guns in Ireland - 1487, is recorded. During the Plantation of Leitrim, the Manor of Carra, that included 1,500 acres of confiscated land, was granted to Tiernan Mac Owen O'Rourke in the 1620's and the castle probably had a make-over around then.[4] In another part of Castletown townland a rath sits on a slight rise on the valley floor, and is now marked by a ring of deciduous trees that were planted on its circular bank and fosse.[5] The rath may have been the usual home of the local chief and the more inhospitable castle only resorted to in war time.

Travelling on eastwards along the N16, on your right the plateau massif of Leean Mountain looms above. It may look barren and inhospitable today, but it must have been densely populated in the past, as recent studies have revealed an archeological complex up there. It's a *"significant prehistoric landscape, potentially in use from the Neolithic period up until the Iron Age, with the presence of over one hundred sites representative of both domestic settlement and ritual practise,"* says Donna Gilligan. There are tombs, standing stones, cairns, a hill fort, enclosures, evidence of cereal cultivation and over 40 hut sites, in an *"uniquely preserved archeological landscape."* [6] More may be revealed from beneath the blanket bog that developed over the top of many sites.

Above the opposite side of the valley, on the high karst plateau, another archeological complex has been discovered in recent years at Aghamore that's spread over an area of some 10 ha of Truskmore. It has both prehistoric settlement and ritual sites, and features a court and a wedge tomb, an enclosure, hut sites and pre-bog walls.[7] The climate was obviously more hospitable in its hey day.

LURGANBOY

Big fortifications and the stain of war are evident around Lurganboy, a village just off the N16, on the left. On the east edge of the village, in Poundhill townland where an east-west stream runs through a couple of prominent hillocks, a battle site was recorded. Here, on April 1st 1643, a group of Irish rebels under Brian McDonough were unfortunate enough to come across some fifty foot soldiers under Frederick Hamilton. Hamilton's men retreated across a bridge into a ditch, then fought back and killed around sixty of the Irishmen.

On a hilltop in the townland of Barrackpark there's a Star Shaped Fort, a walled enclosure with an area of 61.5 m by 61.5 m, that now has a church inside its grounds. Originally it housed a garrison of soldiers, hence the name Barrackpark. Military forts of the day needed to have strong earth and stone embankments to absorb the impact of pounding from cannon fire. At the four corners of these forts large diamond shaped projecting bastions were built to strengthen the structure, thus giving them the name of Star Fort. The design goes back to Michelangelo and it was first used in Florence in 1475.[8] The principles of this design continued as a successful standard up until the 19th century. Of the three Star Forts in Leitrim, the one here and at Manorhamilton are the best preserved. In Barrackpark the small church and graveyard are within the northern, now levelled bastion of the fort. The three remaining diamond shaped corner bastions, at 13 m by 9.5 m across, are defined by earth banks 3 m high on the outside, set on a masonry plinth.[9]

BENBO

Heading back onto the N16 towards Manorhamilton, the rolling hills around you take varying shapes, the tallest and most impressive being Benbo. This great hulking Hill of the Cow towers steeply above the rolling landscape and is the north-western end of the Ox Mountains. Its smooth rounded form shines with metamorphic rocks such as pre-Cambrian quartzite, gneiss and schist. From the summit, at a height of 518 m, spectacular views over much of north Leitrim including the Truskmore massif, glens and uplands around Lough Allen, plus neighbouring counties, can all be seen. It has a strong mythic legacy as well.

"In old Irish writings it is called Beanno-bo. It is so called because of its double peak resembling the horns of a cow... The herds minding sheep on the mountain were called Lords Benbo". [10] The hill has also a well known folktale (in several versions) about a magic cow associated with a supernatural lake on the top.

"The tale goes that a man living at the base of Benbo dreamt three nights running that if he went up to the summit at a certain time then he'd see a cow emerging from a lake. This small round pond of black bog water never dried up and never flooded out. He was told to stand in-between the emerging cow and the lake, and that if he spat at the cow three times, he could possess it. He did this and won the cow". [11]

Folklore also has the hill inhabited by giants, plus a lake guardian spirit with shape-shifting forms. Gold (as well as copper) has been mined on the mountain historically and many tales are of treasures hidden there, but they always warn not to upset the spirits of place by seeking them!

"Giants-Rock got its name because long ago the two giants who were living on Benbo mountain had a quarrel. One of them lifted a large stone and threw it at the other. It hurled down the mountain and it is there still... On the top of Benbo mountain there is a small lake, the water of which is red. It is also said to be bottomless. In this lake we are told there is a pot of gold. Years ago a giant lived on the top of the mountain and...when he was attacked by the [other] giant, he having a pot of gold went immediately to the lake and hid the gold in it. There is an enormous eel in this lake and we are told that he was left minding the gold." [12]

MANORHAMILTON

Manorhamilton, originally called Cluainín, the Little Meadow, is the second town of importance in Leitrim, after Carrick on Shannon. With a population of around 1,600, it's set in the convergence of the Five Glens and is a popular area for hill walkers.

Frederick Hamilton, for whom the town is named, was its founding father socio-path, a professional soldier remembered for inflicting great cruelty upon the populace, while flaunting the dubious distinction of being from a 'nobleman' family. His knighthood was apparently purchased from the king for as much as 400 British pounds.[13] He claimed to have killed 1,200 Irish rebels during the rebellion of 1641 (though it might be an exaggeration).[14] The ruins of his castle dominate the town, as a sobering reminder that even the so-called elite and all-powerful will fall in the end.

"After the confiscation of the Cluainín lands in 1607 a man named Sir Fredrick Hamilton built a castle. This man was a Scotch planter. He built this castle thinking he would be safe from all attacks and he had a tree outside the castle from which he executed a great many people. Sir Fredrick was very cruel and was not liked by the people over whom he ruled. It is said that he killed twenty families of Catholics who lived in Glencar." ...

"Sir Frederick Hamilton...was probably the greatest ruffian of them all. His pastime was adorning the walls of his castle with the heads of all who opposed his way". [15]

By 1631 Hamilton controlled lands of over 16,00 Irish acres. His castle in the townland of Clooneen, constructed between 1634 and 1636, replicated the design of Rathfarnham Castle in Dublin. It has been described as having been an elegant, fortified mansion *"and one of the most imposing 17th century houses in Ireland"*, in its day.[16] It was 30 m long, 25 m wide and 15 m high, and was surrounded by a bawn wall 4 m high with two-storey towers on the four corners. Five years later the town was fairly substantial, having up to twenty five stone houses, a population of one hundred, a Protestant Church, at least one inn and two corn mills. During the Rising of 1641 the Castle was besieged and defended three times, but not taken. During one of the sieges, Manorhamilton was burned and the townspeople were given shelter within the bawn walls. [17]

In retaliation for the uprising, Hamilton *"undertook a scorched earth policy in Leitrim and its hinterland, burning crops and houses, taking prisoners and killing rebels and their supporters....and non-combatants, including women were* [also] *attacked,"* wrote Brendan Scott.[18] He bragged that *"the rebels had 'not so much left as a cabin to camp in' within a six mile radius of Manorhamilton"*. Hamilton went on to make lightning raids in Donegal and he burnt Sligo town, slaughtering its monks and anyone else he encountered, while the public gallows at Hamilton's Castle claimed 58 victims between 1641-43. When he returned to Scotland in 1647, Hamilton, who was heavily in debt, died suddenly aged 57. His castle continued its military presence until 1652, when it was finally burned down by Irish rebels.[19]

From the car park you can look up at the foreboding ruin (on the previous page). It's a three-storey rectangular stone structure, with most of the top floor gone. Two wings project on the north side and there are four slightly rhomboid corner towers with windows, gunloops and fireplaces. With its large fireplace, the north east tower was probably the kitchen. All windows, doors and fireplaces have been robbed of dressed stonework. The main house must have been a chilly home in winter, as only a few small fireplaces are evident.[20] A visitor centre beside the castle opens in the summer, together with cafe, garden and picnic tables.

Not far away, St. Clare's Roman Catholic church sits on an elevation above the centre of town. It was built in 1883, replacing an earlier church of 1810. However on the night of a great wind storm of January 26th 1884, its roof and tower collapsed.[21] Looking out from across the road, on the hilltop opposite you can view St Clare's church and wide vistas from another, more elevated church site. As at Lurganboy, it's an unusual setting, with a Church of Ireland church and graveyard here replacing a military establishment.

The large site on the hill top is within a Star Fort (seen right), that's defined by mighty coursed masonry walls enclosing an area of 73 m by 73 m. Built into the hill by Sir Ralph Gore, a great grandson of Frederick Hamilton, the thick walls, that soar 3-6 m high on their exterior, are on a plinth over bedrock, with stone bastions 17 m by 17 m that project out from each corner.[22] The barracks on this site was in use for about 35 years from 1716. After its demolition, the site was then used for the present Church of Ireland, built in 1783.[23] To get to the Star Fort, take a short walk up Church Lane from the main street. To access the graveyard, go through the big metal gates on the right, beside an old school building.

I found it a delightful, tranquil spot to rest, have a picnic, enjoy the wide views and spring flowers. A picturesque place with dark undercurrents, because I also experienced a Memory Field of warring soldiers that lingered there, in the battle-scarred emotional records of the place. Later, contemplating the brutality of the colonial era, I found a pertinent comment on the futility of the war mentality that created such ever-evolving fortifications as the Star Fort. *"It is often our mightiest projects that most obviously betray the degree of our insecurity."* [24]

Bucking the bleakness of Manorhamilton's colonial past, today's town is alive with the arts, a vibrant reflection of the high percentage of artists, writers and musicians that live in this small county. The Glens Centre runs an exciting programme of events, including theatre and music, while the Leitrim Sculpture Centre offers courses and training.[25]

TULLYSKEHERNY

Two Neolithic tombs can be visited on a remote plateau above Manorhamilton in Tullyskeherny townland. From Manorhamilton, take the road east towards Glenfarne. After 500 m take a right turn onto a country lane, then 1.5 km or so later, when you reach a fork in the road, keep to the left. Then, at the top of the plateau, the road bends sharp left. Park at the top there, or go through the farm gate, driving or walking south along the farm track for 500 m or so. Or drive a further 100 m and on your right is another gate. If the way is open, go through this gate and after about 200 m you'll see the tombs on the left (- it wasn't accessible when I visited in September 2024).

The highland karst-landscape of limestone pavements and weathered rock outcrops is very exposed to the elements, so ideally pick a nice weather day for a visit. It's an Other-worldly location, with wonderful views of hills and distant glens, especially the Glenade u-shaped glacial valley, Benbo to the west; and towards Sligo in the north-west - Truskmore and Tievebaun. Here, if you leave your car at the gate, the modern world is pretty much out of sight. Only the mouldering ruins of a few old stone homesteads are visible, tucked into rough fields of sheep pasture. It must have had a significant population in times past, as the presence of ancient tombs attests.

After passing the clump of conifer trees, the track winds downwards and soon you arrive at the two large and impressive tombs, beside the track on the left. Created out of the karst landscape, both tombs are made from limestone slabs and merge into the stoney site. Only 5m apart, the northern tomb is a long cairn with remnants of a long narrow forecourt leading into an antechamber, with two main chambers. It was robbed of much stone to build the track going past it. (Road builders of the day had to carry rocks on their backs, so they didn't pass up the opportunity to strip the tomb.) In the south end of this cairn are at least six subsidiary chambers, some in good condition.

The southern tomb, some 25 m across (photo overleaf), is a large oval cairn with a gallery of two chambers, each about 2.5m wide. Another chamber at the rear of the gallery is now filled with loose cairn material. The forecourt part is at the southern end. Much of the cairn material is strewn across the south eastern side of the tomb. In adjacent bog covered parts of the plateau, more tombs lie hidden.[26] Here in big sky country you can see far. And there is a visual alignment - from the tomb to a notch in nearby hills to the southwest. So, perhaps they counted time as well here, by sky gazing and noting cyclic celestial alignment events. [27]

Glenfarne

Glenfarne village is set in a picturesque mountain valley close to Lough MacNean Upper. Long an important location in the political scene, bordering Fermanagh to the north and Tullyhaw to the east, the Irish name Gleannfarna means Glen of the Alder Trees. During O'Rourke's rule, Glenfarne belonged to Breifne and then West Breifne.

This area north of Lough Allen is a real hot spot for sweat-houses, with a notable concentration along the Glenfarne Valley. In a 10 km radius surrounding Glenfarne village there are some 30 - 40 known sweat-house sites. Adjacent to the R281 Glenfarne to Kiltyclogher Road there are also three bullaun stones in Laghty Barr, but little is known of them, says the Glenfarne Historical Society. [28]

Close to Glenfarne village, near the Cornavannoge River and within Glenfarne demesne, is an alignment of three standing stones (one fallen) at Brockagh Lower. This stone row could well have been part of a network of significant ritual sites. It can be accessed off the N16 near Clancys Shop and Restaurant.

The Black Pig's Dyke has long embankments running from the north-western shore of Lough MacNean Upper towards the south-eastern shore of Lough Melvin. Some are accessible to view, as at Corracloona, south east of Kiltyclogher.

Lough MacNean Upper

Lough MacNean Upper is a border lake 4.5 km long and 1.5 km wide. Glenfarne demesne lies on its Leitrim shore. Once part of the Tottenham Estate, that in the 1870s included over 14,500 acres of Leitrim land, it was the private hunting grounds of the elite. Nowadays it's a public recreation area and walking trails run from the car park along the edge of Lough MacNean, going through woodland and featuring eleven sculptures. There is a picnic area and boat quay at the lake.[29] On the lake there are four possible crannogs and two of these are close to the shoreline beside Glenfarne demesne. These are Crannoge Island and Creevaghern Island, but they have no evidence of being man made.[30]

The McGoverns, rulers of Tullyhaw, are plentiful here, and also from Dowra to Swanlinbar, Bawnboy to Blacklion. One of their ancestral burial places was the old Abbey of Killinagh near Blacklion. Within the ancient walls of Killinagh Abbey, set in green pastures beside the lake shore, their numerous gravestones can be seen. A bullaun and holy well are nearby.[31]

CORRACLOONA

The most impressive megalith in the area is a court (or possibly wedge) tomb at Corracloona, beside the R281 Glenfarne to Kiltyclogher road and 3.3km south east of Kiltyclogher village. The site, locally known as Prince Connell's Grave and the Giants Grave, is next to the old Corracloona school (now a home) and a brown sign points to it at the field gate. The road is narrow here, but you can park in front of a house around the corner, in Corracloona Road, which is a right turn just after the site. To access the tomb, go through a small wooden gate into the field.

The boggy hill setting overlooks Lough Macnean Upper. The huge chunky boulders nestled amidst wild gardens of blooming heather and bilberries, made it a glorious site to behold on my visit there. It's largely intact, but for the missing cairn that once covered it over. (Perhaps the cairn material was recycled into the school house.) A large displaced roof stone, 2.5 m by

1.8 m sits beside it. The tomb's courtyard opens onto a single burial chamber to the west, through an unique feature - a 'kennel-hole' entrance in the front portal stone. It's the only example of such in Ireland, however they are common in the south of France and Belgium. [32] The site was excavated and re-constructed by Howard Kilbride-Jones in 1953. He reported finding hollow scrapers, thumb-nail scrapers, a leaf shaped arrow-head and a small amount of coarse pottery from the excavation.[33] No human remains were found and no report published. Dated as circa 4,000 years old, it's a couple of thousand years older than Prince Connell, an Iron Age warrior-hero, who is also said to be buried at Fenagh.

To see some of the Black Pig's Dyke, go down the small lane, the Corracloona Road. After taking the left fork, at about one kilometre down from the R281 there is a small woodland area, surrounded by conifer forest, with a visible section of the dyke accessible.

KILTYCLOGHER

Kiltyclogher, in Irish Coillte Clochair, the Stony Woods, is a small village in Leitrim close to the border with Northern Ireland. It was once on the front line in the war of independence, which saw it become much de-populated. Nowadays it's a tranquil place and, when I visited, like a charming still life painting. An estate village that was designed by the local landlord (like Drumsna), the streets are wide and stone buildings elegant. In this area are several megalithic tombs, while west of here, substantial remains of the Black Pig's Dyke can be seen in the Gleann na Muice Duibhe, the Glen of the Black Pig, all marked on OS map 17.

"A section of the Black Pig's Dyke is located to the east of Dough Mountain in the County River valley, beginning 1 km south of Lough Melvin and extending intermittently in a general northwest to southeast direction towards Lough MacNean Upper, a distance of 10.36 km. It was first depicted on the second edition OS map and many of the gaps in the monument correspond to areas of marshy wetland.... Kane included this section as being part of his No. 1 Frontier and he refers to it being broken up into several sections, claiming that local farmers had levelled the earthwork in the past ...Kane also records that it was termed Bohereen-Wan and the Great Man's Track." [34]

Searching for the Black Pig's Dyke, the tiny labyrinthine back roads can be easy to get lost in. And some of the locations (plus that of the Corracloona tomb and other monuments) have been incorrectly marked on maps! To see these local sites, it may be better to go on a tour with the knowledgable staff of Kiltyclogher's Heritage Centre, in the middle of the village. A great asset to the community, the centre was opened in the restored sandstone courthouse building in 2015. Beneath the MacDiarmada statue's stony gaze it houses an exhibition about the 1916 uprising, plus local history. One of the leaders of the uprising and a signatory of the Proclamation of Irish Independence, MacDiarmada was one of the executed martyrs. The centre offers a one hour tour of his restored cottage in the townland of Corranmore, around 5 km from Kiltyclogher and not far from the Corracloona tomb, where the old school beside it was his school. The thatched cottage, maintained in its original condition by the Office for Public Works, is a fine example of a traditional home and it gives an insight into what life was like over a century ago.

The Heritage Centre does not charge for tours, but they accept donations. It's an oasis of hospitality too and the only place in town where you can get a hot drink (while around the corner there's a shop and post office). The centre is not always open, so it's best to book a tour in advance by phoning 0719 854865 or email kiltyclogherheritagecentre@gmail.com

A little south of Kiltyclogher village a court tomb at Carrigeengeare is adjacent to the R283 Manorhamilton road. A simpler structure of four standing stones, it's not as well preserved as Corracloona court tomb. The remains of two more can be accessed either side of the N16 in the townlands of Gortaquill and Killycarney, just over the county border in Cavan.

ROSSINVER

Continuing west-north-west of Kiltyclogher along the R281, Rossinver village is near the lower end of Lough Melvin, and its name means the Promontory of the River Mouth. Lakeshores were popular places for early settlements, as water was the main means of getting to them. The land was otherwise thick with forests, hills and bogs, making water transport ideal. Nearly a century ago, the following description of former times was recorded by a Rossinver school pupil. (The presence of the Crane in it may denote a time pre-1600, before they were wiped out.)

"An old native of Rossinver told me the following story of his native place, as told to him by his grandfather. When his forefathers came to Rossinver it was almost all a forest, from a place in Dartry called Straemor, to a place southwards called Linncullin, and that a boy might get up on a tree at the former place and not come down until he came to the latter place. So dense was the forest, and it abounded with wild game and wild animals such as Wild Cats, Martins, Foxes, Hares, Rabbits, Otters and Deer. On the east of the forest lay the beautiful Lake Melvin abounding with salmon and also perch and eels and different kinds of water fowl, such as the swan, cormorant, crane and common black and white breasted waterhen. Thousands of songbirds filled the forest while their beautiful music resounded over the lake, mountain and forest." [35]

Here, on the southern shore of Lough Melvin, it was an ideal location for the early monastic site that was founded by St Mogue (aka St Aidan) in the 6th or 7th century, in the townland of Gubalaun. The site of Rossinver's Old Church and Holy Well of St Mogue can be visited from Kiltyclogher, by turning right at the intersection with the Manorhamilton R282 road, then turn left back onto the R281 and take the first right, just before the bridge, to the signposted graveyard site. The remains of the medieval St Aidan's Church of the Parish of Ballaghmeehan are here and they are less dilapidated since conservation works were undertaken in 2020.[36] A succession of several churches have been here over a long history and a 13th century east window is incorporated into the current structure. The presence of it's coarbs was recorded up until 1438.

In the adjacent rectangular walled graveyard, which is still in use, the saint, who died in 632 it's believed, is said to be buried. However, we don't know his grave's whereabouts. The site certainly goes back to early times, as a 9th century grave slab with carved cross was found just inside the gate.[37] Another ancient grave slab that sports three cup-marks,[38] was described as a *"strangely shaped bullaun stone"* by archeologist Sam Moore, at a talk on the Black Pig's Dyke in Mohill in March 2024.

"Rossinver Graveyard ...situated in the townland of Gublaun beneath the shade of Sheawn mountain... is considered one of the best burial grounds in Ireland. It is very flat and it lies beside the river. ...It is covered over with a large number of beautifully carved and decorated tombstones and marble and granite headstones and artistic crosses some which are beautiful colours and some in Irish... According to tradition...here dwelt St. Mogue and his monks, and companions until the time of the Plantation... It was the greatest of our schools in the past [and] *it is the most interesting of our ruins at present in this locality...The Fair of St. Mogue's, once the greatest event of the year, was held on the 31st January, up until 1869."* [39]

Nearby, St Mogues Well (seen left) is situated close to the lakeshore and handy to St. Mogues Church. It was where *"formerly a great devotion and pilgrimages were performed... This well is situated under a whitethorn bush... At this well the stations of the cross were performed and many people were cured of various diseases."* [40]

ST MOGUES HOLY WELL EXPERIENCE

You can access the beautiful lakeshore by going through a small gate in front of the abbey ruin. The well, now just a watery hole, is on private land. On the sunny day that I visited the lake waters were deep blue and dreamily serene. But when I found the well, a weedy hole in the ground, the site felt so neglected and sad. Tuning my 'second sight' to the well, I happily observed a still-powerful water spirit, like an angel, who then rose up from the murky wet hole and expressed her surprise and joy to be recognised by me. From above the well several metres in the air, she showered down on me ethereal blessings from out of her water bucket.

ROSSINVER AREA

Today Rossinver is probably best known as the location of the Organic Centre, which is less than a kilometre from the graveyard. Go back to the R281, turn right, cross the bridge and just after it, take the first turn left. This place is a modern day legend, where organic farming and gardening have been promoted and taught for the last 30 years. Display gardens and polytunnels, a shop for produce and plants, as well as the only place to get a coffee in town, make it a must-visit location. The cafe operates on weekends, but hot drinks are available any day and cold drinks and snacks, plus wholefoods are also always available.

You can also access Fowley's Falls river walk from here, by following the signs from the Organic Centre car park area. One of Rossinver's top beauty spots, Fowley's Falls are about 2 km west of the village. On the Glenaniff River in a steeply incised V-shaped river valley, it's a series of stepped waterfalls with curtains of water cascading gloriously over the rocks. [41]

This region has a low population but, like elsewhere, was more populous before the Great Famine. Steep de-population allowed the waterfalls to be forgotten and nature was left happily undisturbed. The river runs through the townland of Dernahemrick, Doire na hImirce - the Oak Wood of the Emigration. It was wildly overgrown and never visited until local people in the late 1980s made a plan to to reveal its long hidden beauty. They created an access track to it from Rossinver village, meandering through forest, and they worked by hand, to preserve the natural beauty. Indeed, *"Such is the other worldliness of the immediate area adjoining these waterfalls, that no words can describe it,"* one of those involved wrote, encouraging visitors to go and experience it. [42] But in the Oak Wood of Emigration, the path grew overgrown again. In 2003 Rossinver Community Development Company (RCDC) decided to restore the walk as per the original vision, keeping it as natural as possible with minimal interference with the landscape, and it has since been extended too. [43]

Heading a little south of Rossinver village, we have St Molaise presiding. Said to be a friend of St Mogue and the patron saint of Rossinver and Kinlough Parishes, St Molaise (533-570AD), was also patron saint of his clan, the Meehans/O'Meighans. However his and Aidan's dates don't match up. Molaise established an abbey here and its erenachs were recorded into the 15th century. His feast day was August 15, date of the old Pagan harvest festival. Before he made his abbey here - *"St Molais went to Devenish in Co. Fermanagh and built a Monastery there."* [44] Devenish is the picturesque island in Lough Erne, near Enniskillen, with substantial monastery ruins including an intact and beautiful Round Tower.

In another story, he wields a sacred book in his spiritual arsenal. *"When St. Molais was leaving Rome the pope gave the gospel to him and this was called the Soilseal Molais and it was enshrined in a case called the Cudac Molais. There are different stories told about this book. It is said if a man swore wrong on this book the leaves would turn up and he would instantly go mad. The Soiseal Moulais was kept in the Meehan family for hundreds of years but was lost. The Cudac Molais is preserved in Trinity College in Dublin."* [45]

Molaise traditionally performed various miracles, including at Tobar Molaise, the second most important holy well in the region. In one legend he was preaching to a group of people who became dehydrated. So he went over to a rock and pushed his hand through it, causing water to flow out out it to quench their thirst. (This generic type of myth enjoys much repetition in the legends of many saints of this world!)

You can visit Tobar Molaise, situated in the southern corner of the townland of Derrynahimmirk/Emigration, and just off the R282 south of Rossinver. The site is at the bottom of the Ballagh River valley. Here cures used to be eagerly sought by pilgrims, who left a stone in thanks, that piled up into a cairn. Still a place of veneration, the well has had a modern well house built around it and the concrete lined well is inside a rectangular roofed stone structure surmounted by a steel cross. [46]

LOUGH MELVIN

With the Leitrim, Fermanagh and Cavan county borders running through it, Lough Melvin was a stronghold of the Mac Glancy clan, rulers of Dartry. Several early monastery sites ring Melvin's shores. The lake is also the home of a rare endemic fish - the Gillyroo, a most curious species that sports a gizzard, like a chicken, for grinding its food!

In the western end of Lough Melvin, the MacGlancys had their royal crannog at Rosclogher, some 100 m from the southern shore. Here, Rosclogher Castle was their power centre through the 13th and 14th centuries. The legendary tower house, that filled up most of the small island, was written about from 1421. It was a strongly built place of retreat and security. An older, cashel-like ring fort is evident around it, with some of the massive walls still standing. The Mac Glancys, who, some say, had a residence on the mainland as well, were kind enough to offer hospitality here to survivors of the shipwrecked Spanish Armada fleet in 1588. They stayed here in safety for two months and defended the castle against English attack. This incurred much wrath from the enemy, but that's another story! [47] A film recently made about MacGlancy's Castle that covers archeology and history of the site is free online. [48]

On the mainland nearby, beside the southern shoreline, an ancient enclosure has been found.

Within it there was a small settlement overlooking the crannog, with earthworks and a church ruin that was built about the same time as the castle. This was Rosclogher Abbey, possibly founded circa 800 by Tigernach of Killeagh. The ruined rectangular sandstone structure has an internal dimension of 11 m by 5.5 m wide. The ancient enclosure bank surrounding the abbey ruin is a sure sign of the site's early importance. [49] The settlement probably serviced the lords on the crannog and its many wooden buildings are attested to by numerous stone foundations remaining. [50] The site is not accessible to the public.

South east of Rosclogher, in the townland of Aghaderrard East, is a bullaun stone, a natural boulder having eight basin hollows, plus a broken fragment of another, on its upper surface. It's situated amidst woodland on the edge of a natural shelf overlooking the lakeshore and 100 m from a court tomb.[51] Locally known as a Giant's Grave, this overgrown megalithic monument sits near the top of a slight rise close to the shore. It's a single chambered, roofless gallery, 5 m by 2 m, with an east facing court with upright slabs up to 1.2 m high, set within a cairn that has jambstones flanking the entrance.[52]

Two large islands on Lough Melvin have ruins on them. Inishtemple/ Innis Teampiull has a church ruin on the south shore, a rectangular structure with sandstone walls 13 m by 6 m, with one slit window, that survives almost complete.[53] Also known as Church Island, the Mac Clancys are traditionally buried here.[54] *"There is an island in Lough Melvin still called Church island, on which are the ruins of a church and* [an informant] *heard that the Monks* [living at Rosfriar] *used to go there for greater safety."* [55] ... *"The oldest burial place in this district was on the Island of Inistemple...This was the burial place for the people north of Lough Melvin up to the 16th century, as the people South of the lake along Dartry district [were] buried in Rossinver graveyard."* [56]

On the island of Inishkeen, near the north lake shore and county border, is a site known as the Friar's Garden. It's set in woodland on the north side. A stone slab with a cross is set in a small stone cairn, with a cut stone pillar base nearby. A second cross-slab is now in the National Museum. A collapsed bank encloses this garden area of some 4 ha and it's best preserved at the east end. Slag was found on the north shore, which may indicate that medieval metal forging also occurred here.[57] During penal times friars are said to have taken refuge on Inishkeen and some were buried in the garden. Stepping stones beneath the water surface connected the island to the mainland and were known as The Friars Pass. [58]

In Lough Melvin, as in Lough Allen, some people have encountered mystical "beautiful ladies" and "mermaids", and also seen "dragons" in recent times. The dragons have been described by clairvoyants as being generally coloured blue, with lovely turquoise wings.[59]

SHEENUN

Overlooking Rossinver and Lough Melvin, Sheenun is a hill that used to be a focus for Lughnasa festivities on Bilberry Sunday, the second Sunday in July. Young people, especially, would meet up there and frolic, with courting and matchmaking a main feature. It was a day for the first meal of new potatoes too.[60] Today Sheenun is a popular for hill walkers and a high hilltop car park is a venue for paragliders to take off from here. The peak is behind it. The next mountain peak to the north has a megalithic tomb on it.

The hill name has various spellings - Sheeaun, Sheehaun, Sheeawn and Sheehawn. Ardagh Sheeran is a townland name on old maps between Sheenan and the lake. (Most maps have no name for the mountain, only the OS maps.) Sidhean - the Fairy Hill, is one suggestion for its original name, from local tourism promoters of the late 1980s. I wondered if this was wishful thinking, however others have also echoed this folk memory. [61]

Around the rest of the mountaintop area there are several ancient tombs. In the townland of Shasgar, on a rock shelf on the edge of a north facing plateau above a steep cliff, there is a court tomb, locally known as a Giant's Grave. This is an oval cairn 17 m by 12 m and 2 m in height. It has a single roofless stone chamber with an entrance 75 cm high flanked by orthostats 90 cm high. [62]

SHEEAUN ENERGIES

Could Sheeaun be north Leitrim's most sacred hill? Whenever I'm in Rossinver my eyes are drawn to it. There are several peaks along the range, at elevations from 250 m to Sheeaun, on the right to the north, at 349 m. From the grounds of the Organic Centre, as in the photo, the range looms large and it's always had a magnetic attraction for me when I've visited there.

At several dowsing and geomancy workshops I taught at the Organic Centre years ago I showed students how to pick up energies remotely and we practised distantly detecting the powerful mountain energies around Sheenun. I showed them a tall and powerful landscape angel stationed on the mountain tops, plus an Energy Ley (aerial energy line) running across them, running north west to south east, that I'd detected. There was something especially vibrant about the massive hills, but I didn't follow it up. To later discover its name - the Hill of the Fairies - was a nice surprise.

More geomantic significance of the mountain came in a description I found online, from fellow geomancer Frank Albrecht, who lived there for several years. *"The Sheenun mountain marks the geomantic centre point for the whole area, it is connected (through a minor line) with the major synchronic line of Ireland that links Ireland with Stonehenge and the Gizeh pyramids,"* he wrote. [63]

Remotely dowsing over a map, I found this linear aerial energy line (that some call 'ley line') to possibly co-incide with the Deerpark Court Tomb in Sligo, Cairn Hill (a probable passage grave and traditional home of the Dagda, near Lough Gill), [64] Knocknashee, the Fairy Hill of south Sligo, and beyond. It sounded like a Ley Hunting adventure would be needed! But that will have to wait for another day.

KINLOUGH

Kinlough, meaning the Head of the Lough, is in Dartry, the ancient territory of the Mac Glancys that corresponded closely with the later Barony of Rosclogher. The Dartraige were an ancient tribe, with branches in places such as Clonmel, Tipperary and west Monaghan. The name comes from Old Irish dart, a heifer. [65] Folklore connects Dartry's chiefs intimately with the landscape here. *"There is a common belief still in Dartry that when one of this Clancy sept dies, a piece of rock falls from the Blue Rock of Dartry Mountain, a peak overhanging or watching over McClancy's famous castle".* [66]

"The Parish of Kinlough...is the most northerly part of Co. Leitrim and of Connaught...[whose] patron saint...is St. Aiden [aka St. Mogue]...This Saint belonged to the O Ruarc family who ruled Breffni Uí Ruairc. He was Bishop of Wexford [and was buried in Rossinver].... The name of the townland [Edenvilla, near Kinlough]..seems to mean the Hill Brow of the Old Tree. An old man, who has since died ...[said] that it was named after St. Aiden, who came to reside there when he retired and who blessed a holy well (and bile [a sacred tree], also) but nobody knows now where this well was.... Two townlands take their names from graveyards. These are Laghta and Fertagh. There are some ancient looking stones in Laughta but an ordinary person would not be able to make anything of them now". [67]

"Laughta got its name in olden times, because there were so many graves in it. The word itself means the place of graves...Most of the land in Laughta is hilly and boggy." [68]

ROSFRIAR

On a wide promontory jutting into the north west end of Lough Melvin there was once a thriving monastery. These days the land is level, overgrown and surrounded by conifer plantations, while the archeology merely records a rectangular enclosure of 52 m by 44 m size, with just a low, 3 m wide earth bank and outer fosse, 2.5 m wide and 60 cm deep. A possible moated site, it has traces of two causeway entrances, about 2 m wide, at the east and west ends. [69] The record of a friary is confirmed by local folklore.

"Long years ago a party of monks landed, in small boats, at Locan na tSaile, an inlet of the sea near Tullaghan. The people of the neighbourhood went down to the sea and received them very kindly...After some time they left Tullaghan and went up the banks of the Drowes River to Lough Melvin [where] they built a small Friary and lived there for a long time. The place chosen by them is now called Rosfriar. It is a long narrow peninsula running out into the lake, situated opposite MacClancy's Castle in Lough Melvin about half a mile away. The place where they built their Friary is lonely and far removed. The stones and bricks used in the building were taken away in latter days to build houses in the locality." [70]

Here at Rosfriar was completed one of Ireland's most well known manuscripts - the Annals of the Kingdom of Ireland, otherwise known as the Annals of the Four Masters. It was a compilation of older manuscripts that recorded history and pseudo-history up until 1616. Peregrine O'Duignan, an ancestor of the Castlefore O'Duignans, was one of these Four Masters who undertook the huge task. A monument celebrating their accomplishment is on the bridge at Mullinaleck, a short distance north of Kinlough.

TULLAGHAN

Heading to the coast, the small village of Tullaghan (An Tulachan, the Small Hillock) is Leitrim's only seaside town on its 4 km long coastline. A modern walking track has been recently made to allow public access to the seashore there. The town sits besides the Drowes River that was once the border between Connaught and Ulster. So it wasn't always quiet, being the scene of many a bloody battle.

Here was a past stronghold of the lords of Carbry, the MacClancys of Duncarbry Castle. Ruins of this probable tower house sit on top of a prominent rise, now seen as a rectangular grassy platform with a collapsed wall around it. The remains of the building are a rocky mound at the north east end, with no architectural features visible.[71] The site is beside a road that goes southwards off the N15 from the village.

"There is an old castle situated near Tullaghan in the townland of Duncarbery, meaning the Fort of Carbery. To the west of the castle there is a big hill…called Carraigh Mór because there is a great big rock on it. The McClancys soldiers used to watch from that rock for Duncarbery castle …Magheracar is situated near the Drowes river, a name meaning the Plain of Slaughter. The O'Donnells [of Donegal] and the O'Connors [of Connaught] fought there. Sarsfield and the English also fought there… Leim an Laoic is where O'Donnell jumped with his horse to save his life, it is on the sea shore near the Drowes river." [72] … *"Tradition speaks of great battles fought in Magheracar (in Donegal) in which hundreds of Leitrim men were killed."* [73]

Remnants of what was once a terminus of Ulster's Black Pig's Dyke can be found here. The archeological record describes a remnant linear bank on a low rise immediately north of the road and south of the Drowes River. *"A fosse, 26 m long by 4 m wide at the base, runs north-south across the centre of the grassy rise, with a bank on either side,"* the Inventory says. [74] This territorial nexus is the stuff of much legend, as well as pseudo-legend, as the following place-lore shows. *"The locality around the rivers Duff and Drowse, near Bundoran, where the Formoire are said to have collected the tribute levied by them on inland populations, preserved the name Magh Cetne na Formoraigh down to the 17th century."* [75]

Next to the village, in the porch of a Roman Catholic church in the townland of Tawnytallan, there are a couple of interesting features. One is a bullaun stone, the other a limestone plaque installed on the wall, with an incised inscription in Latin on it from the 1770s. The flat topped sandstone boulder bullaun has a single basin with traces of stone pecking, that may have been used as a stoup (holy water basin) and could be of pre-Christian significance. Both are believed to have originally come from a cashel (stone ring fort) at Doobally, south east of Duncarbry Castle. [76]

Beyond the village, the Tullaghan Cross is a stone high cross that was found in 1778 on the seashore after a storm and re-erected by the local landlord. It's thought to have originated from a long-vanished monastery there.[77] *"There are some pillar stones or Dolmens in the Tullaghan part of [Kinlough] parish along the sea coast and smaller stones in Donegal across the Drowes."* [78] Indeed, several standing stones and megalithic tombs are on the record for Wardhouse, just west of Tullaghan, and it is considered an archeological complex.[79] The sites are set in undulating pastures with rock outcrops, concentrated in a 4 ha area, with some close to the shore of Donegal Bay. Locally called Giant's Graves, the tombs include a couple of court tombs, a wedge and two portal tombs, plus another couple of possible ruined megalithic structures. [80] There are seven standing stones also recorded in the Wardhouse area. [81]

GLENADE

Heading back from Tullaghan towards Manorhamilton on the R280 you can follow the wide U shaped glacial valley of Glenade. It's considered one of the finest examples of a glacial valley in all of Europe. Like Glencar, Glenade was shaped and moulded by glacial action during the Ice Age. Uplands flanking the valley are also amongst Ireland's best looking upland karst landscapes (with limestone pavements and outcrops), renowned for the quantity and complexity of its karst features in a relatively small area.

Eagle's Rock is a free standing 330 m high limestone pillar, once part of the valley wall that broke away to become this much photographed feature of the Glenade Valley. It formed after the glacier that provided support for the valley's steep walls had retreated. (There are other similar 'collapse features' visible at Peakadaw to the south, and at Swiss Valley in Glencar.) A popular area for hill walking, the walking trail that leads up the cliff face on Eagle's Rock (on private land) has been recently closed. [82]

The valley of Glenade, a name meaning the Glen of Jealousy, has lush pastures that were the traditional haunt of the Holy Cow, or Glas Cow, who could never be milked dry.[83] Perhaps it was the lushness of the valley that created jealousy in others? There are several completely different accounts in the folklore of how Glenade got its name, but cow envy could also be a contender. Glenade school students reported in the 1930's on their local Glas Cow's impressive credentials.

"A long time ago, there was a strange cow seen in Glenade. The story goes that she fed in Crumpawn where the best grazing for miles around is supposed to be. She drank of the water in Loughmarron because it is the purest and best in the Parish, and she slept on the dry hills of Uragh. It was said that this cow could fill with milk any vessel that ever was put under her ... Glasnevin is the name that was given to this cow here." [84]

On the floor of the glen, Glenade Lough is nestled below the towering peaks of the Dartry Mountains. Wildlife is diverse here and the lake and its immediate surroundings were designated a Special Area of Conservation in 1997. Critically endangered European Eels and White Clawed Crayfish make the lake their home. Streams enter it at the northern end, while its waters drain away southwards into the Bonet River. [85]

It may be calmly picturesque today, but a sinister tale is attached to Glenade Lough. A legendary monster called the Dobhar Chú (pronounced Dow-ar-coo), or Water Dog, was said to inhabit the waters. It was accused of mauling to death a woman who was washing clothes on the shore. At the nearby Conwell Cemetery, a stone grave slab sports the carving of a Dobhar Chú with a spear through it, as the alleged killer of Grace Connelly, buried here in 1722. It's been suggested that the story, with its over-the-top supernatural elements, is a fabrication. The Dobhar Chú was scapegoated, perhaps, to cover up murder by the husband. If so, it certainly wouldn't be the first pseudo-legend to have obscured the truth. And I'm sure it won't be the last.

References

Introduction - Time Travelling Leitrim

1. Leitrim History & Society, edited by Liam Kelly & Brendan Scott, Geography Publications, Dublin, 2019, page 21.
2. The Ancient Celts, 2nd edition, by Barry Cunliffe, Oxford University Press, 2018, UK, page 377.
3. Archeological Inventory of Co. Leitrim, Michael J. Moore, Government of Ireland, 2003, page ix.
4. Leitrim History & Society, edited by Liam Kelly & Brendan Scott, Geography Publications, Dublin, 2019, page 21.
5. Leitrim Observer 26.3.25 page 5.
6. See www.geomantica.com

Chapter 1 - Setting the Scene

1. Fairy Haunts of Ireland, Alanna Moore, Python Press, 2023, Ireland, page 29.
2. Hand of History, Burden of Pseudo History, Touchstone of Truth, Trafford Publishing, Tom O'Connor, Ireland, 2005, page 327.
3. Fairy Haunts of Ireland, Alanna Moore, Python Press, 2023, Ireland, page 24.
4. https://balkancelts.wordpress.com/2015/07/04/cernunnos-and-the-ram-headed-serpent/
5. Hand of History, Burden of Pseudo History, Touchstone of Truth, Trafford Publishing, Tom O'Connor, Ireland, 2005, page 80.
6. The Dictionary of Celtic Mythology - James MacKillop, Oxford University Press, UK, 2004 page 413.
7. The Schools' Collection, Volume 0252, Page 010 © National Folklore Collection, UCD.
8. Hand of History, Burden of Pseudo History, Touchstone of Truth, Trafford Publishing, Tom O'Connor, Ireland, 2005, page 7.
9. Hand of History, Burden of Pseudo History, Touchstone of Truth, Trafford Publishing, Tom O'Connor, Ireland, 2005, page 23.
10. The Black Pig's Dyke Regional Project 2014 Volume 1, Coilin Ó Drisceoil, Mary Leenane, Stephen Davis, Barry Fitzgibbon and Mary Teehan.
11. Hand of History, Burden of Pseudo History, Touchstone of Truth, Trafford Publishing, Tom O'Connor, Ireland, 2005, page 188.
12. The Ancient Celts, 2nd edition, by Barry Cunliffe, Oxford University Press, 2018, UK.)
13. The Black Pig's Dyke Regional Project 2014 Volume 1, Coilin Ó Drisceoil, Mary Leenane, Stephen Davis, Barry Fitzgibbon and Mary Teehan.
14. Hand of History, Burden of Pseudo History, Touchstone of Truth, Trafford Publishing, Tom O'Connor, Ireland, 2005, page 217.
15. A Reconstruction of the Cycle of Celtic Myths Current in the Atlantic Iron Age Culture of France, Britain and Ireland circa 60-55BCE, at the time of Caesar's Conquest of Gaul, by Garrett Olmsted, Professor Emeritus Bluefield State University, online.
16. The Gundestrup and Chiemsee Cauldrons: Witnesses to the Art and Iconography of the Celtic Veneti, by Prof. Garrett Olmsted, online.
17. The Ancient Celts, 2nd edition, by Barry Cunliffe, Oxford University Press, 2018, UK.
18. Hand of History, Burden of Pseudo History, Touchstone of Truth, Trafford Publishing, Tom O'Connor, Ireland, 2005, page 187
19. The Schools' Collection, Volume 0214, Page 117 © National Folklore Collection, UCD.
20. The Ancient Celts, 2nd edition 2018, Barry Cunliffe, Oxford University Press, UK.
21. The Doon Of Drumsna - A Celtic Iron Age Frontier, by Tom Condit And Victor M. Buckley, via the 1997 Leitrim Guardian and https://genelach.org/article-doon_of_drumsna.xhtml

References

Chapter 2 - Through the Gateway to the North West

1. An Introduction to the Architectural Heritage of County Leitrim, Dept. of the Environment, Heritage and Local Government, page 20, Ireland.
2. The Schools' Collection, Volume 0213, Page 128 © National Folklore Collection, UCD.
3. https://en.wikipedia.org/wiki/Irish_elk
4. Archeological Inventory of Co. Leitrim, Michael Moore, Government of Ireland, 2003, page 88.
5. The Schools' Collection, Volume 0213, Page 019 © National Folklore Collection, UCD.
6. Hand of History, Burden of Pseudo-History, Touchstone of Truth, Tom O'Connor, Trafford Publishing, 2005, Ireland, page 79.
7. The Schools' Collection, Volume 0210, Page 391, © National Folklore Collection, UCD, .
8. Archeological Inventory of Co. Leitrim, by Michael J. Moore, Government of Ireland, 2003, page 158.
9. The Schools' Collection, Volume 0210, Page 391, © National Folklore Collection, UCD.
10. Archeological Inventory of Co. Leitrim, Michael J. Moore, Government of Ireland, 2003, page 97.
11. The Schools' Collection, Volume 0210, Page 206 © National Folklore Collection, UCD.
12. https://en.wikipedia.org/wiki/Maigh_Nissi
13. Leitrim History & Society, edited by Liam Kelly & Brendan Scott, Geography Publications, Dublin, 2019, page 209.
14. The Plantation of Leitrim 1585-1670 by Gerard MacAtasney, Carrick on Shannon Heritage Group, 2013, Ireland, page 98.
15. Archeological Inventory of Co. Leitrim, Michael J. Moore, Government of Ireland, 2003, page 210.
16. Historic Kiltoghert - the story of its monastic foundation, church, graveyard, townland and parish, by J J Guckian, Co Leitrim, page 117.
17. An Introduction to the Architectural Heritage of County Leitrim, National Inventory of Architectural Heritage, Government of Ireland, 2004, page 61.
18. An Introduction to the Architectural Heritage of County Leitrim, National Inventory of Architectural Heritage, Government of Ireland, 2004, page 22.
19. Historic Kiltoghert - the story of its monastic foundation, church, graveyard, townland and parish, by J J Guckian, Co Leitrim, page 116.
20. Archeological Inventory of Co. Leitrim, Michael J. Moore, Government of Ireland, 2003 page 181.
21. Archaeological Impact Assessment for a Proposed Footpath & Associated Works at Jamestown, Co. Leitrim on behalf of Leitrim County Council, by Tamlyn McHugh, January 2022 www.fadoarchaeology.com page 33.
22. Archeological Inventory of County Leitrim, Michael Moore, page 181.
23. https://www.findagrave.com/cemetery/2639644/jamestown-abbey
24. The Plantation of Leitrim 1585-1670 by Gerard MacAtasney, Carrick on Shannon Heritage Group, 2013, Ireland, page 76.
25. Archaeological Impact Assessment for a Proposed Footpath & Associated Works at Jamestown, Co. Leitrim on behalf of Leitrim County Council, by Tamlyn McHugh, January 2022 www.fadoarchaeology.com page 33.
26. Archeological Inventory of Co Leitrim, Michael J. Moore, Government of Ireland, 2003, page 216.
27. Archaeological Impact Assessment for a Proposed Footpath & Associated Works at Jamestown, Co. Leitrim on behalf of Leitrim County Council, by Tamlyn McHugh, January 2022 www.fadoarchaeology.com page 33.
28. Historic Kiltoghert - the story of its monastic foundation, church, graveyard, townland and parish, by J J Guckian, Co Leitrim, page 119.
29. Leitrim History & Society, edited by Liam Kelly& Brendan Scott, Geography Publications, Dublin, 2019, page 214.
30. Leitrim History & Society, edited by Liam Kelly & Brendan Scott, Geography Publications, Dublin, 2019, page 215.
31. https://www.franciscans.ie/our-friaries/former-friaries/connaught/jamestown-co-leitrim/
32. http://www.carrickonshannonparish.com/jamestown.htm
33. Historic Kiltoghert - the story of its monastic foundation, church, graveyard, townland and parish, by J J Guckian, Co Leitrim, page 119.

34. Leitrim History & Society, edited by Liam Kelly & Brendan Scott, Geography Publications, Dublin, 2019, page 208.
35. Archeological Inventory of Co. Leitrim, Michael J. Moore, Government of Ireland, 2003, page 127.
36. Archeological Inventory of Co. Leitrim, Michael J. Moore, Government of Ireland, 2003, page 27.
37. Archeological Inventory of Co. Leitrim, Michael J. Moore, Government of Ireland, 2003, page 27.
38. Leitrim History and Society, edited by Liam Kelly and Brendan Scott, Geography Publications, Dublin, 2019, page 32.
39. Archeological Inventory of Co. Leitrim, Michael J. Moore, Government of Ireland, 2003, page 19.
40. Archeological Inventory of Co. Leitrim, Michael J. Moore, Government of Ireland, 2003, page 128.
41. Early Medieval Archeology in Co. Leitrim AD 400-1100, in Leitrim History & Society, edited by Liam Kelly & Brendan Scott, Geography Publications, Dublin, 2019, page 52.
42. The Schools' Collection, Volume 0210, Page 484 © National Folklore Collection, UCD.
43. Archeological Inventory of Co. Leitrim, Michael J. Moore, Government of Ireland, 2003, page 156.
44. Historic Kiltoghert - the story of its monastic foundation, church, graveyard, townland and parish, by J J Guckian, Co Leitrim, page 118.
45. Fairy Haunts of Ireland, Alanna Moore, Python Press, 2023, Ireland, page 24.
46. Historic Kiltoghert - the story of its monastic foundation, church, graveyard, townland and parish, by J J Guckian, Co Leitrim, page 118-119.
47. The Schools' Collection, Volume 0208, Page 204 © National Folklore Collection, UCD.
48. Historic Kiltoghert - the story of its monastic foundation, church, graveyard, townland and parish, by J J Guckian, Co Leitrim, page 16.
49. Archeological Inventory of Co. Leitrim, Michael J. Moore, Government of Ireland, 2003, page 69.
50. Historic Kiltoghert - the story of its monastic foundation, church, graveyard, townland and parish, by J J Guckian, Co Leitrim, page 16.
51. Historic Kiltoghert - the story of its monastic foundation, church, graveyard, townland and parish, by J J Guckian, Co Leitrim, page 17.
52. A Case Study: Clochar Macc nDaimini, by R B Warner, Dept Antiquities, Ulster Museum, Belfast. Irish place-names and archaeology III. A case study: Clochar Mace nDaimini. Bulletin of the Ulster Place-Name Society, series 2, vol. 4, 1982, 27-31, online.
53. Leitrim History & Society, edited by Liam Kelly & Brendan Scott, Geography Publications, Dublin, 2019, page 47-48.
54. The Schools' Collection, Volume 0213, Page 106 © National Folklore Collection, UCD.
55. Fairy Haunts of Ireland, Alanna Moore, Python Press, 2023, Ireland, page 14.
56. The Schools' Collection, Volume 0213, Page 104 © National Folklore Collection, UCD.
57. The Schools' Collection, Volume 0213, Page 145 © National Folklore Collection, UCD
58. A History of Drumsna and its Environs, Tony Ward, Co Leitrim.
59. The Schools' Collection, Volume 0210, Page 503 © National Folklore Collection, UCD.
60. Archeological Inventory of Co. Leitrim, Michael J. Moore, Government of Ireland, 2003, page 213.
61. Trollope, Anthony, The Macdermots of Ballycloran, 1847, Thomas Cautley Newby, UK.

Chapter 3 - River Crossings

1. Place names of south Leitrim and north Roscommon in 1270AD - A research submission to the Irish Placenames department Noel MacLochlainn, 2020, Second Edition, online.
2. Place names of south Leitrim and north Roscommon in 1270AD, A research submission to the Irish Placenames department Noel MacLochlainn, 2020, Second Edition, online.
3. Hand of History, Burden of Pseudo History, Touchstone of Truth, Trafford Publishing, Tom O'Connor, Ireland, 2005, page 344.
4. Archeological Inventory of Co. Leitrim, Michael J. Moore, Government of Ireland, 2003, page 2.
5. Journeys from the Centre of the Earth, Ian Stewart, Century, 2005, UK.
6. The Prehistoric Archeology of Ireland, John Wadell, 2022 edition, Wordwell, Ireland, page 298.
7. Leitrim History & Society, edited by Liam Kelly & Brendan Scott, Geography Publications, Dublin, 2019, page 45.
8. The Plantation of Leitrim 1585-1670 by Gerard MacAtasney, Carrick on Shannon Heritage Group,

References

2013, Ireland, page 7.

9. Leitrim History & Society, edited by Liam Kelly & Brendan Scott, Geography Publications, Dublin, 2019, page 262.

10. The Plantation of Leitrim 1585-1670 by Gerard MacAtasney, Carrick on Shannon Heritage Group, 2013, Ireland, page 98.

11. Leitrim History & Society, edited by Liam Kelly & Brendan Scott, Geography Publications, Dublin, 2019, page 46.

12. Fairy Haunts of Ireland, Alanna Moore, Python Press, 2023, Ireland, page 14.

13. Leitrim History & Society, edited by Liam Kelly & Brendan Scott, Geography Publications, Dublin, 2019, page 55.

14. Leitrim History & Society, edited by Liam Kelly & Brendan Scott, Geography Publications, Dublin, 2019, page 53.

15. Leitrim Guardian 2019, no. 51, Ireland, page 8.

16. The Annals of Annaduff, Des Guckian, Leitrim, Ireland, page 2.

17. The Annals of Annaduff, Des Guckian, Leitrim, Ireland, page 3.

18. Leitrim History & Society, edited by Liam Kelly & Brendan Scott, Geography Publications, Dublin, 2019, page 57.

19. The Annals of Annaduff, Des Guckian, Leitrim, Ireland, page 9.

20. Leitrim History & Society, edited by Liam Kelly & Brendan Scott, Geography Publications, Dublin, 2019, page 57.

21. Leitrim History & Society, edited by Liam Kelly & Brendan Scott, Geography Publications, Dublin, 2019, page 46.

22. The Annals of Annaduff, Des Guckian, Leitrim, Ireland, page 3.

23. A History of Drumsna and its Environs, Tony Ward, no date.

24. Archeological Inventory of Co. Leitrim, Michael J. Moore, Govt of Ireland, 2003, pages 171-172.

25. Leitrim's Greatest Treasure, the King & Queen Sculpture at Annaduff, Sept. 2022, Leitrim Observer.

26. A History of Annaduff and Dromod by Tony Ward, self published, Co Leitrim, 1993.

27. Archeological Inventory of Co. Leitrim, Michael J. Moore, Government of Ireland, 2003, page 14.

28. The Schools' Collection, Volume 0210, Page 496 © National Folklore Collection, UCD.

29. A Sign Posted Walking Tour of Carrick on Shannon, Leitrim County Council, page 3.

30. An Introduction to the Architectural Heritage of County Leitrim, Dept of the Environment, Heritage and Local Government, page 23.

31 Place names of south Leitrim and north Roscommon in 1270AD, A research submission to the Irish Placenames department Noel MacLochlainn, 2020, Second Edition, online.

32 The Schools' Collection, Volume 0232, Page 040 © National Folklore Collection, UCD.

33. The Schools' Collection, Volume 0209, Page 307 © National Folklore Collection, UCD.

34. The Schools' Collection, Volume 0209, Page 355 © National Folklore Collection, UCD.

35. Archeological Inventory of Co. Leitrim, Michael J. Moore, Government of Ireland, 2003, page 172.

36. Leitrim History & Society, edited by Liam Kelly & Brendan Scott, Geography Publications, Dublin, 2019, page 56.

37. The Schools' Collection, Volume 0210, Page 040 © National Folklore Collection, UCD.

38. Leitrim History & Society, edited by Liam Kelly & Brendan Scott, Geography Publications, Dublin, 2019, page 123.

39. The Schools' Collection, Volume 0210, Page 474 © National Folklore Collection, UCD.

40. The Schools' Collection, Volume 0210, Page 375 © National Folklore Collection, UCD.

41. Place names of south Leitrim and north Roscommon in 1270AD - A research submission to the Irish Placenames Department, Noel MacLochlainn, 2020, Second Edition (also) Battle of Connacht 1270: Aedh O'Conchobar's victory at Áth an Chip, 22 Feb 2020, Noel MacLochlainn, (online).

42. Leitrim History & Society, edited by Liam Kelly & Brendan Scott, Geography Publications, Dublin, 2019, page 58.

43. Leitrim History & Society, edited by Liam Kelly & Brendan Scott, Geography Publications, Dublin, 2019, page 46.

44. Leitrim History & Society, edited by Liam Kelly & Brendan Scott, Geography Publications, Dublin, 2019, page 58.

45. The Plantation of Leitrim 1585-1670 by Gerard MacAtasney, Carrick on Shannon Heritage Group, 2013, Ireland, page 98.
46. Archeological Inventory of Co. Leitrim, Michael J. Moore, Government of Ireland, 2003, page 205.
47. https://www.drumhiernyhideaway.ie/en/history/
48. Archeological Inventory of Co. Leitrim, Michael J. Moore, Government of Ireland, 2003, 146.
49. The Schools' Collection, Volume 0231, Page 208 © National Folklore Collection, UCD.
50. The Schools' Collection, Volume 0207, Page 495 © National Folklore Collection, UCD.
51. The River Shannon - journey down Ireland's longest river, Aileen Cooper, Collins Press, Cork, 2011.
52. The Schools' Collection, Volume 0231, Page 261 © National Folklore Collection, UCD
53. The Schools' Collection, Volume 0232, Page 54 © National Folklore Collection, UCD
54. The Schools Collection, Volume 0232, Page 100 © National Folklore Collection, UCD.
55. The Schools' Collection, Volume 0232, Page 100 © National Folklore Collection, UCD.
56. The Schools' Collection, Volume 0232, Page 075 © National Folklore Collection, UCD.
57. The Schools' Collection, Volume 0232, Page 192 © National Folklore Collection, UCD.
58. The Schools' Collection, Volume 0232, Page 54 © National Folklore Collection, UCD.
59. The Schools' Collection, Volume 0210, Page 301 © National Folklore Collection, UCD.
60. The Schools' Collection, Volume 0232, Page 105 © National Folklore Collection, UCD.
61. The Schools' Collection, Volume 0232, Page 126 © National Folklore Collection, UCD.

CHAPTER 4 - KINGS OF HOSPITALITY

1. Place names of south Leitrim and north Roscommon in 1270AD - A research submission to the Irish Placenames department', Noel MacLochlainn, 2020, Second Edition, online.
2. Historic Kiltoghert - the story of its monastic foundation, church, graveyard, townland and parish, J J Guckian, Co Leitrim.
3. The Celts - uncovering the mythic and historic origins of western culture', Jean Markale, Inner Traditions, VT, USA, 1978.
4. The Epic of Gilgamesh, a new translation by Andrew George, Penguin Books, 1999, UK.
5. Leitrim History and Society, edited by Liam Kelly and Brendan Scott, Geography Publications, Dublin, 2019, page 55.
6. Leitrim History & Society, edited by Liam Kelly & Brendan Scott, Geography Publications, Dublin, 2019, page 59.
7. The Schools' Collection, Volume 0210, Page 107 © National Folklore Collection, UCD.
8. The Schools' Collection, Volume 0210, Page 547 © National Folklore Collection, UCD.
9. Leitrim History & Society, edited by Liam Kelly& Brendan Scott, Geography Publications, Dublin, 2019, page 136.
10. Leitrim History & Society, edited by Liam Kelly & Brendan Scott, Geography Publications, Dublin, 2019, page 59.
11. Leitrim History & Society, edited by Liam Kelly & Brendan Scott, Geography Publications, Dublin, 2019, page 61.
12. Kiltoghert - towards the millennium, Kiltoghert Millennium Committee, Carrick on Shannon, 1999, Ireland, page 14.
13. Historic Kiltoghert - the story of its monastic foundation, church, graveyard, townland and parish, by J J Guckian, Co Leitrim, page 14.
14. http://www.carrickonshannonparish.com/kiltoghertgraveyard.htm
15. Kiltoghert - Towards the Millennium, Kiltoghert Millennium Committee, 1999.
16. The Festival of Lughnasa, Maire MacNeill, University College Dublin, 2008, page 606-607.
17. Historic Kiltoghert - the story of its monastic foundation, church, graveyard, townland and parish, by J J Guckian, Co Leitrim, page 14.
18. The Schools' Collection, Volume 0231, Page 279 © National Folklore Collection, UCD.
19. The Schools' Collection, Volume 0207, Page 492 © National Folklore Collection, UCD.
20. The Schools' Collection, Volume 0210, Page 023 © National Folklore Collection, UCD
21. The Schools' Collection, Volume 0210, Page 563 © National Folklore Collection, UCD.

References

22. Historic Kiltoghert - the story of its monastic foundation, church, graveyard, townland and parish, J J Guckian, Co Leitrim.
23. The Prehistoric Archeology of Ireland, John Waddell, Ireland, 2022, page 76.
24. Breifne before the Ui-Briuin, John P Dalton, in Breifny Antiquarian Society's Journal, 1925-26, Cavan.
25. The Schools' Collection, Volume 0231, Page 263 © National Folklore Collection, UCD.
25. Historic Kiltoghert - the story of its monastic foundation, church, graveyard, townland and parish, by J J Guckian, Co Leitrim.
26. The Schools' Collection, Volume 0210, Page 190 © National Folklore Collection, UCD.
27. The Main Manuscript Collection, Volume 0465, Page 0201 © National Folklore Collection, UCD.
28. The Schools' Collection, Volume 0209, Page 311 © National Folklore Collection, UCD.
29. The Schools' Collection, Volume 0231, Page 263 © National Folklore Collection, UCD.
30. Archeological Inventory of Co. Leitrim, Michael J. Moore, Government of Ireland, 2003, page 20.
31. Archeological Inventory of Co. Leitrim, Michael J. Moore, Government of Ireland, 2003, page 18.
32. Archeological Inventory of Co. Leitrim, Michael J. Moore, Government of Ireland, 2003, page 18.
33. The Schools' Collection, Volume 0211, Page 218 © National Folklore Collection, UCD.
34. Archeological Inventory of County Leitrim, compiled by Michael J. Moore, Government of Ireland, 2003, page 189.
35. The Schools' Collection, Volume 0211, Page 258 © National Folklore Collection, UCD.
36. The Schools' Collection, Volume 0211, Page 216 © National Folklore Collection, UCD.
37. Archeological Inventory of Co. Leitrim, Michael J. Moore, Government of Ireland, 2003, page 88.
38. The Schools' Collection, Volume 0211, Page 243 © National Folklore Collection, UCD.
39. The Schools' Collection, Volume 0210, Page 031 © National Folklore Collection, UCD.
40. Bailiúchán na Scol, Imleabhar 0210, Leathanach 11 Íomhá agus sonraí © Cnuasach Bhéaloideas Éireann, UCD.
41. Mentioned by archeologists in the Pre-history of Leitrim episode of a podcast series here - www.youtube.com/@connectingthroughleitrimsh9903/videos
42. Leitrim Guardian 2018 no 50, J J McDermott, page 140.
43. Archeological Inventory of Co. Leitrim, Michael J. Moore, Government of Ireland, 2003, page 51.
44. Battle of Connaught 1270, Noel MacLochlainn, Ireland, 2020, online.
45. The Schools' Collection, Volume 0220, Page 286 © National Folklore Collection, UCD.
46. Archeological Inventory of Co. Leitrim, Michael J. Moore, Government of Ireland, 2003, page 207.
47. Leitrim History & Society, edited by Liam Kelly & Brendan Scott, Geography Publications, Dublin, 2019, page 118.
48. Archeological Inventory of Co. Leitrim, Michael J. Moore, Government of Ireland, 2003, page 10.
49. The Schools' Collection, Volume 0208, Page 204 © National Folklore Collection, UCD
50. https://en.wikipedia.org/wiki/Keshcarrigan
51. Archeological Inventory of Co. Leitrim, Michael J. Moore, Government of Ireland, 2003, page 17.
52. Leitrim History & Society, edited by Liam Kelly & Brendan Scott, Geography Publications, Dublin, 2019, page 137.
53. Archeological Inventory of Co. Leitrim, Michael J. Moore, Government of Ireland, 2003, page 182.
54. Folk-Lore, Volume 4, Folk-lore Gleanings from County Leitrim. by Leland L. Duncan https://en.wikisource.org/wiki/Folk-Lore/Volume_4/Folk lore_Gleanings_from_County_Leitrim#top
55. The Schools' Collection, Volume 0207, Page 036 © National Folklore Collection, UCD.
56. https://en.wikipedia.org/wiki/Kiltubbrid_Shield
57. Archeological Inventory of Co. Leitrim, Michael J. Moore, Government of Ireland, 2003, page 6.
58. Archeological Inventory of Co. Leitrim,Michael J. Moore, Government of Ireland, 2003, page 189.
59. Archeological Inventory of Co. Leitrim, Michael J. Moore, Government of Ireland, 2003, page 16.
60. Archeological Inventory of Co. Leitrim, Michael J. Moore, Government of Ireland, 2003, page 173.
61. Archeological Inventory of Co. Leitrim, Michael J. Moore, Government of Ireland, 2003, page 206.
62. The Plantation of Leitrim 1585-1670 by Gerard MacAtasney, Carrick on Shannon Heritage Group, 2013, Ireland, page 98.
63. Leitrim History & Society, edited by Liam Kelly & Brendan Scott, Geography Publications, Dublin, 2019, page 221.
64. Leitrim History & Society, edited by Liam Kelly & Brendan Scott, Geography Publications, Dublin,

2019, page 222.
65. Rosclogher to Roosky, the Leitrim Story, by Lorcan O Runai.
66. Archeological Inventory of Co. Leitrim, Michael J. Moore, Government of Ireland, 2003, page 214.
67. The River Shannon- a journey down Ireland's longest river, Aileen Cooper, Collins Press, Cork, 2011.
68. http://irisharchaeology.ie/2013/03/the-keshcarrigan-bowl/#goo
69. Historic Kiltoghert - the story of its monastic foundation, church, graveyard, townland and parish,' by JJ Guckian, Co Leitrim, page 18.
70. The Black Pig's Dyke Regional Project 2014 Volume 1 by Coilin Ó Drisceoil, Mary Leenane, Stephen Davis, Barry Fitzgibbon and Mary Teehan.
71. Historic Kiltoghert - the story of its monastic foundation, church, graveyard, townland and parish, J J Guckian, 2000.
72. Historic Kiltoghert - the story of its monastic foundation, church, graveyard, townland and parish, J J Guckian, 2000.
73. Fairy Haunts of Ireland, Alanna Moore, Python Press, 2023, Ireland, page 24.
74. O'Donovan, John, Ordnance Survey of Ireland: Letters, Cavan and Leitrim, 1836.

CHAPTER 5 - SAINTLY ENVY

1. https://en.wikipedia.org/wiki/Muintir Eolais
2. The Annals of Annaduff, Des Guckian, Co Leitrim, page 10.
3. https://celt.ucc.ie/published/T100010A/index.html
4. O'Donovan, John, Ordnance Survey of Ireland: Letters, Cavan and Leitrim, 1836.
5. https://www.houseofnames.com/shanley-family-crest/Irish-Alt
6. A History of Annaduff and Dromod, Tony Ward, Co Leitrim, 1993.
7. From Rosclogher to Roosky - the Leitrim Story, Loran o Runai, Co. Leitrim.
8. https://www.petersommer.com/blog/another-thing/saint-manchans-shrine
9. Memories from Cartron and Eslin Schools, 2016, Co. Leitrim, 2016.
10. Fairy Haunts of Ireland, Alanna Moore, Python Press, 2023, Ireland, page 85.
11 .https://irp.cdn-website.com/9a9d8ae7/files/uploaded/Mohill%20history%20-%20a%20chronology.pdf
12. The Schools' Collection, Volume 0214, Page 327 © National Folklore Collection, UCD.
13. https://en.wikipedia.org/wiki/Manch%C3%A1n_of_Mohill
14. The Schools' Collection, Volume 0237, Page 027 © National Folklore Collection, UCD.
15. The Schools' Collection, Volume 0220, Page 112 © National Folklore Collection, UCD.
16. The Schools' Collection, Volume 0220, Page 135 © National Folklore Collection, UCD.
17. https://www.loughrynn.net/
18. The Schools' Collection, Volume 0214, Page 333 © National Folklore Collection, UCD.
19. The Schools' Collection, Volume 0214, Page 351 © National Folklore Collection, UCD.
20. The Schools' Collection, Volume 0220, Page 230 © National Folklore Collection, UCD.
21. Archeological Inventory of Co. Leitrim, Michael J. Moore, Government of Ireland, 2003, page 6.
22. http://aughavascloone.ie/content.aspx?par=8&ContentId=28
23. The Archeological Inventory of Co. Leitrim, Michael J Moore, 2003, Govt of Ireland, page 174.
24. The Schools' Collection, Volume 0221, Page 359 © National Folklore Collection, UCD.
25. The Schools' Collection, Volume 0221, Page 359 © National Folklore Collection, UCD.
25. Leitrim History & Society, edited by Liam Kelly & Brendan Scott, Geography Publications, Dublin, 2019, page 36.
26. http://aughavascloone.ie/content.aspx?par=8&ContentId=28
27. The Festival of Lughnasa, Maire MacNeill, University College Dublin, 2008, page 606.
28. Archeological Inventory of Co. Leitrim, Michael J. Moore, Government of Ireland, 2003, page 189.
29. The Schools' Collection, Volume 0221, Page 636 © National Folklore Collection, UCD.
30. The Schools' Collection, Volume 0221, Page 145 © National Folklore Collection, UCD.
31. The Schools' Collection, Volume 0221, Page 145 © National Folklore Collection, UCD.
32. The Schools' Collection, Volume 0221, Page 635 © National Folklore Collection, UCD.

References

33. Archeological Inventory of Co. Leitrim, Michael J. Moore, Government of Ireland, 2003, page 16.
34. The Schools' Collection, Volume 0221, Page 143 © National Folklore Collection, UCD.
35. The Schools' Collection, Volume 0221, Page 016 © National Folklore Collection, UCD.
36. Archeological Inventory of Co. Leitrim, Michael J. Moore, Government of Ireland, 2003, page 11.
37. Carrigallen Parish - a history, edited by Raymond Hackett and Michael Reilly, Leitrim, 1996.
38. The Schools' Collection, Volume 0221, Page 617 © National Folklore Collection, UCD.
39. Archeological Inventory of Co. Leitrim, Michael J. Moore, Government of Ireland, 2003, page 6.
40. http://www.shee-eire.com/Sites&Monuments/Megalithic-tombs/Leitrim/Aghavas/aghavas.htm
41. Archeological Inventory of Co. Leitrim, Michael J. Moore, Government of Ireland, 2003, page 23.
42. Carrigallen Parish - a history, edited by Raymond Hackett and Michael Reilly, 1996, Ireland.
43. http://homepage.eircom.net/~vscallen/html/body_carrigallen.html
44. http://homepage.eircom.net/~vscallen/html/body_carrigallen.html
45. Archeological Inventory of Co. Leitrim, Michael J. Moore, Government of Ireland, 2003, page 22.
46. Carrigallen Parish - a history, edited by Raymond Hackett and Michael Reilly, Leitrim, 1996.
47. http://homepage.eircom.net/~vscallen/html/body_carrigallen.html
48. Archeological Inventory of Co. Leitrim, Michael J. Moore, Government of Ireland, 2003, page 43.
49. Carrigallen Parish - a history, edited by Raymond Hackett and Michael Reilly, Leitrim, 1996.
50. Carrigallen Parish - a history, edited by Raymond Hackett and Michael Reilly, Leitrim, 1996.

Chapter 6 - Lakes of the Holy Cow

1. The Schools' Collection, Volume 0214, Page 048 © National Folklore Collection, UCD.
2. Leitrim History & Society, edited by Liam Kelly & Brendan Scott, Geography Publications, Dublin, 2019, page 10.
3. Fairy Haunts of Ireland, Alanna Moore, Python Press, 2023, Ireland, page 84-86.
4. The River Shannon- a journey down Ireland's longest river, Aileen Cooper, Collins Press, Cork, 2011.
5. Archeological Inventory of Co. Leitrim, Michael J. Moore, Government of Ireland, 2003, page 15.
6. Place names of south Leitrim and north Roscommon in 1270AD - A research submission to the Irish Placenames department Noel MacLochlainn, 2020, Second Edition (online).
7. Archeological Inventory of Co. Leitrim, Michael J. Moore, Government of Ireland, 2003, page 91.
8. Eanac Dub - a history of Annaduff and Roosky by Tony Ward, 1993.
9. Rosclogher to Roosky - the Leitrim story, by Lorcan o'Runai, no date.
10. Archeological Inventory of Co. Leitrim, Michael J. Moore, Government of Ireland, 2003, page 192.
11. The Schools' Collection, Volume 0217, Page 003 © National Folklore Collection, UCD.
12. The Annals of Annaduff, Des Guckian, Leitrim, Ireland, page 17.
13. https://en.wikipedia.org/wiki/Dromod
14. Eanac Dub - A History of Annaduff and Dromod, Tony Ward, 1993.
15. The Schools' Collection, Volume 0217, Page 112 © National Folklore Collection, UCD.
16. Archeological Inventory of Co. Leitrim, Michael J. Moore, Government of Ireland, 2003, page 43.
17. Archeological Inventory of Co. Leitrim, Michael J. Moore, Government of Ireland, 2003, page 51.
18. Archeological Inventory of Co. Leitrim, Michael J. Moore, Government of Ireland, 2003, page 209.
19. https://www.loughrynn.ie/history/
20. The Schools' Collection, Volume 0214, Page 331 © National Folklore Collection, UCD
21. Places, stories and a cyclists memories of County Leitrim, Leon O'Cathasaigh https://www.irishcentral.com/travel/best-of-ireland/cycliing-county-leitrim
22. The Celts - uncovering the mythic and historic origins of western culture, Jean Markale, Inner Traditions, VT, USA, 1976, page 294.
23. Place names of south Leitrim and north Roscommon in 1270AD, A research submission to the Irish Placenames department Noel MacLochlainn, 2020, Second Edition, online.
24. Battle of Connaught 1270, by Noel MacLochlainn, Ireland, 2020.
25. Battle of Connaught 1270, by Noel MacLochlainn, Ireland, 2020.
26. Rosclogher to Rooskey - the Leitrim story, by Lorcan o'Runai, no date.
27. Gortleletteragh National School, Farnaught, Reunion 2009, Longford, Ireland.

28. The Schools' Collection, Volume 0220, Page 142 © National Folklore Collection, UCD.
29. The Schools' Collection, Volume 0217, Page 127 © National Folklore Collection, UCD.
30. The Schools' Collection, Volume 0220, Page 128 © National Folklore Collection, UCD.
31. The Schools' Collection, Volume 0220, Page 127 Image and data © Nationa
32. Gortletteragh National School, Farnaught, Reunion 2009, Longford, Ireland.
33. Archeological Inventory of Co. Leitrim, Michael J. Moore, Government of Ireland, 2003, page 9.
34. Gortletteragh National School, Farnaught, Reunion 2009, Longford, Ireland.
35. The Schools' Collection, Volume 0214, Page 336 © National Folklore Collection, UCD.
36. Archeological Inventory of Co. Leitrim, Michael J. Moore, Government of Ireland, 2003, page 22.
37. Archeological Inventory of Co. Leitrim, Michael J. Moore, Government of Ireland, 2003, page 6.
38. The Schools' Collection, Volume 0222, Page 562 © National Folklore Collection, UCD.
39. The Schools' Collection, Volume 0222, Page 618 © National Folklore Collection, UCD.
40. The Schools' Collection, Volume 0222, Page 652 © National Folklore Collection, UCD.
41. The Schools' Collection, Volume 0222, Page 663 © National Folklore Collection, UCD.
42. De Vismes Kane, William F. M. The Black Pig's Dyke: The Ancient Boundary Fortification of Uladh. Proceedings of the Royal Irish Academy. Section C: Archaeology, Celtic Studies, History, Linguistics, Literature 27 (1908-1909): 322-28.
43. Folk-lore - A Quarterly Review. Volume 29, 1918, djvu/241.
44. The Main Manuscript Collection, Volume 0521, Page 399, © National Folklore Collection, UCD.
45. The Schools' Collection, Volume 0222, Page 589 © National Folklore Collection, UCD.
46. The Main Manuscript Collection, Volume 0521, Page 398 © National Folklore Collection, UCD.
47. The Schools' Collection, Volume 0220, Page 096 © National Folklore Collection, UCD.
48. Annals of Annaghduff, Des Guckian, Leitrim, Ireland, page 7.
49. The Schools' Collection, Volume 0219, Page 149 © National Folklore Collection, UCD.
50. The Annals of Annaduff, Des Guckian, Leitrim, Ireland, page 7.
51. Medieval Parish Churches in Muintir Eolais, in Leitrim History and Society, edited by Liam Kelly and Brendan Scott, Geography Publications, Dublin, 2019, page 142.
52. An Introduction to the Architectural Heritage of County Leitrim, National Inventory of Architectural Heritage, Government of Ireland, 2004, page 9.
53. The Annals of Annaduff, Des Guckian, Leitrim, Ireland, page 8.
54. Leitrim History & Society, edited by Liam Kelly & Brendan Scott, Geography Publications, Dublin, 2019, page 144.
55. The Schools' Collection, Volume 0217, Page 127 © National Folklore Collection, UCD.
56. The Schools' Collection, Volume 0219, Page 149 © National Folklore Collection, UCD
57. Between the Meadows - the archeology of the N4 Dromod - Roosky Bypass, Catriona Moore, TII, Ireland, 2021.
58. The Schools' Collection, Volume 0219, Page 155 © National Folklore Collection, UCD.
59. Meandering through Bornacoola, by the Active Age Group, Bornacoola, Leitrim circa 1999.
60. The Schools' Collection, Volume 0219, Page 080 © National Folklore Collection, UCD.
61. The Schools' Collection, Volume 0229, Page 269 © National Folklore Collection, UCD.
62. The Schools' Collection, Volume 0225, Page 146 © National Folklore Collection, UCD.
63. Hand of History, Burden of Pseudo History, Touchstone of Truth, Trafford Publishing, Tom O'Connor, Ireland, 2005, page 79.
64. Annals of Annaduff, Des Guckian, Leitrim, Ireland, page 8.

Chapter 7 - Land of the Dagda

1. Leitrim Guardian 2023, no. 55, page 8-9.
2. Rosclogher to Rooskey - the Leitrim Story, Lorcan o' Runai.
3. The Schools' Collection, Volume 0237, Page 023 © National Folklore Collection, UCD.
4. The Head Sheaf - the life and times of the people of Sliabh an Iarainn, 2010.
5. The Schools' Collection, Volume 0212, Page 376 © National Folklore Collection, UCD.
6. Leitrim Guardian 2023 no. 55, page 8-9.

References

7. Archeological Inventory of Co. Leitrim, Michael J. Moore, Government of Ireland, 2003, page 47.
8. The Schools' Collection, Volume 0214, Page 076 © National Folklore Collection, UCD.
9. The Schools' Collection, Volume 0212, Page 377 © National Folklore Collection, UCD.
10. Leitrim History & Society, edited by Liam Kelly & Brendan Scott, Geography Publications, Dublin, 2019, page 52.
11. The Schools' Collection, Volume 0220, Page 262 © National Folklore Collection, UCD.
12. Talk by Sam Moore in Mohill, Leitrim on 14.3.2024.
13. Bailiúchán na Scol, Imleabhar 0212, Leathanach 378 © Cnuasach Bhéaloideas Éireann, UCD.
14. An Introduction to the Architectural Heritage of County Leitrim, National Inventory of Architectural Heritage, Government of Ireland, 2004, page 8.
15. The Main Manuscript Collection, Vol. 0465, Page 0220 © National Folklore Collection, UCD. 1937
16. The Schools' Collection, Volume 0223, Page 300 © National Folklore Collection, UCD.
17. Rogers, R S, The Folklore of the Black Pig's Dyke, Ulster Folklife 3.1 (1957): 33.
18. Leitrim History & Society, edited by Liam Kelly & Brendan Scott, Geography Publications, Dublin, 2019, page 321.
19. Leitrim Story - Celebrating Leitrim, Cormac Hill, www.sliabh-an-Iarainn'sstory.com
20. Archeological Inventory of Co. Leitrim, Michael J. Moore, Government of Ireland, 2003, page 183.
21. Patrick Logan, The Holy Wells of Ireland, Colin Smythe, 1980, Ireland, page 22.
22. The Schools' Collection, Volume 0966, Page 156 © National Folklore Collection, UCD.
23. The Schools' Collection, Volume 0966, Page 164 © National Folklore Collection, UCD.
24. Rosclogher to Roosky, the Leitrim Story, Lorcan o Runai.
25. Mountain Echoes, Sliabh an Iarainn's Story, St. Patrick's Well at Miskaun Glebe, by Katherine Keaney.
26. Archeological Inventory of Co. Leitrim, Michael J. Moore, Government of Ireland, 2003, page 190.
27. Sliabh an Iarainn Slopes - history of the town and parish of Ballinamore, Co Leitrim, by Father Dan Gallogly, 1991, Ireland.
28. Sliabh an Iarainn Slopes - history of the town and parish of Ballinamore, Co. Leitrim by Fr Dan Gallogly, 1991.
29. Archeological Inventory of Co. Leitrim, Michael J. Moore, Government of Ireland, 2003, page 204
30. Archeological Inventory of Co. Leitrim, compiled by Michael J. Moore, Government of Ireland, 2003, page 173.
31. Carrigallen Parish - a history, edited by Raymond Hackett and Michael Reilly, Leitrim, 1996.
32. Archeological Inventory of Co. Leitrim, Michael J. Moore, Government of Ireland, 2003, page 206.
33. Carrigallen Parish - a history, edited by Raymond Hackett and Michael Reilly, Leitrim, 1996.
34. The Schools' Collection, Volume 0968, Page 296 © National Folklore Collection, UCD.
35. Sensitive Permaculture, Alanna Moore, Python Press, 2011, Australia, page 129.
36. Plain of Blood, A Study of the Ritual Landscape of Magh Slécht, Co. Cavan, thesis by Kevin White 2013, page 12, (online).
37. https://en.wikipedia.org/wiki/Battle_of_Magh_Slecht
38. Plain of Blood, A Study of the Ritual Landscape of Magh Slécht, Co. Cavan, thesis by Kevin White (online), 2013, page 1.
39. Plain of Blood, A Study of the Ritual Landscape of Magh Slécht, Co. Cavan, thesis by Kevin White (online), 2013, page 20.
40. The Schools' Collection, Volume 0964, Page 316 © National Folklore Collection, UCD.
41. The Schools' Collection, Volume 0964, Page 395 © National Folklore Collection, UCD
42. Plain of Blood, A Study of the Ritual Landscape of Magh Slécht, Co. Cavan, thesis by Kevin White, 2013, page 1, (online).
43. John O'Donovan, Ordnance Survey of Ireland: Letters, Cavan and Leitrim, 1836.
44. Leitrim Stor - celebrating Leitrim, circa 1980, page 177, www.sliabh-an-iarann'sstory.com
45. The Schools' Collection, Volume 0968, Page 298 © National Folklore Collection, UCD.
46. The Schools' Collection, Volume 0964, Page 273 © National Folklore Collection, UCD
47. Plain of Blood, A Study of the Ritual Landscape of Magh Slécht, Co. Cavan, thesis by Kevin White, 2013, page 37.
48. Fairy Haunts of Ireland, Alanna Moore, Python Press, 2023, Ireland, page 13.
49. The Schools' Collection, Volume 0964, Page 359 © National Folklore Collection, UCD.

50. The Festival of Lughnasa, Maire MacNeill, University College Dublin, 2008, page 120.
51. Plain of Blood, A Study of the Ritual Landscape of Magh Sléct, Co. Cavan, thesis by Kevin White (online), 2013, page 62.
52. Festival of Lughnasa, Maire MacNeill, University College Dublin, 2008, page 121.
53. Plain of Blood, A Study of the Ritual Landscape of Magh Slécht, Co. Cavan, thesis by Kevin White (online), 2013, page 37.
54. Plain of Blood, A Study of the Ritual Landscape of Magh Slécht, Co. Cavan, thesis by Kevin White (online), 2013, page 78.
55. Plain of Blood, A Study of the Ritual Landscape of Magh Slécht, Co. Cavan, thesis by Kevin White (online), 2013, page 33.
56. Plain of Blood, A Study of the Ritual Landscape of Magh Slécht, Co. Cavan, thesis by Kevin White (online), 2013, page 14.
57. https://en.wikipedia.org/wiki/Kilnavert
58. Plain of Blood, A Study of the Ritual Landscape of Magh Slécht, Co. Cavan, thesis by Kevin White (online), 2013, pg 43.
59. Plain of Blood, A Study of the Ritual Landscape of Magh Slécht, Co. Cavan, thesis by Kevin White (online), 2013, page 26.
60. Plain of Blood, A Study of the Ritual Landscape of Magh Slécht, Co. Cavan, thesis by Kevin White (online), 2013, page 45.
61. Archeological Inventory of Co. Leitrim, Michael J. Moore, Government of Ireland, 2003, page 171.
62. Plain of Blood, A Study of the Ritual Landscape of Magh Slécht, Co. Cavan, thesis by Kevin White (online), 2013, page 34.
63. https://www.bawnboy.com/History-Heritage-Folklore/pages/christianity-to-templeport.html
64. Plain of Blood, A Study of the Ritual Landscape of Magh Slécht, Co. Cavan, thesis by Kevin White (online), 2013, page 38.
65. Plain of Blood, A Study of the Ritual Landscape of Magh Slécht, Co. Cavan, thesis by Kevin White (online), 2013, page 31.
66. The Schools' Collection, Volume 0968, Page 296 © National Folklore Collection, UCD.
67. The Schools' Collection, Volume 0963, Page 311 © National Folklore Collection, UCD.
68. The Schools' Collection, Volume 0964, Page 177 © National Folklore Collection, UCD.
69. (The Schools' Collection, Volume 0963, Page 311 © National Folklore Collection, UCD.
70. The Schools' Collection, Volume 0963, Page 311 © National Folklore Collection, UCD.
71. The Schools' Collection, Volume 0964, Page 318 © National Folklore Collection, UCD.
72. https://www.templeport.ie/pages/lisanover-gold-collar.html
73. The Schools' Collection, Volume 0963, Page 312 © National Folklore Collection, UCD.
74. The Schools' Collection, Volume 0963, Page 315 © National Folklore Collection, UCD.
75. The Schools' Collection, Volume 0724, Page 449 © National Folklore Collection, UCD
76. https://www.jampaling.org
77. The Death Of Conall Cernach At Ballyconnell, County Cavan by Tom Smith, online.
78. https://www.irishcultureandcustoms.com/ACounty/Cavan.html
79. The Death Of Conall Cernach At Ballyconnell, County Cavan by Tom Smith, online.
80. Plain of Blood, A Study of the Ritual Landscape of Magh Slécht, Co. Cavan, thesis by Kevin White (online), 2013, page 40.
81. The Schools' Collection, Volume 0964, Page 174 © National Folklore Collection, UCD.
82. The Last Hero of Ulster: An Alternative to the Heroic Biography Tradition of Conall Cernach, A thesis presented by Emmet Taylor, Nova Scotia, March 2019, online.
83. The Festival of Lughnasa, Maire MacNeill, University College Dublin, 2008, page 174.
84. https://www.anglocelt.ie/2023/02/12/all-eyes-on-the-tomregan-stone-an-unusual-history/
85. Plain of Blood, A Study of the Ritual Landscape of Magh Slécht, Co. Cavan, thesis by Kevin White (online), 2013, page 47.
86. Stone Age Farming (3rd edition 2025), Alanna Moore, Python Press, Ireland, page 123.
87. Plain of Blood, A Study of the Ritual Landscape of Magh Slécht, Co. Cavan, thesis by Kevin White (online), 2013, page 47.

References

CHAPTER 8 - IRON MOUNTAIN

1. The Ancient Celts, 2nd edition, by Barry Cunliffe, Oxford University Press, 2018, UK, page 256.
2. The Schools' Collection, Volume 0207, Page 109 © National Folklore Collection, UCD.
3. https://leitrimtourism.com/walks-and-trails/canal-lakeside-walks/acres-lake-boardwalk/
4. The River Shannon- journey down Ireland's longest river, Aileen Cooper, Collins Press, Cork, 2011.
5. https://www.leitrim.ie/council/services/heritage-and-conservation/natural-heritage/leitrim-geology-publication/leitrims-geological-heritage.pdf
6. The Schools' Collection, Volume 0206, Page 441 © National Folklore Collection, UCD.
7. Historic Kiltoghert - the story of its monastic foundation, church, graveyard, townland and parish, by J J Guckian, Co Leitrim, page 115.
8. Historic Kiltoghert - the story of its monastic foundation, church, graveyard, townland and parish, by J J Guckian, Co Leitrim, page 115.
9. Ulster Journal of Archeology, 1970.
10. Leitrim Story - Celebrating Leitrim, circa 1980, page 177, www.sliabh-an-iarann'sstory.com page 164.
11. Leitrim History & Society, edited by Liam Kelly & Brendan Scott, Geography Publications, Dublin, 2019, Susan Hegarty, page 10.
12. https://www.leitrimadventure.ie/news-events/a-history-of-leitrim-part-1/
13. Leitrim Story - Celebrating Leitrim, circa 1980, page 163, www.sliabh-an-iarann'sstory.com
14. Leitrim Story - Celebrating Leitrim, circa 1980, page 165, www.sliabh-an-iarann'sstory.com
15. The Schools' Collection, Volume 0206, Page 002 © National Folklore Collection, UCD.
16. The River Shannon - journey down Ireland's longest river, Aileen Cooper, The Collins Press, Cork, 2011.
17. Water Spirits of the World, Alanna Moore, Python Press, 2013, Australia, page 41.
18. Sacred Ireland, Cary Meehan, Gothic Image, UK, 2005, page 689.
19. The Schools' Collection, Volume 0207, Page 141 © National Folklore Collection, UCD.
20. In a 2024 forum on a Leitrim WhatsApp group called Sowing the Seed.
21. The Schools' Collection, Volume 0209, Page 513 © National Folklore Collection, UCD.
22. Leitrim History & Society, edited by Liam Kelly & Brendan Scott, Geography Publications, Dublin, 2019.
23. Place names of south Leitrim and north Roscommon in 1270AD - A research submission to the Irish Placenames department Noel MacLochlainn, 2020, Second Edition, online.
24. https://www.leitrim.ie/council/services/heritage-and-conservation/natural-heritage/leitrim-geology-publication/leitrims-geological-heritage.pdf
25. The Schools' Collection, Volume 0207, Page 106 © National Folklore Collection, UCD.
26. The Schools' Collection, Volume 0219, Page 352 © National Folklore Collection, UCD.
27. The Festival of Lughnasa, Maire MacNeill, University College Dublin, 2008, page 121.
28. Archeological Inventory of Co. Leitrim, Michael J. Moore, Government of Ireland, 2003, page 187.
29. The Festival of Lughnasa, Maire MacNeill, University College Dublin, 2008, page 122.
30. The Schools' Collection, Volume 0207, Page 148 © National Folklore Collection, UCD.
31. The Schools' Collection, Volume 0207, Page 108 © National Folklore Collection, UCD.
32. The Schools' Collection, Volume 0206, Page 464 © National Folklore Collection, UCD.
33. Leitrim Guardian 2017, no 49, page 51.
34. The Leitrim Guardian, 2022, no. 54, Ireland and issue 2023 no 55, page 81.
35. Leitrim History & Society, edited by Liam Kelly & Brendan Scott, Geography Publications, Dublin, 2019, page 51.
36. https://www.leitrimireland.com/listings/it-is-located-just-before-the-village-of-ballinaglera-close-to-dowra-village-and-about-10-kilometres-from-drumshanbo-and-is-on-the-route-of-the-leitrim-way-walking-trail-st-hughes-sweathouse/
37. The Festival of Lughnasa, Maire MacNeill, University College Dublin, 2008, page 182.
38. The Schools' Collection, Volume 0206, Page 013 © National Folklore Collection, UCD.
39. The Black Pig's Dyke Project 2014, volume 2, by Coilin O Deisceoil, Mary Leeann, Stephen David, Barry Fitzgibbon and Mary Teehan.

40. Fairy Haunts of Ireland, Alanna Moore, Python Press, 2023, Ireland, page 89.
41. The Schools' Collection, Volume 0964, Page 038 © National Folklore Collection, UCD.
42. https://en.wikipedia.org/wiki/Glangevlin
43. The Schools' Collection, Volume 0964, Page 008 © National Folklore Collection, UCD.
44. https://www.swanlinbar.ie/maguires-chair/
45. https://www.bawnboy.com/History-Heritage-Folklore/pages/christianity-to-templeport.html
46. The Festival of Lughnasa, Maire MacNeill, University College Dublin, 2008, page 176.
47. https://www.glangevlin.com/2021/07/30/the-lost-village-of-tobar/
48. Hand of History, Burden of Pseudo History, Touchstone of Truth, Trafford Publishing, Tom O'Connor, Ireland, 2005, page 80.
49. The Schools' Collection, Volume 0210, Page 159 © National Folklore Collection, UCD.
49. Water Spirits of the World, Alanna Moore, Python Press, Australia, 2013, page 43.

CHAPTER 9 - WILD WEST BREIFNI

1. The Schools' Collection, Volume 0205, Page 268 © National Folklore Collection, UCD.
2. The Schools' Collection, Volume 0205, Page 268 © National Folklore Collection, UCD.
3. Ulster Journal of Archeology, 1970.
4. Archeological Inventory of Co. Leitrim, Michael J. Moore, Government of Ireland, 2003, page 230.
5. The Schools' Collection, Volume 0205, Page 215 © National Folklore Collection, UCD.
6. The Schools' Collection, Volume 0205, Page 217 © National Folklore Collection, UCD.
7. Archeological Inventory of Co. Leitrim, Michael J. Moore, Government of Ireland, 2003, page 200.
8. Leitrim History & Society, edited by Liam Kelly & Brendan Scott, Geography Publications, Dublin, 2019, page 116.
9. Archeological Inventory of Co. Leitrim, Michael J. Moore, Government of Ireland, 2003, page 200.
10. Archeological Inventory of Co. Leitrim, Michael J. Moore, Government of Ireland, 2003, page 204.
11. Archeological Inventory of Co. Leitrim, Michael J. Moore, Government of Ireland, 2003, page 192.
12. Archeological Inventory of Co. Leitrim, Michael J. Moore, Government of Ireland, 2003, page 192.
13. MacNeill, Mairie, The Festival of Lughnasa, Oxford, UK, 1962, page 182.
14. The Schools' Collection, Volume 0202, Page 238 © National Folklore Collection, UCD.
15. The Schools' Collection, Volume 0203, Page 069 © National Folklore Collection, UCD.
16. Archeological Inventory of Co. Leitrim, Michael J. Moore, Government of Ireland, 2003, page 41.
17. The Festival of Lughnasa, Maire McNeill, University College Dublin, 2008, page 184.
18. https://www.leitrim.ie/council/services/heritage-and-conservation/natural-heritage/leitrim-geology-publication/leitrims-geological-heritage.pdf
19. https://www.leitrim.ie/council/services/heritage-and-conservation/natural-heritage/leitrim-geology-publication/leitrims-geological-heritage.pdf
20. Geological Survey Ireland. Leitrim - County Geological Site Report, Geological Survey Ireland, 2020. https://gsi.geodata.gov.ie/downloads/Geoheritage/Reports/LM008_Creevelea.pdf
21. https://www.leitrim.ie/council/services/heritage-and-conservation/natural-heritage/leitrim-geology-publication/leitrims-geological-heritage.pdf
22. The Schools' Collection, Volume 0203, Page 305 © National Folklore Collection, UCD.
23. Archeological Inventory of Co. Leitrim, Michael J. Moore, Government of Ireland, 2003, page ?
24. The Schools' Collection, Volume 0202, Page 008 © National Folklore Collection, UCD.
25. Leitrim History & Society, edited by Liam Kelly & Brendan Scott, Geography Publications, Dublin, 2019, page 320.
26. Archeological Inventory of Co. Leitrim, Michael J. Moore, Government of Ireland, 2003, page 218.
27. Drumlease - two centuries of a Church of Ireland parish in County Leitrim, Desmond A. Gillmor, Gillmor Publications, 2021, Ireland, page 11.
28. Drumlease - two centuries of a Church of Ireland parish in County Leitrim, Desmond A. Gillmor, Gillmor Publications, 2021, Ireland, page 15.
29. Drumlease - two centuries of a Church of Ireland parish in County Leitrim, Desmond A. Gillmor,

References

Gillmor Publications, 2021, Ireland, page 19.
30. https://www.historyireland.com/dervorgilla-scarlet-woman-or-scapegoat/
31. O'Rourke Strongholds of West Breifne and some other chieftaincies, Dunta Ui Ruairc, 1994, online.
32. https://dromahairheritage.wordpress.com/plantation/
33. Archeological Inventory of Co. Leitrim, Michael J. Moore, Government of Ireland, 2003, page 203.
34. Leitrim History & Society, edited by Liam Kelly & Brendan Scott, Geography Publications, Dublin, 2019, page 111.
35. https://dromahairheritage.wordpress.com/2017/05/06/notes-on-orourkes-hall/
36. Leitrim History & Society, edited by Liam Kelly & Brendan Scott, Geography Publications, Dublin, 2019, page 115.
37. Leitrim History & Society, edited by Liam Kelly & Brendan Scott, Geography Publications, Dublin, 2019, page 116.
38. Archeological Inventory of Co, Leitrim, Michael J. Moore, Government of Ireland, 2003, page 214.
39. The Faith We Inherited, The Millenial Liturgical Committee, 2000.
40. https://leitrimtourism.com/heritage/creevelea-abbey/
41. The Plantation of Leitrim 1585-1670 by Gerard MacAtasney, Carrick on Shannon Heritage Group, 2013, Ireland, page 99.
42. Rosclogher to Roosky, the Leitrim Story, Lorcan o Runai.
43. Sam Moore talk, 14/3/24, Mohill.
44. Archeological Inventory of County Sligo, Volume 1, South Sligo, Archeological Survey of Ireland, Government of Ireland, 2005, page 413-414.
45. The Faith We Inherited, The Millennium Liturgical Committee, Ireland, 2000.
46. Archeological Inventory of County Sligo Vol. 1, South Sligo, Archeological Survey of Ireland, Government of Ireland, 2005, page 444.
47. Archeological Inventory of County Sligo Vol.e 1, South Sligo, Archeological Survey of Ireland, Govt of Ireland, 2005, page 438.
48. Sacred Ireland, Cary Meehan, Gothic Image, UK, 2002, page 690.
49. Archeological Inventory of County Sligo, Volume 1, South Sligo, Archeological Survey of Ireland, Government of Ireland, 2005, page 444.
50. Fairy Haunts of Ireland, Alanna Moore, Python Press, 2023, Ireland, page 57.
51. https://heritageireland.ie/places-to-visit/parkes-castle/
52. https://www.yeatstrail.ie/deerpark/   http://www.carrowkeel.com/sites/sligo/deerpark.html
53. https://www.coillte.ie/site/deerpark/
54. https://leitrimtourism.com/treasured-landscapes/glencar-waterfall/
55. Leitrim Guardian page 115, 2018, no 50.
56. https://www.discoverireland.ie/leitrim/glencar-lake

CHAPTER 10 - BASTIONS OF THE NORTH

1. The Schools' Collection, Volume 0190, Page 313 © National Folklore Collection, UCD.
2. Between the Meadows - the archeology of Edercloon on the N4 Drimod- Roosky Bypass, by Caitriona Moore, Transport Infrastructure Ireland, 2021.
3. Fairy Haunts of Ireland, Alanna Moore, Python Press, 2023, Ireland, page 85 - 89.
4. Archeological Inventory of Co. Leitrim, Michael J. Moore, Government of Ireland, 2003, page 206.
5. Archeological Inventory of Co. Leitrim, Michael J. Moore, Government of Ireland, 2003, page 68.
6. Leitrim History & Society, edited by Liam Kelly & Brendan Scott, Geography Publications, Dublin, 2019, page 38.
7. Archeological Inventory of Co, Leitrim, Michael J. Moore, Government of Ireland, 2003, page 19.
8. https://manorhamilton.ie/wp-content/uploads/2021/11/Manorhamilton-heritage-bk-v8.pdf
9. Archeological Inventory of Co. Leitrim, Michael J. Moore, Government of Ireland, 2003, page 216.
10. The Schools' Collection, Volume 0197, Page 057 © National Folklore Collection, UCD.
11. The Schools' Collection, Volume 0195, Page 289 © National Folklore Collection, UCD.
12. The Schools' Collection, Volume 0200, Page 130 © National Folklore Collection, UCD.

13. Leitrim History & Society, edited by Liam Kelly & Brendan Scott, Geography Publications, Dublin, 2019, page 262.
14. Leitrim History & Society, edited by Liam Kelly & Brendan Scott, Geography Publications, Dublin, 2019, page 274.
15. The Schools' Collection, Volume 0192, Page 300 © National Folklore Collection, UCD.
16. Leitrim History & Society, edited by Liam Kelly & Brendan Scott, Geography Publications, Dublin, 2019, page 259.
17. https://manorhamilton.ie/wp-content/uploads/2021/11/Manorhamilton-heritage-bk-v8.pdf
18. Leitrim History & Society, edited by Liam Kelly & Brendan Scott, Geography Publications, Dublin, 2019, page 287.
19. Leitrim History & Society, edited by Liam Kelly & Brendan Scott, Geography Publications, Dublin, 2019, page 271.
20. Archeological Inventory of Co. Leitrim, Michael J. Moore, Government of Ireland, 2003, page 212.
21. Margaret Connolly, The Changing Names of Manorhamilton's New Line, Leitrim Guardian 2021, vol 53.
22. Archeological Inventory of Co. Leitrim, Michael J. Moore, Government of Ireland, 2003, page 216.
23. https://manorhamilton.ie/wp-content/uploads/2021/11/Manorhamilton-heritage-bk-v8.pdf
24. Leitrim Guardian 2020, no. 52, page 40, Ireland.
25. https://leitrimtourism.com/towns-villages/manorhamilton/
26. https://www.leitrimireland.com/listings/manorhamilton-tullyskeherney-archaeology-site/
27. http://www.megalithicireland.com/Tullyskeherny%20Court%20Tombs.html
https://www.themodernantiquarian.com/site/3277/tullyskeherny
28. https://leitrimdoc.ie/wp-content/uploads/2021/09/Glenfarne-A-History_wm.pdf
29. https://leitrimtourism.com/treasured-landscapes/glenfarne-demesne/
30. Archeological Inventory of Co. Leitrim, Michael J. Moore, Government of Ireland, 2003, page 44.
31. https://www.glangevlin.com/2021/05/13/the-kingdom-of-the-mcgoverns/
https://leitrimdoc.ie/wp-content/uploads/2021/09/Glenfarne-A-History_wm.pdf
32. https://visionsofthepastblog.com/2018/06/07/corracloona-megalithic-tomb-leitrim-ireland/
33. Archeological Inventory of Co. Leitrim, Michael J. Moore, Government of Ireland, 2003, page 5.
34. The Black Pig's Dyke Project 2014, volume 2, by Coilin O Deisceoil, Mary Leeann, Stephen David, Barry Fitzgibbon and Mary Teehan.
35. The Schools' Collection, Volume 0191, Page 274 © National Folklore Collection, UCD.
36. https://en.wikipedia.org/wiki/Rossinver.
37. Leitrim Guardian, 2025, no. 57, page 80.
38. Archeological Inventory of Co. Leitrim, Michael J. Moore, Government of Ireland, 2003, page 180.
39. The Schools' Collection, Volume 0191, Page 357 © National Folklore Collection, UCD.
40. The Schools' Collection, Volume 0191, Page 386 © National Folklore Collection, UCD.
41. https://www.leitrim.ie/council/services/heritage-and-conservation/publications/leitrims-geological-heritage.pdf
42. Rossinver Waterfall by Una Breeding and Grainne McGuinness, Leitrim Guardian, 1990, page 108.
43. https://www.theorganiccentre.ie/page/rossinver
44. The Schools' Collection, Volume 0195, Page 286 © National Folklore Collection, UCD.
45. The Schools' Collection, Volume 0195, Page 286 © National Folklore Collection, UCD.
46. Archeological Inventory of Co. Leitrim, Michael J. Moore, Government of Ireland, 2003, page 188.
47. Rosclogher to Roosky, the Leitrim Story, by Lorcan O Runai.
https://www.leitrimireland.com/listings/rossclogher-castle/
48. https://www.youtube.com/watch?v=ZDgFAAx-Dm8
49. Archeological Inventory of Co. Leitrim, Michael J. Moore, Government of Ireland, 2003, page 183.
50. Leitrim History & Society, edited by Liam Kelly & Brendan Scott, Geography Publications, Dublin, 2019, pages 95 + 103.
51. Archeological Inventory of Co. Leitrim, Michael J. Moore, Government of Ireland, 2003, page 192.
52. Archeological Inventory of Co. Leitrim, Michael J. Moore, Government of Ireland, 2003, page 2.
53. Archeological Inventory of Co. Leitrim, Michael J. Moore, Government of Ireland, 2003, page 181.
54. From Rosclogher to Roosky, the Leitrim Story, by Lorcan O Runai.

References

55. The Schools' Collection, Volume 0190, Page 027 © National Folklore Collection, UCD
56. The Schools' Collection, Volume 0190, Page 320 © National Folklore Collection, UCD.
57. Archeological Inventory of Co. Leitrim, Michael J. Moore, Government of Ireland, 2003, page 180.
58. http://www.rossinveryouthcommunity.com/the-history-heritage-of-rossinver/
59. In a forum on a Leitrim WhatsApp group called 'Sowing the Seed', January 2024.
60. The Festival of Lughnasa, Maire McNeill, University College Dublin, 2008, page 184.
61. Leitrim Guardian 1990, Rossinver Waterfall, by Una Bredin and Grainne McGuinness.
62. Archeological Inventory of Co. Leitrim, Michael J. Moore, Government of Ireland, 2003, page 10.
63. https://sheenunhouse.wordpress.com/
64. Fairy Haunts of Ireland, Alanna Moore, Python Press, 2023, Ireland, page 83.
65. Leitrim History & Society, edited by Liam Kelly & Brendan Scott, Geography Publications, Dublin, 2019, page 325.
66. The Schools' Collection, Volume 0190, Page 312 © National Folklore Collection, UCD.
67. The Schools' Collection, Volume 0190, Page 027 © National Folklore Collection, UCD.
68. The Schools' Collection, Volume 0189, Page 379 © National Folklore Collection, UCD
69. Archeological Inventory of Co. Leitrim, Michael J. Moore, Government of Ireland, 2003, page 202.
70. The Schools' Collection, Volume 0190, Page 058 © National Folklore Collection, UCD.
71. Archeological Inventory of Co. Leitrim, Michael J. Moore, Government of Ireland, 2003, page 204.
72. The Schools' Collection, Volume 0190, Page 108 © National Folklore Collection, UCD.
73. The Schools' Collection, Volume 0190, Page 027 © National Folklore Collection, UCD.
74. Archeological Inventory of Co. Leitrim, Michael J. Moore, Government of Ireland, 2003, page 38.
75. L O'Clery's Life of Hugh Roe O'Donnell pg 264 via Breifne before the Ui-Briuin, part 3 by John P Dalton, in The Breifny Antiquarian Society's Journal, 1925-26, Cavan.
76. Archeological Inventory of Co. Leitrim, Michael J. Moore, Government of Ireland, 2003, page 193.
77. https://leitrimtourism.com/towns-villages/tullaghan/
78. The Schools' Collection, Volume 0190, Page 027 © National Folklore Collection, UCD.
79. Archeological Inventory of Co. Leitrim, Michael J. Moore, Government of Ireland, 2003, page 39).
80. Archeological Inventory of Co. Leitrim, Michael J. Moore, Government of Ireland, 2003, page 12.
81. Archeological Inventory of Co. Leitrim, Michael J. Moore, Government of Ireland, 2003, page 24.
82. https://www.leitrim.ie/council/services/heritage-and-conservation/publications/leitrims-geological-heritage.pdf
83. Fairy Haunts of Ireland, Alanna Moore, Python Press, 2023, Ireland, page 85.
84. The Schools' Collection, Volume 0189, Page 014 © National Folklore Collection, UCD
85. https://en.wikipedia.org/wiki/Glenade_Lough

ABOUT THE AUTHOR

Alanna Moore comes from Sydney Australia and currently lives in Ireland. She has had a life long interest in history, geomancy, dowsing and the environment. A co-founder of the New South Wales Dowsing Society in 1984, this is her eleventh book. Her books have been published around the world and translated into several languages. Her previous book was Fairy Haunts of Ireland, 2023.

Alanna also teaches the art of dowsing environmental energies and provides professional dowsing services, generally by remote surveys, divining the subtle energies and spirits of place, and tours, via her website at www.geomantica.com

FAIRY HAUNTS OF IRELAND
- a guide to magical, uplifting and supernatural sites, where one can access the ancient spiritual heritage of Ireland and participate in her ever-luminous Other-world continuum

by Alanna Moore, November 2023
ISBN 9780645285437   125 A5 pages, paperback, colour

What is the nature of the Other-dimensional world of fairyland? Since ancient times, seers have described the parallel world of nature spirits and deities. Peeling away the biased accounts of medieval monks, one finds archaic fragments of mythos of the Other, also in children's stories. Best of all, we can encounter their presences at locations around the magical island of Ireland.

This is a guide to some of Ireland's standout supernatural sites and it's richly illustrated in full colour. Included are some of the author's fairy experiences, such as at the source of the Shannon River; seven years of observing and interacting with fairy queens in Leitrim; journeying with Cow goddess Boinn and dancing with the Daghda.

What has been said about this book -

*A well written and thoughtful piece of work...
positive and sincere....It is animism for the 21st century.*
   Rob Vance, 'Pagan Ireland', vol 3 issue 3 spring 2024.

Alanna has a huge amount of knowledge about the energies of the land and spiritual beings that live in Ireland, making this an informative, fascinating and entertaining book.
   Ruth Elisabeth Hancock, author of 'Work Your Energy'.

*This could become one of my favourite books.
It's up there with the great Michael Dames.*
   Laurence Main, Ley Hunters, UK

Books like this, that merge history and folklore of the old with messages coming up out of the land, in these new times are essential.
   Yolande Hyde, author 'Soul Evolution', Australia.

www.ingramcontent.com/pod-product-compliance
Lightning Source LLC
Chambersburg PA
CBHW051157290426
44109CB00022B/2494